D0923134

中國新疆古代藝術

THE ANCIENT ART IN XINJIANG，CHINA

主編　穆舜英　副主編　祁小山　張平

新疆美術攝影出版社出版
Published by The Xinjiang Art and Photography Press

First Edition 1994

ISBN7—80547—223—8/J · 180

Published by:

    Xinjiang Fine Arts and Photo Pub-
lishing House, China

    (118 Xihong Road, Urumqi, China)

Distributed by:

    China International Book Trading
Corporation

    (35 Chegongzhuang Xilu, Beijing 100044,
China P. O. Box 399, Beijing, China)

Printed in the People's Republic of China

目録　CONTENTS

前　言

　　新疆，古稱西域，是中國西部邊疆省區，面積為一百六十五萬平方公里。在其北面和西面分別與蒙古、俄羅斯、哈薩克斯坦、吉爾吉斯斯坦、塔吉克斯坦、阿富汗、巴基斯坦等國接壤，是中國通向中亞、西亞、南亞，甚至遠達地中海各國的陸上門戶，古代絲綢之路就曾經過這裡。由於它地處亞洲腹地這一特殊地理位置，不僅使這一地區成為溝通舊大陸東西各國的重要通道，而且也成為世界四大古代文明（即黃河流域古代文明、印度河流域古代文明、兩河流域古代文明及地中海區域古代文明）的交流薈萃之地，這就使得這一地區的古代藝術文化呈現出一幅色彩繽紛、絢麗多姿的畫面。

　　西域歷來就是中國一個多民族聚居的地區。在歷史上曾有許多古老的部落、民族在此活動，如在天山以北草原上有著名的游牧部族塞人（西方史料中稱為塞克或斯基泰人）、月氏、匈奴和烏孫等，在天山以南各沙漠綠洲有羌人、樓蘭人、車師人、焉耆人、龜茲人、疏勒人、于闐人，以及後來活躍在天山南北的鮮卑人、柔然人、突厥人、吐蕃人、點戛斯人、回鶻人和蒙古人等等。至今在新疆境內仍居住著維吾爾族、漢族、哈薩克族、柯爾克孜族、蒙古族、塔吉克族、回族、錫伯族、滿族、塔塔爾族、烏孜別克族、達斡爾族和俄羅斯族等十三個民族。這些民族在歷史長河中，雖然都有其本身歷史發展的興衰變遷，但都為西域文明藝術的發展做出了重要的貢獻，創造了各自不朽的藝術作品。

　　藝術是人類為追求生存和發展，探索〝盡善盡美〞的人類社會生活的形象反映。歷史上人類創造的極為豐富的各種藝術品都是人類社會物質文明和精神文明發展的產物。西域地區有著悠久的歷史，又是東西方文化交流滙合的中心。古代眾多民族創造的精美絕倫的古代藝術品，不僅是古代文明寶庫中的重要組成部分，而且對世界古代文明的創造和發展也有著不可磨滅的貢獻，並產生了巨大的影響。今天我們循著歷史發展的軌跡，尋覓西域藝術的精華，將在人們面前展示出西域藝術發展的光輝燦爛的歷史及其不朽的藝術魅力。

　　西域的古代藝術發展淵源，最早可以追溯到距今一萬年至七千年的舊石器時代晚期和中石器時代。這時候的人類已從原始打擊粗重石器的自然狀態下解放出來，學會了使用間接打擊法和剝制法來製造更精巧的細小石器，有了細石鏃、細石矛和細石葉石器（細刃片石器），出現了弓箭、長矛和石刀。恩格斯在《家庭、私有制和國家的起源》一書中就曾指出：〝弓箭對於蒙昧時代，正如鐵器對於野蠻時代和火器對於文明時代一樣，乃是決定性的武器〞。這標示著原始社會生產技術的發展和生產工具的重大革新，並且有了原始畜牧業和種植業，也開始出現了原始藝術的萌芽。人類在原始社會階段的漫長歲月中，首先是與自然鬥爭，為爭取生存而奮鬥，其追求生活美的意願，也只能是蘊育於這一鬥爭之中，故原始藝術品往往也是生產工具，實用與欣賞的審美性融為一體，這是原始藝術表現的重要特徵。

　　在今新疆石器時代遺址中，人們在哈密七角井細石器遺址和烏魯木齊柴窩堡細石器遺址中曾發現一類石核石器，其底部打製成錐狀體、柱狀體和船底形體等，呈現出一定的幾何形狀，這些特徵不僅具有劃分時代意義，而且表現了人類在追求著形狀的變化，注意了〝美〞的體現，它透視了古代西域原始藝術的啟端。在新疆的羅布泊洼地和吐魯番盆地的細石器遺址中，人們還發現了一類製作極為精緻的〝桂葉形〞細石鏃和石矛（圖2），其外觀製作得與桂花樹葉極為相似，鏃或矛兩端呈尖狀，中間略鼓，有立體感。更令人感嘆的是鏃（矛）表面被通體加工精雕細琢出的凹凸面，似片片魚鱗，在陽光照射下閃閃發亮，顯示了一種原始的神秘力。當然這些細石鏃鏃面修琢成魚鱗狀，首先是為了加強石鏃的殺傷力，但這一枚枚桂葉形石鏃也無疑地凝結了古人探索美的心願。它們是原始石器藝術中的精品。

進入新石器時代（約距今五、六千年），人類在石器製作中又出現了新技術——磨光技術、磨製石器成為新石器時代石器的典型特徵。在新疆新石器時代遺址中出土的磨光石鐮、磨製石斧、玉斧和琢製的石球等，表面光滑細膩，尤其是用羊脂玉磨製的玉斧（圖4），更是加工精細，晶瑩光潔，幾乎可以和近代玉器媲美。而遺址中發現的石球（圖3）製作規整，琢製勻稱，充分反映了這一時期雕鑿石器的工藝水平。

在原始石器藝術中，作為獨立藝術品出現的是在木壘四道溝發現的一件石祖（圖334），雕鑿異常逼真，這是對男性生殖力的崇拜的物質形象表現。石祖的出現表示了古代人對人的自身力量的認識和追求，也是石器藝術中寫實風格的作品。這裡要說明的是新疆新石器時代遺址中有的還發現了少量小銅刀或小銅片，有些學者認為這些遺址可能已進入青銅文化時期。

新疆原始石器藝術具有在粗獷中透示出一種神秘色彩的美的風格，這反映了古人對自然的和人的力量的追求和探索。

新疆歷史進入金石並用時期和青銅文化時期（約距今三、四千年），藝術的發展已出現了地區的差異和藝術風格的多樣性。這個時代的遺址在全疆各地都有發現。在羅布泊的孔雀河北岸古墓溝古墓地，出土了豐富的石、骨器和草編器等文物，人們發現極有特點的木雕和石雕半身女俑像（圖295、圖333），以及用蘆葦、草杆、香蒲草葉編織的帶花紋的簍筐，其時代為距今3800年左右。這些木、石雕半身人像，整體雕鑿刀法很粗獷，但卻細緻地雕鑿出修長的臉龐，頭頂的毛織帽，甚至其毛線的紋路也清晰可辨，女俑頭後鑿出辮狀的短髮髻，胸部雙乳突出。這些在羅布泊古墓溝地區發現的木、石雕半身人像，為探索古墓溝人的形象、習俗，及其原始崇拜提供了重要的資料，同時也是這一地區的獨有的藝術珍品。值得注意的是在古墓溝墓區出土的文物中沒有發現陶器，也不見大型青銅器，僅在墓區發現過兩個很小的銅卷片。

較古墓溝時期要晚，大約在距今二千六、七百年左右，相當於中原的春秋戰國時期，在新疆的許多地方發現了以出土彩陶為特徵的考古文化。這類遺址多分布在天山東部的哈密地區和吐魯番盆地，近年來在焉耆盆地（含輪台和庫車地區）也有重要發現。在天山以北的伊犁河流域曾有少量發現。這批彩陶器從器形的製作，色澤的調配，花紋的布局和紋樣圖案的變化，都具有各個地區或不同民族的獨特藝術風格。如在哈密盆地發現的一批雙耳彩陶罐（圖22.25.26），在紅色陶衣上繪黑色花紋，滿身塗彩，紅黑色澤調配十分醒目。其花紋圖案有：蔓藤枝葉紋、三葉草紋、水波S紋，還有菱形紋，橫豎線紋，垂幛紋和填以折線的倒三角紋。在吐魯番盆地及在這一地區的天山谷地發現的彩陶器、典型器形是單耳彩陶罐，有紅衣黑彩或紅衣紅彩，大部分滿身塗彩，花紋圖案多見的是弧形三角紋、網狀紋、渦卷紋和針葉紋。而在焉耆盆地的和靜、輪台和克孜爾河水庫地區發現的彩陶器，典型器形則是單耳帶流陶罐（杯），其裝飾圖案的布局，常見的是在罐的頸部或口腹部的一側繪有一條斜或橫的寬帶（圖36），在寬帶內繪飾不同的圖案花紋，大部分為紅衣紅彩，也有在紅衣上部分塗白黃色彩，再塗紅或紫彩。其花紋圖案常見的有方棋盤格紋、山形紋、網狀紋和變化多端的動物紋、幾何紋等。其中有兩件彩陶罐，圖案花紋極為罕見，一件是在和靜察吾呼溝古墓出土的單耳帶流彩陶罐，在罐的頸部繪有一橫排跪伏的雙峰駱駝（圖20），細線輕描，筆觸細膩，形象極其逼真；另一件是在輪台群巴克古墓中發現的單耳帶流彩陶罐，在罐的腹部的一個側面繪有一幅人頭側面像（圖27），古代的彩繪工只用寥寥數筆，用橫豎斜線就勾畫了出來，這種運用描象素描技巧的熟練程度，是令人驚嘆的。在伊犁河流域發現的彩陶器，多見的是高頸弧腹的彩陶壺和矮腹圓底的彩陶鉢，紅衣紅彩，滿身塗彩，常見花紋有虛實方格、菱形紋、曲折紋、網狀紋和針樹葉紋。將上述新疆的彩陶文化與周緣地區的比較，便可發現哈密地區的彩陶器，從器形特徵及其花紋布局，與甘肅河西地區的火燒溝彩陶文化極為相似，這一地區的彩陶藝術風格似乎受到河西地區古代文化的影響。但在新疆的吐魯番、焉耆等地發現的彩陶，則無論從器形還是圖案花紋方面看，都與甘肅河西地區和中亞、西亞　地區發現的彩陶文化其主體完全不同，明顯地具有本身獨有的藝術特點。從彩陶的圖案花紋上，還可以看到其藝術風格具有很強的寫實性，如其山形紋、網狀紋和變形鳥紋等，明顯受到新疆盆地高山地形和漁獵放牧生活的影響。藝術的形象往往來源於生活的直觀，這是寫實風格形成的根源。新疆彩陶文化藝術的發展是新疆古代藝術中的一枝燦爛的花卉，而這些分布在各個地區的彩陶藝術其不同的藝術風格正反映了新疆古代多民族的特點和藝術的地區性多樣化的發展。

　　與上述彩陶藝術大致同時代或較早的歷史時期中，還有兩類藝術，一類是新疆各大山系中發現的岩石刻畫，從北部的阿爾泰山、中部的天山，到南部的崑崙山、阿爾金山都有發現，這些為世人矚目的岩畫，大都分布於高山牧場、中低山區及牧民轉場的路線的附近岩壁上，是新疆古代游牧民族的藝術文化遺存。岩畫採用粗線條陽刻手法鑿刻在岩石壁上，也有少量彩繪岩畫發現於洞穴內，岩畫主題多見動物畫、放牧畫和狩獵畫，畫中常見的動物是鹿、山羊、馬、狼、牛。其原始質樸的畫風顯露在畫面之上。岩畫藝術中最令人驚異的是1987年在呼圖壁縣西南天山中康家石門子發現的大幅生殖崇拜岩畫，位於東經86°19′，北緯43°51′，海拔1500米處，畫面鑿刻在距地面約10米的岩壁上，面積達120多平方米，整幅畫面布滿了男女人物像，或站或臥，或衣或裸，總數約二三百人，畫面有人物舞蹈的場面和男女交媾的形象，採取了誇張的手法，突出了畫的主題。其畫面之大、人數之眾，為新疆岩畫之冠，是一幅罕見的大幅岩畫（圖155·156·157·158），已引起學術界的廣泛注意，具有重大的社會和藝術價值。關於新疆岩畫的斷代問題是一個複雜的問題，其中大部分岩畫可能早到銅石並用時期，一部分則可能在公元前後，但也有的可能晚到公元十二、十三世紀的蒙古時期，延續時間較長。

　　另一類是八十年代以來在伊犁河流域發現的青銅藝術品。其中最突出的是新源縣發現的一組銅器，有銅武士俑、對虎銅環、對翼獸銅環和昭蘇縣發現的人面駝足銅方盤等，都是罕見的青銅藝術珍品。銅武士俑（圖74），通高40厘米，重約3公斤，採用了澆模焊製法，武士頭戴尖頂彎勾大沿帽，單膝跪地，上身裸露，下身圍短裙，兩手在胸前作空握執物狀（物已不見）。武士雙目前視，臉部神態莊重端凝，造型極其生動，是古代少數民族的形象，這是目前在新疆境內僅有的一件。與銅武士俑同時發現的對虎銅項圈（圖76），對翼獸銅項圈（圖77），也是新疆境內所僅見，虎、獸造型粗獷，其環的直徑約為40厘米，環圈粗8厘米，可作為項圈戴在脖頸處，似是古代部落酋長的權力象徵，均為澆模製成。在吐魯番盆地南山阿拉溝古墓中發現的雙獸方盤高座銅器（圖75），銅方盤中鑄兩只小獅，盤下為一喇叭形高方座，為澆模焊接，相類似之物在中亞地區也曾發現，可能是古代塞人的遺存，已經有了高水平的冶煉鑄造技術，同時也為人們認識和研究新疆北部草原青銅文化的藝術風格提供了珍貴的實物資料。新疆伊犁河流域的青銅文化似與中亞、西亞的草原青銅文化互相有著密切的聯繫。

　　近年在天山地區，還陸續發現了一批雙耳深腹高足銅鍑，一般通高50-60厘米（圖79·80·81），體形較大，顯然澆灌鑄造這樣大型銅器，要求其更高的技術。與此類相似的器物在中亞、西亞地區也有發現，是一種實用器皿。古人在製作這些銅鍑時，普遍在雙耳和口沿部分，作了藝術加工，有的加鑄成蘑菇狀，是一種純粹裝飾美的表現。

除此之外，新疆境內還發現了一批具有濃厚鄂爾多斯草原藝術風格的獸紋銅飾牌，主要發現地點在哈密、巴里坤、吐魯番、木壘等地。獸紋銅飾牌製作均極為精巧，在一塊長形或圓形的銅牌上，用雕刻鏤空的技法，鑄刻出野豬、虎、馬的形象，其中的野豬紋透雕團形飾牌（圖88），野豬搏馬銅飾牌（圖83），以及包金虎形銅牌（圖87）等等，都是極為罕見的藝術珍品。它們都是新疆古代青銅藝術品中佼佼者。

　　新疆原始石器藝術、彩陶藝術、岩畫藝術、青銅藝術等等眾多的藝術類型，表現了多姿多采的藝術傳統，充分反映了新疆歷史上的多民族性。各個民族在新疆這一寬廣的歷史舞台上，創造了和留下了自己不朽的藝術作品。

　　公元前二世紀，中國西漢王朝派張騫首次通西域，開闢了絲綢之路，又於公元前六十年在今新疆的輪台地區設立政權機構〝西域都護府〞。歷史的發展變化，使得古代新疆的文化藝術進入一個新的發展階段，在人們面前展現了一幅極為燦爛的畫面。由於絲綢之路的開闢，伴隨著商品貿易的發展，促進了東西方之間經濟文化的直接交流。代表中亞、西亞、南亞甚至地中海地區的優秀文化藝術流傳到了新疆，並通過新疆傳播到中國的內地；而中國傳統的經濟文化也隨著商業交通的發展，流傳到了西方。人們在新疆境內發現了許多公元前後漢朝時的絲織工藝品，同時也發現了具有濃厚西方文化風格的毛織工藝品，如：在古代絲路重鎮樓蘭遺址發現的東漢王朝時期的絲織品，這確是一批難得的古代絲織工藝精品，雖然距今已達二千年的歲月，發現時也已成了殘片，但仍然可以看出東漢絲織工藝的高超水平。這些錦綢用各種不同的顏色的絲線織出繁縟的蔓藤枝葉紋，在圍繞著的雲紋中夾織各類珍禽祥獸和吉祥語，這些被神化的虎、龍、豹等走獸和鴨、鳥、孔雀等飛禽圖案，和吉祥語〝永昌〞、〝長壽明光〞和〝延年益壽大宜子孫〞（圖261‧262‧263）等等均夾織在圖案中，與其他花紋滙為一體，織造異常精緻，這些典型的東漢絲織工藝品，是古代東方文化的優秀代表，東漢絲織品在民豐尉犁等地也有發現。而人們在已發表的洛浦山普拉古墓出土的兩件緙毛（圖267‧268）製品的圖案中，則明顯地看到了西方文化的影響，在該墓中發現的一件〝人首馬身〞緙毛，其圖案花樣設計完全取材於希臘羅馬的神話故事。另一件〝武士像〞緙毛，武士頭扎白額帶，深目高鼻，明顯具有白種人的特點，其側面立豎一長矛。這兩件毛織品都是古代絲路上罕見的珍品，其圖案花紋也值得人們注意。另棉織品是在民豐尼雅遺址中發現的，是一件織有花紋的藍色棉布（圖260），其左面的圖案花紋是裸體菩薩像，右側是一條龍的尾巴，龍的頭部已殘缺不見。棉織品最早起源於東非，後流傳到印度、中國，而佛教的傳入中國當在公元一世紀之後，故這件棉織品反映的織造工藝圖案已受到南亞古印度文化的影響。東西方文化藝術之間的交互滲入影響，是新疆古代文化藝術的特點之一。

　　公元二、三世紀後，起源於印度的佛教文化越來越滲入新疆境內各地，對新疆的文化藝術產生了重大的影響。在新疆南疆沙漠邊緣各綠洲地區分布的古樓蘭鄯善文化、古焉耆文化、古龜茲文化、古于闐文化、古疏勒文化和古高昌文化等，其主要內涵無不與佛教文化有關。考古學家在這些地區發現了許多佛教石窟和佛寺遺址，新疆的佛教石窟藝術，成為新疆中世紀文化藝術的重要組成部分。新疆佛教藝術品主要是壁畫和塑像，包括佛像和供養人像。在這兩個方面人們也可看到外來文化的影響，如：在若羌米蘭佛寺中發現的有翼天使壁畫（圖178）；在于闐、拜城、焉耆等佛寺中發現的各類供養人泥塑頭像，其形象或是突眼張口，或滿頭卷髮，或深目高鼻，梳有髮髻（圖379），明顯具有中亞和西亞人的特徵。但是新疆佛教藝術的主要方面還表現了新疆本地區的傳統藝術風格，如著名的克孜爾石窟（圖429‧430），這是目前在新疆境內保存壁畫數量最多的石窟。壁畫的題材以宏揚佛教為主，但表現手法和風格卻是新疆的藝術傳統。人們從克孜爾石窟壁畫中看到了這些特色，如壁畫中繪的大量佛本生故事畫，佛傳故事畫，說法圖，菩薩像等等，內容是佛教的，但所繪佛和菩薩的形象卻具有古龜茲人的特徵。至於壁畫中還有相當數量的世俗因緣故事畫，各類供養人畫，那就完全是本地人的形象了。又如從繪畫技巧來看，在克孜爾石窟壁畫中，以線條勾畫出人物，突出表現了人物強壯的骨骼和肌肉，同時著色採用了暈染法，使畫面增加了凹凸的立體感。繪畫技法上所使用的這種線描法和凹凸法就是古代著名的新疆畫家尉遲跋質那父子創立的〝屈鐵盤絲〞的繪畫技法傳統。再從克孜爾石窟壁畫的布局來看，克孜爾石窟的畫師們採取了用菱形格畫面，將一組組佛本生故事，繪於一個又一個菱形格畫面中（圖194），更令人感到嘆服的是每個菱形格畫面的邊緣都以山樹來裝飾，讓人感到其畫面既有區分又有聯繫，這種布局是克孜爾石窟在壁畫藝術中獨創的。克孜爾石窟壁畫保存了大量佛本生故事畫，據調查其類型有80種之多，是世界上保存佛本生故事畫最多的地區。而克孜爾石窟在窟形建築上也獨創了〝龜茲石窟形〞。新疆境內石窟佛教藝術的研究，正在引起人們的重視，這是打開古代時期新疆藝術大門的鑰匙，需要進一步的發掘和研究。

到了中國隋唐時期，新疆古代藝術文化又進入了一個新的發展階段。無論在木雕、泥塑、板畫、紙畫、石刻和織造工藝等等方面，都受到了中原隋唐先進文化藝術的影響，出現了新疆古代藝術發展的繁榮時期。人們在吐魯番地區就曾發現大批具有盛唐藝術風格的藝術品，有織錦、絹畫、泥塑、彩繪陶器等等，如在吐魯番古墓中發現的唐朝〝仕女奕棋圖〞絹畫（圖210），係在素面絹綢上繪一貴婦女正手執棋子、神情專注棋盤，作欲下未下之狀。此婦女身著紅底藍黃白小花的織錦衫裙，髮梳高髻，額貼金黃，臉龐塗脂抹粉，畫風細膩，是典型的盛唐藝術風格。與此相似的還有〝舞伎圖〞絹畫（圖214），〝侍馬圖〞絹畫（圖216），都是極其珍貴的絹畫工藝品。在此批古墓中還出土了大量彩色泥塑，其中彩色打馬球俑（圖393），打球手騎在一匹奔馳的駿馬上，手揚球捧正作擊球狀，形象生動逼真，與此同時出土的還有〝牽駝俑〞、〝武士俑〞、〝帶帷帽盛裝女騎馬俑〞、〝舞女俑〞、〝宦官俑〞（圖385），還有〝天王踏鬼俑〞（圖328）、〝人首豹身鎮墓獸〞（圖386）等等，真是色彩斑爛，琳琅滿目，美不勝收，在藝術上都達到了很高的造詣。有意思的是這批泥塑形象有漢人，也有少數民族；有的泥塑如舞女俑和宦官俑，僅頭部和帽冠是泥塑，彩繪臉部，其身軀部分以草把為骨，兩臂用紙條卷成，外穿織綢衫裙袍，舞女還身披織錦或彩紗披巾（圖382）。這種工藝製作技術應是古高昌地區獨創的。

在與此歷史階段大致相當的時期中，新疆民族藝術文化也有獨創性的發展。在新疆遼闊的草原地區有一批相當數量的突厥石人，這些用整塊高達1-2米的沙岩石鑿刻成的石人，有的比真人還大，其中典型的有溫泉阿爾卡特草原石人（圖341），在整塊沙岩石上面雕鑿出一個高約1.9米的石人，臉龐寬闊，顴骨高，上唇蓄八字鬍，身著翻領大衣，腰部束帶，右手持酒杯，舉至胸前，左手按刀劍，腳蹬皮靴，雕鑿刀法粗獷有力，儼然是一位屹立在草原上的威嚴的武士。草原石人，有鑿刻全身的，也有十分簡陋的，只鑿刻出頭部的，中國史料中記載突厥族有用石人作墓碑的埋葬習俗，故草原地區的石人有相當部分應是突厥藝術文化的遺存，是新疆民族藝術中的不朽珍品。古代回鶻人的藝術文化主要發現在今吐魯番和吉木薩爾地區，是西州回鶻汗國時期的遺存，從目前已發表的材料看主要的代表作是在柏孜克里克佛教石窟和北庭故城西大寺中發現的一批供養人壁畫，身著盛裝的回鶻男女貴族手持吉祥花束成群地排列繪在石窟寺院牆面上。貴族男子都穿著窄袖長袍，腰上懸掛各類配件（圖231），但這些貴族男子，頭上所戴的帽子各有不同，有桃形，有扇面形，還有山叉戟形，女貴族則頭戴花冠。在北庭故城西大寺發現的回鶻王和王妃供養畫，也都是各人手持一束吉祥花，王冠為桃形冠，王妃頭戴高桃形花冠，其形態莊嚴高貴，富有王者風度。而在回鶻王畫同一地點發現的《王者出行圖》畫（圖248），畫面戰旗林立，戰馬跳躍，其動態與前幅畫中的靜態恰成對比，這些都是古代回鶻藝術文化中的珍品。令人感到十分有意思的還有他們兩人所穿的錦袍，其錦面花紋為聯珠環形，與波斯薩珊朝所盛行的聯珠紋飾十分相似。古代回鶻藝術從人物造型及其藝術風格，都可看到中原唐朝和中亞地區藝術風格的影響。可惜的是柏孜克里克石窟中的回鶻人壁畫已流散到國外，人們現在只能從已發表的畫冊上一窺其真跡。

　　新疆地區的藝術文化，尤其是伊斯蘭教傳入之後，顯著地受到了伊斯蘭教藝術文化風格的滲透和影響。突出的是至今在新疆境內仍可見到的那些宏偉壯麗的建築，如吐魯番市〝蘇公塔〞（圖443）、霍城縣的〝吐虎魯鐵木耳麻札〞（圖422）、喀什市的〝艾提尕爾清真寺〞（圖438）和〝阿巴霍加麻扎〞（即香妃墓）（圖440），這些建築都用彩色琉璃磚瓦裝飾，外牆和穹窿形塔頂在陽光照射下熠熠發光，顯得莊嚴肅穆，富麗堂皇，這是一批獨具藝術風格的建築紀念物。

　　藝術是人類社會思維文化的形象表現，具有明顯的意識形態的和民族文化的特徵，因此藝術與人類歷史中哲學、宗教、美學、雕塑和繪畫工藝等等都有密切的聯繫，研究藝術、透過藝術，可以使人們了解過去和展望未來。絢麗多彩的新疆藝術，是中國多民族藝術寶庫中的重要組成部分，也是世界藝術文化藝苑中一朵奇葩。

穆舜英　於烏魯木齊新疆文物考古研究所

1993.06.16

Preface

Xinjiang, called the Western Regions in ancient times, is situated in the northwestern part of China. It has an area of 1.6 million square kilometres. It is contiguous to the People's Republic of Mongolia, Russia, Kazakhstan, Kirghizstan, Tajikstan, Afghanistan, Pakistan and India. Xinjiang is the land gateway of China to Central, Western and Southern Asia, and so far as to the Levant through the ancient "Silk Road". This special geographical position makes it not only an important passageway linking up the East and the West, but also a place where the four civilizations of the ancient world met. As a result, the ancient art here are various in style.

Xinjiang has been a multi - ethnical region of China from the time immemorial. During historical ages, it had been inhabited by many peoples,e.g. the grassland north Tianshan was lived by the well - known Rouzhi,Xiongnu(Hun)and Wusun, etc.; the oases south Tianshan lived by the peoples of Qiang, Loulan, Cheshi, Yanqi, Qiuzi, Sule, and Yutian; and later on, Tubo(Tibetan), Kirgiz, Huihe (Ouigour) and Mongolian, etc. Up to now, it has been still inhabited by Uygur, Han, Kazak, Kirgiz, Mongol, Tajik, Hui, Xibe,Manchu, Tatar, Uzbek, Daur and Russian, totaling 13 nationalities. All of them have made important contributions to the development of the civilization in the Western Regions, especially in the field of ancient art.

Art is a reflection of social activities. The works of art produced in all past dynastities can represent the material and vigorous civilizations of that times. As a centre of cultural exchange between the East and the West, Xinjiang has innumberable elegant works of art produced by peoples lived there, which had exerted a tremendous influence to the development of ancient civilizations of the world. Now let us look for the cream of the works of art along the orbit of development of the history and show people the glorious course of the art in the Western Regions.

The history of the ancient art in the Western Regions can be traced back to the latter Paleolithic Age and the Mesolithic period, i.e. 10,000-7,000 years ago, when human can make microstone wares with skills of indirect striking and stripping. The microstone wares of those times are mainly arrowhead, microhead, microspear, microblade and microknife. It was also in this period that bow and arrow were made out, which, as the sign of developement in technic and tools, means that primitive herdism and cultivation appeared, and the seeds of primitive art arose also. It's not only beautiful but also pratical. This is the important characteristic of primitive art, because during the primitive society, people must fight for existence, the works of art are sometimes tools of production.

At the sites of Qijiaojin in Hami and Chaiwopu in Urumqi, we found a kind of necleuses, of which the base was shaped like geometric figures such as awl, column, etc. It has an epoch - making significance, meanwhile gives a sense of beauty.   It means the origin of the primitive art in the Western Regions.

There are some microstone arrowheads and spears shaped like a laurel -leaf (Pl. 2) found at the sites in Lopnor and the Turfan Basin.   Their ends are pointed, middle parts bulged, and surfaces processed in the shape of fish scale, showing some mysterious power. They are the cream of the works of stone art.

During the Neolithic Age (about 5,000~6,000 years ago), a new skill --polishing craft began to be used to process stonewares, and polished stonewares had become a typical characteristic.   Many polished stonewares, such as sickles, axes and bolas etc.   with surface fine and smooth, were unearthed at ancient sites of Xinjiang.   One of them is a jade axe (Pl. 4) which can almost compare favorably with that of modern times.   It represent the technological level of that time.

Among the works of primitive art, a stone penis model, found at the Sidaogou Site in Mori County, was made as trust work of art (Pl. 34).   It makes clear that human began to think about themselves.   It also reflects a kind of thought of reproduction worship.   Some scholars hold that the sites may belong to the Bronze Age because of a little bronze wares such as small blades of flakes unearthed there.

Since the Bronze Age (about 3,000~4,000 years ago), the art of Xinjiang had appeared various local styles.   Many ancient sites of this period were found.   At the graveyard of Gumugou (ancient tombs gully) at the north of the Lopnor near the Peacock River, many stone wares, bonewares, wooden wares,and straw articles, dating to 3,800 years ago, were found.   Among them there are some wooden and stone busts (Pl. 295, 323) and masks crudely made out of proportion.   One is a female which was made of wood and carved crudely with a beautiful face.   Her head is capped with a woollen cap, of which we can see clearly the lines; hair of the back of the head weaved in short braids; breasts plentiful.   All these support important materials for researching the image,custom, and primitive worship of the Gumugou people.   It merits attention that in this area we have never found any earthenware or large bronze ware except two bronze miniflakes.

Later than the times of Gumugou, about 2,600~2,700 years ago, equal to the Spring and Autumn Period, the Warring States Period of China, at many areas in Xinjiang, pottery cultures have been found.   These sites are mainly in Hami and Turfan east Tianshan.   Now some are also found in Yanqi (including Luntai and Kuqa) and the Ili River Basin north Tianshan.

These painted pottery reflect the unique styles of art and culture of different areas or nationalities in the production of wares, the mixture and matching of colors, the pattern arrangements and the variety of patterns and designs.   A number of painted pottery jars with two handles, found in Hami Basin, have black painted patterns on the red coat (Pl. 22, 25, 26).   They were painted all over the surface with red and black matched strikingly. Their patterns include vines, clovers, flameshapes, curves, lozenges, vertical and horizontal lines, triangles filled with broken lines.   The typical shape of the painted pottery found in

Turfan Basin and the valleys of the Tianshan Mountains nearby is painted jar with single handle. They have black or red patterns on the red coat and most of them were painted all over. The patterns are mainly meshes, spirals, leaves. However, among the painted pottery found at Hejing, Luntai in Yanqi Basin and in the area around Kizil reservoir, painted pottery jars or cups with spouts are typical ones. The usual arrangement of decorative patterns is to draw a band slantingly or vertically on one side of the neck or belly (Pl.36). Various patterns and designs are painted within the band. Usually they have red patterns on red coat, but some have white or yellow on red coat first, then have red or purple painted on again. The popular patterns are chessboards, mountains, meshes and various kinds of animal designs and geometric designs. Two of these painted pottery jars bear seldom seen patterns. One is a painted single - handled pottery jar with spout unearthed from the ancient tomb at Chawuhu Gully, Hejing. A row of kneeling two - humped camels were painted around its neck (Pl. 20). The camels are described lively with fine lines and exquistie brushwork. Another one is a painted single - handled pottery jar with spout discovered at the Qunbake Ancient Tombs, Luntai (Pl. 27). The jar bears a person's profile on one side of its belly. The ancient painter drew the figure only with several horizontal, vertical or oblique lines. The skillfulness of his abstract sketching technique is very impressive. The most popular shapes of the painted pottery found in the Ili Valley are pottery ewer with long neck and arc belly, and pottery bowl with low belly and circular bottom. They are painted all over, with red patterns on the red coat. The patterns on them are usually chessboards, lozenges, broken lines, meshes and leaves. When comparing the painted pottery culture of Xinjiang with those of adjoining areas, one can find that the painted pottery found in Hami are very similiar to those found at Huoshaogou Gully, Hexi area in Kansu, both in shape and pattern arrangement. This suggests that the ancient culture of Hexi area had influenced the style of the painted pottery culture in Hami. But the painted pottery found in Turfan and Yanqi, etc. are completely different from those of the painted pottery cultures in Hexi area, Central and Western Asia either in shape or in pattern. They bear their own characteristics of artistic styles. We can see clearly profound realistic nature of their artistic styles from the patterns and designs of these painted pottery. Some designs are obviously influenced by the mountains and basins in Xinjiang and fishing, hunting and herding life style. The subject of art always comes from the object of life, and this is the origin of the realistic artistic style. The development of the painted pottery culture of Xinjiang is a wonderful work of the ancient art in Xinjiang, and different artistic styles of the painted pottery cultures in various areas reflect the multi - ethnical characteristic in ancient Xinjiang and the development of art in different manners and regions.

Almost at the same time, there appeared two sorts of artistic forms. One is the rock carving found at the great mountain system of Xinjiang, namely the Altay Mountains in the north, the Tianshan Mountains in the middle and the Kunlun and Altun Mountains in the south. Mostly distributed on the cliffs around Alpin ranches, mid - high and low mountainous areas etc., these notable rock carvings are the artistic and cultural remains of the ancient nomadic peoples in Xinjiang. The rock carvings were incised on the surfaces of cliffs in broad lines. Occasionally, they were found inside caves. The usual subjects of rock carvings are the pictures of animals and secenes of herding and hunting.The animal figures are chiefly deer, goats, horses, wolves and cows. It's very interesting that the pictures of carriages have also been found. The carriage usually was described as two circles with a linking line, sometimes a driver was drown on it. The primitive and simple style was fully revealed in these pictures. The most striking discovery is the great - sized"re-production worshipping" rock carving found in Kangjiashimenzi, Hutubi County, in the southwest of the Tianshan Mountains in 1987. Located at 43° 51' N and 86° 19' E with an elevation of 1500m, the picture was engraved on the cliff 10m square metres with almost 300 male and female figures, standing or lying, dressed or naked. They are dancing or having sex. The exaggerated description makes the subject of the picture displayed impressively. It tops the rock carvings in Xinjiang both in size and the number of figures (Pl. 155,156,157, 158). This rarely seen rock carving bears high social and artistic values and has been noticed widely by scholars.But the date of the rock carvings in Xinjiang remain a complicate problem.

Another artistic form is the bronze works found at the Ili Valley. A great number of large- sized bronzes have been discovered here since the 1980s.These bronzes, especially the group of bronzes including figures of warrior, twin-tiger necklace, winged twin -beast and twin -beast tray with high base found in Xinyuan County and man-camel tray in Zhaosu County, are seldom-seen treasures of bronze art. The figure of warrior (Pl. 74), H. 40cm, W. 3kg, was made by pouring and welding. With the upper part of his body naked and an apron on the lower part of the body, the warrior is in the gesture of squatting, wearing a wide-brimmed hat with a conic top. This bronze figure of warrior, in the image of certain minority people, was shaped vividly. He looks forward seriously with his hands in the gesture of holding something in front of his chest. This bronze figure, along with the bronze twin-tiger necklace (Pl. 76) and the bronze winged twin-beast necklace (Pl. 77) are the only ones found in Xinjiang. These two roughly-made neck-laces, about 30cm in diameter and 5cm in thickness, seem to be the symbol of the power of the leaders of ancient tribes. At both ends of the twin-tiger necklace there are two figures of tigers glaring at each other. The twin-beast necklace is similiar with the twin-tiger neckalce both in basic shape and method of making, i. e. pouring. The bronze twin-beast tray with high base has also been found at the Alagou Ancient Tombs, Nanshan, Turfan Basin (Pl. 75). It has two small beasts cast on the top and a horn-shaped high base. Its parallels have been found in Central Asia too. They were regarded as the remains of Sakas, or the religious implements of Zoroastrianism. The discovery of these bronze works shows that the technique of melting and casting had been fully developed in the bronze culture era of Xinjiang, It also provides precious testimony for us to recognize and study the artistic style of the bronze culture of the prairie in northern Xinjiang. The bronze culture of the prairie in the Ili Valley is probably related to those of Central and Western Asia very closely.

Recently, a group of double-handled bronze caldrons with deep belly and high legs have been found in the Tianshan Mountains.　The height of these large- sized caldrons is usually up to 50-60cm　(Pl. 79,80,81).　Obviously, it requires excellent technique to make the bronzes in this size by pouring.　The artistic variations made by ancient craftsmen, usually on the double handles and lips of the caldrons, endow these bronzes with pure beauty, however, some similar bronzes found in Central and Western Asia are mainly household utensils.

Besides, a number of bronze plaques with animal designs possessing strong artistic style of Ordos have been found in Xinjiang. Mainly discovered in Hami, Barkol, Turfan, Mori, etc. , these bronze plaques were made exquisitely with hollowed-out figures of wild boars, tigers and horses. Among them, the bronze plaque with wild boar design (Pl.88), the bronze plaque with fighting wild boar and camel design (Pl. 83) and the tiger-shaped gilded bronze plaque (Pl. 87),etc., are all seldom-seen artistic treasures.　In brief, all of these bronze plaques are outstanding works of ancient Xinjiang bronze art.

The numerous forms of ancient Xinjiang art, e. g., the primitive stone art, the painted pottery art, the rock carving art and the bronze art all reflect the rich and colorful artistic tradition and the multi-ethnical characteristic of Xinjiang's history.　They prove that all peoples in Xinjiang have created and reserved their own everlasting art on the wide historical stage of Xinjiang.

After the 2nd century B.C., Xinjiang art went into a new historical period.The opening-up of the "Silk Road" and the development of the commerce and trade promoted the direct economic and cultural interflows between the East and the West. Some excellent works of art from Central, Western and Southern Asia, and so far as the Mediteranean regions were introduced into the interior of China via Xinjiang.　Meanwhile, the traditional art of China was introduced into the West.　Not only the silk fabrics of China in the Han Dynasty, but also the woollens with marked artistic style of the West were found in Xinjiang, e.g., from some silk fabrics of the Latter Han found at Loulan Site on the ancient Silk Road, we can see the high level of spinning and weaving of the Latter Han; on the other hand, from the patterns of two pieces of woollens unearthed from a tomb at Sampula Cemetery, Lop County, we can see clearly the cultural influence of the West.　The former was woven with designs of tree- branches, rattan, cloud and patterns of birds and beasts such as tigers, dragons, leopards, duck, peacocks, chickens, etc. In addition, some of which were decorated with chinese characters such as "永昌"(Pl. 261)"長壽明光"(Pl. 262)"延年益壽大宜子孫"(PL. 258),etc.　All of these had meanings of lucky in ancient China, reflecting the cultural and artistic styles of China.　Silk fabrics of this kind were also found at Minfeng County and Yuli County. The latter (Pl. 267, 268)were decorated with centaur design which was from a tale of Rome or Greece, and warrior design.　The warrior with deep eyes and high nose, fore head tied a white band, and a long spear by the side, had clearly the feature of the white race. This kind of woollens are seldom seen on the "Silk Road".　There is still more a cotton fabric found at Niya Site, Minfeng County.　This is a piece of blue cotton cloth (Pl.260) with designs of a boddhisttva figure on the upper and a dragon tail (head was damaged) on the lower.   Cotton fabric first originates from Eastern Africa.   Later it was introduced into India and China.   The Buddhism was introduced into China in the lst century A.D. From this, we can say that the style of patterns of this cotton fabric was influenced by ancient Indian culture.   One of the characteristics of the ancient art of Xinjiang is that the works of art were influenced by both the cultures of the East and West.

After the 2nd and 3rd century B.C., the Buddhist culture originated from India spread to all parts of Xinjiang and greatly influenced the art and culture in Xinjiang.   The ancient culture of Loulan, Shanshan, Yanji, Kuqa, Hotan, Shule and Gaochang scattered over the oases along the rim of the desert in Southern Xinjiang, are related to Buddhist culture invariably. Many sites of Buddhist grottoes and temples have been found in these areas by archaeologists.   Indeed, the Buddhist grotto art has become an important part of the art and culture in medieval Xinjiang.   The main works of Xinjiang Buddhist art are wall paintings and clay figures, including figures of Buddha and donors.   These two artistic forms reveal the external influences.   For instance, the wall paintings of winged angels have been found at the Buddist temples in Khotan, Baicheng and Yanqi bear the characteristics of the people in Central and Western Asia with deep-set eyes, high-bridged noses and curved hair, etc. (Pl. 379).   But the main stream of the Buddist art in Xinjiang is traditional local artistic style, such as the famous Kizil Grottoes (Pl. 429,430).   Kizil Grottoes rank lst within Xinjiang in the number of the wall paintings preserved.   Although the subjects of the wall paintings concentrate on expanding the Buddhism, the technique and style of expression belong to the artistic tradition of Xinjiang.   For example, even the figures of Buddha and boddhisattvas in the wall paintings of Kizil Grottoes have the characteristic of ancient Kucha people, not to mention the figures in the pictures of donors and secular stories.   They are completely the figures of native people.   Farther more, the technique of painting applied in the wall paintings of Kizil Grottoes is the traditional technique pioneered by the famous painters in ancient Xinjiang, i.e. Yuchibazhina and his son, and the rhomboid seperation of the pictures of the wall paintings is the unique method of the traditional arrangement in Kizil Grottoes (Pl. 194).   Finally, the shape of the grottoes in Kizil painting is unparalleled, known as the Qiuzi Grottoes type.   According to investigation, more than eighty pictures of Jataka stories have been preserved in the wall paintings, and this ranks Kizil Grottoes lst area in the world in the variety of the preserved pictures of Jakata stories. Today, more and more attention is paid on the research of the Buddhist Grotto art in Xinjiang.

The ancient art and culture of Xinjiang entered a new phase of development.   During the Sui and Tang Dynasties, the developed art and culture of the Central Plains pushed the ancient art of Xinjiang forward with influences on wooden carving, clay sculpture, wall painting, painting on wooden board, paper painting, silk painting, stone inscription and weaving, etc.   Many works of art with the artistic style of the Prosperous Tang Period have been found in Turfan, such as brocades, silk paintings, clay sculptures, painted pottery, golden and silver objects.   A typical case is the silk painting of a beautiful woman playing chess(Pl. 210).   This exquisitely painted picture, along with the silk paintings of a rich dressed woman

(Pl. 214)and a groom leading a horse (Pl. 216)show the typical artistic style of the Prosperous Tang Period vividly. They are all precious works of art. There are also numerous painted clay sculptures found in Turfan. Among them, the figure of a man playing polo is all true to life and shows great vitality and vividness (Pl. 393). In the meantime, figures of a man leading a camel, warriors, female riders, dancers, officials (Pl. 385), lokapalas (Pl. 328)and tomb guards (Pl. 386), etc., have been found here too. It's very interesting that these clay sculptures include both figures of Han people and minorities. It also should be mentioned that some clay sculptures found in ancient Gaochang area, such as figures of dancers, are very special. Their heads and hats are made by clay, bodies mainly by straw, hands by twisted papers and their faces were painted in colours. They are all dressed in silk, and female dancers have brocade draped over their shoulders and colorful gauze shawls (Pl. 382). This technique is an original creation in ancient Gaochang area.

Almost during the same historical period, the national art and culture of Xinjiang developed too. There are quite a few of Turkic stone status found in the wide prairie of Xinjiang. They usually were made out of pieces of sandy rock, one to two meters high. Some of the statues are taller than real person. The stone statue found in Aerkate grassland, Wenquan (Pl. 341) is typical among them. Made out of a whole piece of sandy rock, this 1. 9m high statue has handlebar moustaches, a broad face and prominent cheekbones. He wears coats with upturned collars and a belt around the waist, and stands in boots with the right hand holding a cup, and the left hand resting on a sword. He looks just like a majestic warrior standing erectly on the grassland. Some stone statues were carved completely, while others were simply cut out with only head being recognized. According to Chinese historical custom of having stone statue as gravestone, most of the stone statues found in the prairie of Xinjiang are probably the remains of ancient Turkic art and culture. They are immortal masterpieces of the art and culture of Xinjiang. The art and culture of ancient Uighurs, i. e. the remains of ancient Xizhou (Khocho) Uighurian Kingdom, are mainly discovered in Turfan and Jimsa. In Bezeklik Grottoes and Western Temple, Beting Ancient City, a number of the wall pintings of donors have been found. The figures of rich dressed Uighurian noblemen and noblewomen were painted in rows on the walls of the grottoes and temple with lucky flowers in their hands. The noblemen wear long robes with narrow sleeves and various pendants at their waists (Pl. 231). The shape of these noblemen's hats varies interestingly, while those noblewomen all have high garlands in the shape of peach. The Uighurian King and his concubine in the picture found at Beting Xidasi (ancient temple) hold a bunch of lucky flowers respectively. The still atmosphere in this picture contrasts finely with the picture of a king in procession found at the same place (Pl. 248). The latter has a strong atmosphere of moving with countless battle banners and leaping horses. Both of the pictures are the treasures of ancient Uighurian art and culture. The shape of figures and the artistic style of ancient Uighurian art all reflect the influences from the Central Plains and Central Asia. Unfortunately, Uygurian wall paintings in Bezeklik Grottoes have scattered abroad, We only can get a glimpse of these arthentic works in some picture albums.

The art and culture of Xinjiang in latter period, especially after Islam spreading to Xinjiang, Were strongly in fluenced by Islamic art and culture. The glaring examples are the Emin Minaret and Mosque found in Turfan (Pl. 443), the Tuguluk—Temur Mazar in Huocheng (Pl. 422), the Idkah Mosque (Pl. 438) and the Apakhoja Tomb (Pl. 440) in Kashgar. All of these structures, decorated with colorful mosaics, show high artistic quality. They are memorial structures with unique artistic style.

Art is a vivid reflection of the intellectual culture of human society. It is closely related to philosophy, religions, aesthetics, sculpture and painting. We can understand the past and look into the future by studying art. The colorful art of Xinjiang is an important part of the national art of our country as well as a wonderful work of the art and culture of the world.

Mu Shunying
(Xinjiang Institute of Archaeology)

圖　版
Photo

石器

在人類物質文明史上，石器時代是一個漫長的歷史發展階段。它經歷了舊石器、中石器和新石器三個文化時期。迄今為止，新疆尚未發現舊石器時代的文化遺存，而屬於中石器至新石器段代的遺物，在天山南北都有所發現。如阿勒泰、喀什噶爾、玉龍喀什等河流域，吐魯番、哈密盆地和羅布泊地區。其中吐魯番盆地和羅布泊地區的細石器文化延續時間長，內容豐富。新疆石器工藝的出現，其歷史可追溯到距今約一萬年至七千年的中石器時代。

新疆中石器時代文化的主要特徵是打製的石器比較細小，器形主要有細石片、石葉、石核、石球等。從所見的石器可以看出，古人系選擇具有一定硬度和韌性的隧石、石英等自然石塊為原料加工製作成細石器，除具有實用價值之外，還具有樸素的審美觀念。如石葉形體多窄而長，正面都有單脊或雙脊，斷面呈三角形或梯形；有的將一端修整成尖狀器，有的則截取一端或兩端作復合工具上的鑲嵌物之用。石片石器有長刮削器、尖狀器等，其中最典型、最具藝術特徵的石器是「桂葉形」、「柳葉形」的石鏃和石矛，採用間接壓剝法進行加工、修整，工藝精細。石鏃和石矛尖端犀利，造型對稱，橫剖面呈三角狀，鏃面通體壓剝呈波浪紋或魚鱗紋，具有樸素的原始藝術美。其中圓錐形、圓柱形和石球等幾何體的石器，對於原始藝術的發展更有普遍的意義。

隨著農耕文化的興起，石材的選擇和石器製作工藝更趨成熟。如石斧的石材硬度大，石鋤則選用長條形的石塊，石刀和石鏃多取材於片頁岩，以便剝離成片狀進行加工。這時期，石器的打製、琢製、磨製以及鑽孔等工藝都有很大進步，應用對稱法則，使各類石器的造型更趨勻稱。如疏勒出土的石鏃、石刀，造型比例合理、弧背凹刃、通體磨光，既實用又美觀。喀什、塔城等地出土的石鋤造型，富有原始粗獷的工藝美。值得特別提及的是和碩、樓蘭等地發現的玉斧，它們的出現是在長期石器製作中對材料性能的掌握以及審美能力提高的產物。玉斧光潤、鋒利，用青玉或白玉磨製而成，造型古樸，不僅是一件實用的生產工具，無疑也是一件新疆早期的藝術珍品，使人充分感受到規則和樸素的美感。

（圖 PL，002）

STONE IMPLEMENT

The cultural remains of Palaeolithic Age have not been found in Xinjiang so far, but there found the remains of Mesolithic Age and Neolithic Age both in the north and south of the Tianshan Mountains. The microlithic cultures found in the Turfan Basin and Lopnur area went on for a long period and had substantial content. The history of the stone implement techhnique in Xinjiang can be traced back to Mesolithic Age between 10,000-7,000 years ago.

The main character of the Mesolithic Culture in Xinjiang is that chipped stone tools, mainly tiny flakes, leaves, cores, bolas, etc. are comparatively fine. The stone implements which have been found already show that the microlithes made out of relatively hard and tough flint quartz by ancient people carry not only practical value, but also unaffected aesthetic ideas. Usually stone leaves are long and narrow. Their obverses are single-ridged or double-ridged, and their sections are often triangular or trapezoid. Some were made into pointed implements with one end being pointed, while others had one end or both ends cut so as to be inlaid on complex tools. Stone flakes include long scrapers, pointed implements and so on. Among them, laurel-leaf-shaped and willow-leaf-shaped implements are typical ones and bear most artistic characteristics, such as stone arroowheads and spears. Finely made and polished by the method of indirect chipping, stone arrowheads and spears have sharp ends, symmetrical shapes and triangular cross sections. Stone implements in geometrical shapes, such as cones, cylinders and bolas, are especially important for the development of primitive art.

Along with the rise of agriculture, the skills of material-choosing and implement-making became more and more mature. For example, materials for stone axes were harder than before, oblong stones were chosen to make stone hoes, and schist was used for stone knives and sickles. As a result of the appliance of the rule of symmetry, the shapes of various kinds of stone implements became more proportional. So they are practical as well as beautiful. The stone hoes found in Kashgar and Tacheng are rich in rough beauty of primitive art. Besides, jade axes found in Hoxud and Loulan should be mentioned here. These axes were smoothly and sharply polished out of green or white jades with antique taste in their shapes. They are not only practical tools, but also early artistic treasures of Xinjiang.

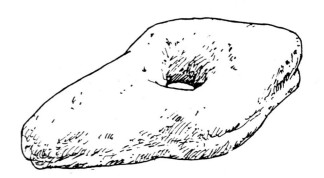

（圖 PL，010）

石器 *Stone Implement*

001 石鏃 Microlithic Arrowheads

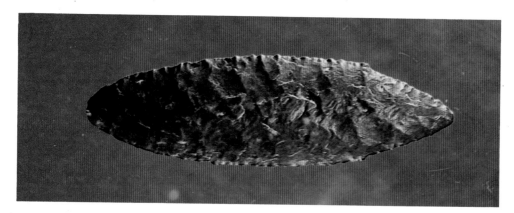

002 桂葉形石矛 Stone Spearhead

003 石球 Bola

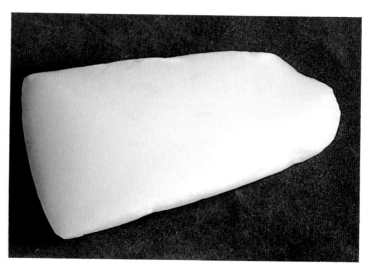

004 白玉斧 White Jade Axe

006　三角形石鋤　The Stone Hoe in the Triangle Shape

007　石鋤　Stone Hoe

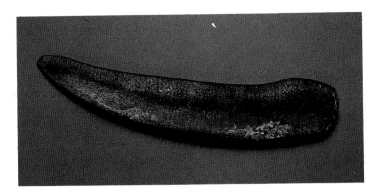

008　石鐮　Stone Sickle

010　鶴嘴鋤　Stone Hoe in the Shape of Crane-Mouth

009　青玉斧　Blue Jade Axe

陶器

　　陶器是古代人們日常生活中必不可少的器物，陶器藝術是新疆古代藝術的主要組成部份。迄今為止的考古發現表明，早在新疆石器時代和青銅時代，新疆陶器就已顯示出豐富多彩的文化面貌和不同的地方風格。在阿爾泰克爾木齊、塔城衛校、木壘四道溝、和碩新塔拉古遺址，出土了新疆最早的陶器，距今有3000年以上的歷史。塔里木盆地沿天山一帶，天山以北和以東的綠洲，如拜城、輪台、和靜、烏魯木齊、吐魯番、哈密、伊吾、巴里坤、木壘、奇台，以及伊犁河流域都出土過彩陶器；而北疆的阿勒泰、塔里木南緣的喀什、和闐等地則未見彩陶出土，這是新疆陶器藝術中的一個地方特點。而北疆和南疆各地出土彩陶的造型與紋樣，都各有些不同，與中亞、西亞和中原相比較，又有根本的區別。東疆地區的哈密的彩陶造型和裝飾藝術，則明顯受到甘青地區彩陶的影響。阿勒泰、塔城的彩陶造型和紋飾又顯然不同，極富地方特色。這些在陶質、陶色和造型方面的特點，正是新疆古代的地理環境、經濟條件和民族文化等差異而顯示出的不同風格。

　　新疆出土彩陶器中有一些共同的特點，如均為手製，夾砂，火候較低，陶胎為磚紅色，器形主要是罐、盆、盤、杯、鉢、豆等，多在器表施紅色陶衣，繪黑彩，也有少量敷施白、黃色陶衣，繪紫色或紅色彩。較典型的紋飾圖案是以粗細、曲折的線條組成的三角紋、網格紋、曲波紋等多變的幾何形紋為主題，繁縟多變的紋樣和豐富的色彩，表現出彩陶淳厚質樸的情感和完美的藝術形式。如新疆和靜察吾乎溝出土的彩陶，其裝飾手法採取疏與密、斜與正的相互陪襯，表現出暗中透亮的鮮明層次。使彩陶紋飾靈活多變，具有很強的感染力，是古代新疆彩陶藝術中水平較高的作品。

　　隨著社會生產的發展和文化交流，新工藝、形式的陶器不斷湧現。如吐魯晉——唐古墓出土的陶器，均為輪製，並在陶器表面施敷黑地上用紅、白、藍等色繪出蓮花、卷雲等圖案。反映出高昌地區魏晉以來受中原文化的影響。

　　南北朝、隋唐時期，新疆各地製陶工藝中出現了模製陶器和外來裝飾紋樣，尤其是波斯藝術的影響和佛教文化的影響。在庫車、巴楚、喀什、和闐等地出土了許多造型新穎、裝飾繁縟的陶器藝術品。其中和闐出土的裝飾陶器，陶土細膩、純淨，火候高，罐、壺和小玩具等，造型和貼塑的裝飾，構思精巧，人和動物的形象寫實，具有濃郁的生活氣息。宋元時期產生的低溫釉陶器和瓷器，不僅是生活中的實用器物，同時也成為建築裝飾材料而用於美化生活了。

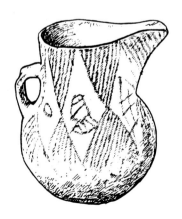

（圖 PL，035）

POTTERY

Pottery was indispensable for ancient people. Pottery art was a main part of the ancient art in Xinjiang. Archaeological finds so far have revealed that the pottery in Xinjiang showed their rich cultural features and different local styles, as early as Stone Age and Bronze Age. The pottery art of Xinjiang has its own characteristics. The oldest pottery of Xinjiang, dating to 3000 years ago, were unearthed from Altay, Tachen, Mori, Hoxud. The painted pottery were only found in the rim of the Tarim Basin along the Tianshan Mountains, the oases in the north and east of the Tianshan Mountains, such as Baicheng, Luntai, Hejing, Urumqi, Turfan, etc. and the Ili Valley; whereas there were no painted pottery found in Altay ,Kashgar and Hotan. The painted pottery found in northern and southern Xinjiang bear varied styles in figure and design according to their locations and are completely different from those of Central and Eastern Asia and inner China. This reflects the diference of geological circumstances, economical conditions and national cultures in ancient Xinjiang.

But, the painted pottery unearthed from Xinjiang enjoy many common characteristics. They are all made of red clay mixed with sand and all by hand. The popular figures are pottery jars, pots, cups, bowls and stemmed vessels. They usually have black painted patterns on the red coats. Occasionally the coat is white or yellow. The typical patterns are triangles, chessboards and curves. The painted pottery found in Chawuhu Gully,Hejing, can be regarded as high level works of the painted pottery art in ancient Xinjiang.

Along with the developing of social production and cultural communication, pottery in new crafts and styles appeared continually. During the Southern and Northern Dynasties and the Sui, Tang Dynasties, model-made pottery and exotic patterns were introduced into Xinjiang. Persian art and Buddhist culture had strong influences, and many pottery works of art in novel shaqes and patterns were found in Kucha, Bachu ,Kashgar, Hotan, etc. Till the Song and Yuan Dynasties, glazed pottery and porcelain of low temperature were made. They were not only practical implements but also building materials.

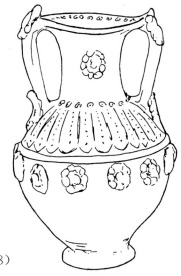

（圖 PL ,058）

陶器 *Pottery*

011　複彩波浪紋彩陶豆　Painted Pottery Dou (stemmed dish)

012　敞口帶流束頸圓腹壺　Pottery Jar with a Wide Flared Mouth

013　幾何紋單耳帶流杯　Painted Pottery Cup with a Single Handle and a Spout

014　夾砂灰陶杯　Grey Pottery Cups

015　倒三角狀錐刺紋陶杯　Pottery Cup with
Triangle Designs

016　四口鼓腹罐　Pottery Pot With Four Mouths (damaged)

017　水波紋環底罐　Stamped Pottery Jar

018　植物紋彩陶罐　Handleless Painted Pottery Pot

019　長流單耳陶杯　Pottery Jug with a Single Handle and a Spout

020　臥駝紋單耳帶流彩陶罐　Painted Pottery Jar with Lying Camel Decorative Design (damaged)

021　變形鳥紋單耳帶流彩陶杯　Painted Pottery Cup with a Single Handle

022 三葉草紋雙耳彩陶罐　Painted Pottery Jar with Double Handles

023 單耳彩陶鉢　Painted Pottery Bowl

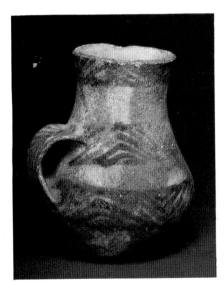

024 環帶折線單耳彩陶壺　Painted Pottery Jar with a Single Handle

025 長頸雙耳彩陶壺　Painted Pottery Pot with a Long Neck and Double Handles

026 連續波狀紋貫耳壺　Painted Pottery Pot with Double Horizonal Ring Handles

028　垂幛紋帶流罐　Pottery Jar with a Single Handle and a Spout

027　高流大彩陶罐　Pottery Jar With a Large　Spout

030　直筒單耳彩陶杯　Painted Pottery Cup with a Single Handle and Flat Belly

029　山川紋彩陶釜　Painted Pottery Jar

031　條紋單耳彩陶杯　Painted Pottery Cup with a Single Handle

032　葫蘆形單耳壺　Pottery Pitcher in the Shape of a Gourd

034　單耳彩陶鉢　Painted Pottery Bowl with a Single Handle

033　長頸壺　Long-necked Pottery Flask

036 斜帶彩陶杯 Painted Pottery Cup

035 人頭像單耳帶流彩陶罐 Painted Pottery Jar with a Spout and Human Figure Decoration

037 單耳彩陶豆 Painted Pottery Dou (Stemmed Dish)

038 弧形三角紋單耳彩陶罐 Painted Pottery Jar with a Single Handle

039 條網紋單耳彩陶罐 Painted Pottery Jar with a Single Handle

041 三角紋渦紋單耳彩陶罐 Painted Pottery Jar with a Single Handle

040 樹叉紋單耳彩陶罐 Painted Pottery Jar with a Single Handle

042　折線紋彩陶壺　Painted Pottery Pot

043　繭形陶壺　Cocoon-shaped Pottery Flask

044　雙孔陶燭台　Pottery Candle Stand with Two Holders

045　連續幾何圖紋鼓腹彩陶壺　Painted Pottery Pot

047 高腹彩陶壺 Painted Pottery Pot

046 網紋單耳彩陶杯 Painted Pottery Cup with a
Single Handle

048 網格紋短頸彩陶罐 Handleless Painted
Pottery Pot

049 樹枝紋彩陶鉢 Painted Pottery Bowl

051　黑陶杯　Pottery Cup with Black Slip

050　黑陶壺　Pottery Pot with Black Slip

053　人面紋細嘴單耳壺　Single - handled Pottery Pot

052　桑葉紋陶壺　Pottery Pot with Incised Decoration

054　雙系扁陶壺　Oblate Pottery Amphora

055　三耳人物罐　Three-Handled Pottery Vase

056　人頭像殘陶片　Pottery Shard with Brahman Figure
　　　Decoration

057　敞口陶薰爐　Pottery Incensory

37

058 貼花雙耳瓶 Pottery Vase with Two Handles and Embossed Decoration

059 猴耳條紋壺 Pottery Jug

060 單耳壺 Pottery Jar with a Single Handle

061 單耳彩繪陶罐 Painted Pottery
pitcher with a Single Handle

062 陶虎子 Pottery Urinal

063 陶博山爐 Pottery Boshan Incensory

065 喙形嘴單耳壺 Pottery Pitcher with a Bird-head-shaped Mouth

064 雙耳黑陶罐 Pottery Jar

067　敛口舍利罐　Pottery Sarira Casket with a Contracted Mouth

068　筒形陶棺　Pottery Coffin

066　人面花瓣贴塑舍利罐　Pottery Sarira Vase with Embossed Decoration

069　彩绘舍利罐　Painted Pottery Sarira Casket

070　龍紋青瓷盤　Celadon Plate

071　龍泉青瓷碗　Celadon Bowl of Longquan Ware

072　山鳥紋黃褐釉陶壺　Yellowish-Brown Glazed
Pottery Vase

073　山水畫青花瓷瓶　Blue and White Porcelain Vase

銅器 （附金銀器）

　　銅器的出現，標誌著人類社會進入了一個新的時代。約在距今3000—2500年左右，在新疆的許多遺址中都發現了銅刀、銅鏃、銅錐、銅斧、銅鏡、銅馬具，以及銅質的各種裝飾品，並發現了採掘銅礦的礦井和冶煉銅塊的窰址。

　　值得注意的是，近年在伊犁地區的新源、察布查爾，天山北麓的巴里坤、奇台、烏魯木齊等地，發現了一些距今約2500年左右的大型青銅器皿，如銅鼎、獸足銅盤、圈足銅鍑、承獸銅盤、獸形銅項圈等，風格獨特、鑄造工藝精湛，實為國內所罕見。

　　在東疆地區所發現的早期銅器中，有一種以動物題材為造型裝飾藝術的實用品。主要表現在銅牌、銅鏡或者是銅刀柄部。這些浮雕、圓雕以及透雕的動物造型，多以簡練、樸拙的線條來刻劃各種動物的外形輪廓。如鹿首柄飾弧背銅刀、羊形柄銅鏡，都反映了草原民族對動物的特殊感情。還如裝飾藝術品：木壘發現的野豬搏馬紋銅飾牌，在長13寬6.5厘米的邊框內，一隻野豬低頭伸頸咬住馬的右前腿，而左面的馬咬住野豬的肩部，力的較量充滿著畫面，是一件造型生動的鄂爾多斯風格的藝術品。

　　公元前126年以後，隨著「絲綢之路」的開通與發展，進一步促進了東西方科技文化間的交流。如中原的銅鏡，中亞兩河流域、伊朗和西亞的金銀器皿，以及佛教、摩尼教等宗教題材的金銀、銅造像在新疆各地都有出土。如烏魯木齊南山礦區古墓出土的金器，其模壓成型的獅、虎等動物造型甚美，雄獅前爪後收騰空躍起，張口揚鬃，生動活潑。阿合奇縣古墓出土的打模的金馬和鑄造的金鷹鹿飾品，都是這一時期黃金工藝品的瑰寶，還有焉耆出土的銀盤，藝術構思新奇高超，中心鏨刻一隻駝鳥，周圍同向環繞6隻姿態各異的駝鳥，栩栩如生，是一件精美的工藝品。這些都是通過「絲綢之路」東西方經濟文化交流的實物見證。

　　新疆青銅文化，代表了當時生產力發展的水平，反映了當時的社會意識形態。其鑄造工藝、造型和紋樣等具有自身的特點，同時也表現出融匯了東西文化而形成的藝術風格。

（圖 PL,077）

BRONZE (including golden and silver objects)

The appearance of bronzes marks a new era of human society. In Xinjiang, bronze knives, arrowheads, awls, axes, mirrors, harness, and ornaments were found in many sites of 3000-2500 years ago. There also found sites of ancient mines and smelters.

Recently, several kinds of large-sized bronzes of 2500 years ago were found in Xinyuan and Qapqal in Ili area, Barkol, Qitai and Urumqi in the north of the Tianshan Mountains. These bronzes, including bronze tripods, basins with animal-leg-shaped legs, cauldrons, trays and animal-shaped necklaces, were made exquistily with unique styles.

Among the early bronzes found in eastern Xinjiang, there is one type of practical articles in animal figures. The patterns are mainly on bronze plaques, mirrors and handles of knives. Animal figures were usually sketched with pithy and simple lines. They reflect the special feelings of nomadic people to animals. Another type is ornament. For example, the bronze plaque with wild boar and horse patterns found in Mori bears the strong artistic style of Ordos.

After 126 B.C. along with the open-up and development of the Silk Road, the cultural communication between the East and West was deepened. Bronze mirrors from China, golden and silver objects from Central, Western Asia and Iran, and bronze, golden and silver statues of Buddhist, Manichean contents have been found all over Xinjiang. Golden objects found in Urumqi, such as mould-madelions, tigers, etc. and in Akqi, such as mould-made horses and cast eagles,etc. are most precious jewel of golden articles of that time, not to say the silver tray found in Yanji. These are all material testimony of economical and cultural communication between the East and West through the Silk Road.

The bronze art of Xinjiang represents the developing level of the productive forces then and reflect the social ideoloical form of that time. Its characteristics in casting technique, figure and pattern revcal the artistic styles of both the eastern and western cultures.

（圖 PL，145）

銅器
Bronze

銅武士俑 Bronze Figure
of a Warrior

075　高方座承獸銅盤　Bronze Tray with High Base

076　對虎銅頸圈　Bronze Necklace

077　對翼獸銅頸圈　Bronze Necklace Decorated with Double Winged Animals

078　三足銅鼎　Copper Cauldron with Three Legs

079　雙耳高足銅鍑　Bronze Cauldron with Two Upright Handles and a Circular Leg

080　雙耳高足銅鍑　Copper Cauldron

081　雙耳高足銅鍑　Bronze Cauldron

082　獸首吞蹄式足雙耳銅方盤　Bronze Tray

083 野豬博馬紋銅飾牌　Copper Plaque

084 雙鳥形銅扣　Bronze Buckle

085 虎噬羊銅牌　Bronze Plaque

086 雙羊銅飾牌　Bronze Plaque

087 包金虎形銅牌、金箔　Copper Plaques Decorated with Tigers' Patterns & Golden Leaves

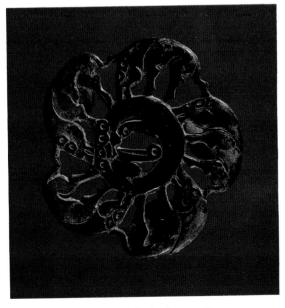

088 野豬紋透雕團形銅飾牌　Copper Plaque

089　銅斧　Bronze Axe

090　銅斧　Bronze Axe

091　銅斧　Bronze Axe

092　銅錛　Bronze Adzes

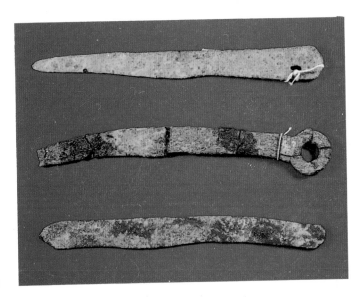

093 銅刀 Bronze Knives

094 銅馬銜 Copper Hamess

095 豎銎銅斧 Bronze Axe with a Perpendicular Handle

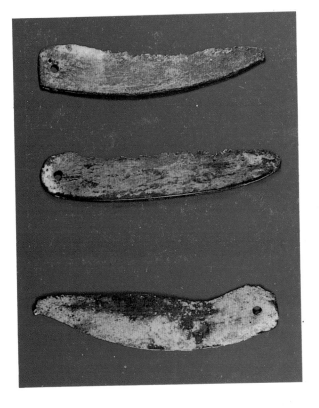

096 銅鐮 Bronze Sickles

49

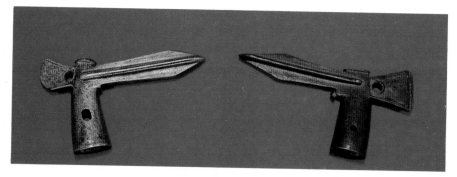

097　銅戈　Copper Dagger - Axes

098　折背羊首柄銅刀　Bronze Knife

099　熊首青銅刀　Bronze Knife

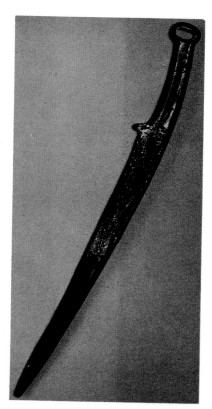

100　弧背鹿首銅刀　Bronze Knife

101　環首銅刀　Bronze Knife

50

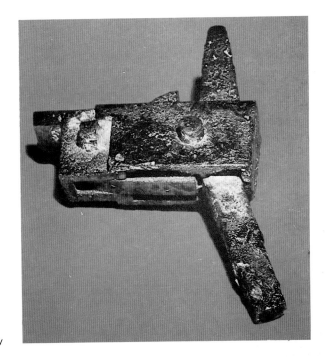

102　銅弩機　Bronze Crossbow

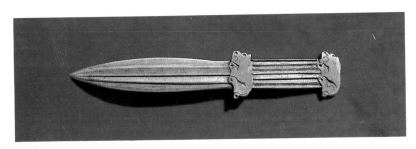

103　野豬柄短劍　Short Sword

104　小銅矛　Small　Bronze Spearhead

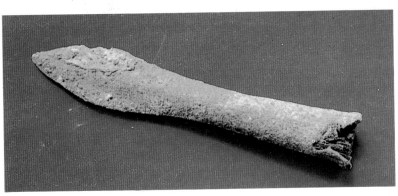

105　銅矛　Bronze Spearhead

106　銅鏃　Copper Arrow - Heads

107 蜷獸紋銅鏡 Copper Mirror Decorated with a Curly Animal Pattern

108 直柄銅鏡 Copper Mirror with a Handle

109 羊飾柄銅鏡 Copper Mirror with a Sheep-Shaped Handle

110 厚緣銅鏡 Copper Mirror

52

111 四神規矩鏡 Copper Mirror

112 許由繅父故事鏡 Copper Mirror with the Story of Xuyou and Saofu

113 柳毅傳書故事鏡 Copper Mirror with the Story of Liuyi

114 草獸紋銅鏡 Copper Mirror Decorated with the Patterns of Plants and Beasts

115 仙騎鏡 Copper Mirror

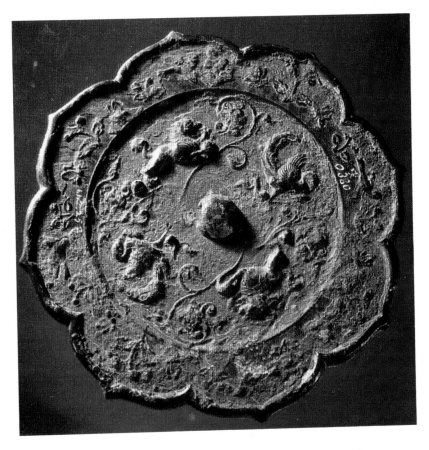

116 瑞獸鸞鳥鏡 Copper Mirror Decorated with Birds and Beasts Patterns

117　銅坐佛像　Seated Buddha

118　鍍金銅佛頭　Head of Buddha

119　銅摩尼神像　Cooper Figure of Mani　　120　鎏金金剛騎馬像　Vajrapani

121　鎏金銅菩薩坐像　Seated Bodhisattva

122　銅立佛像　Standing Buddha

123　鎏金銅菩薩立像　Standing Bodhisattva

124　鎏金銅菩薩　Gilt Bronze Bodhisattva

125　銅香爐　Copper Incense Burner

126　銅獅　Copper Lion

127　阿拉伯文宣德爐　The Xuan De Incense Burner
　　with Arabian Characters

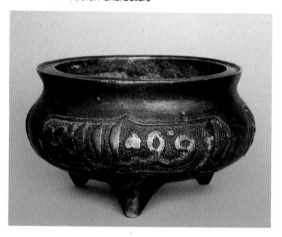

128　刻花銅碗　Copper Bowl

129　銅獅鎮子　Copper Paperweight

130　銅洗手壺和銅盆　Copper Pot and Basin

131 黑汗朝錢幣 Karakhanid Coin

132 漢佉二体錢 Sino - Kharosthi Coin

133 貴霜錢 Kushan Coin

134 高昌吉利錢 Gaochang "jili" Coin

135 龜茲五銖錢 Kuchean Wu-chu Coin

136 突騎施錢 Turgis Coin

137　金馬飾　金鷹鹿飾　*Golden Horse and Eagle - Deer*

138　嵌寶石金戒指　*Golden Fingerring Inlaid with Rubies*

139　八龍紋金帶扣　*Golden Buckle with Dragons' Patterns*

140　葡萄墜金耳環　*Golden Earring*

143 虎紋圓金牌 金飾帶 Golden Plaques and Belt

141 六菱形金花飾片 Golden Flower

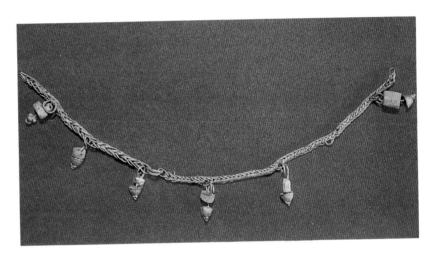

144 金鏈飾 Golden Chain

145 獅形金牌飾 Golden Plaque in the Lion Shape

142 金耳環 Golden Earring

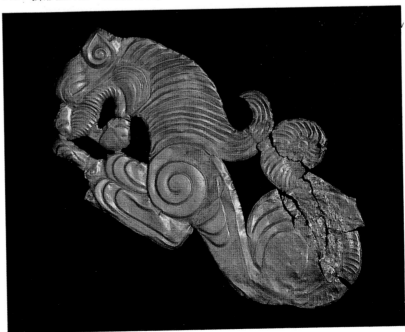

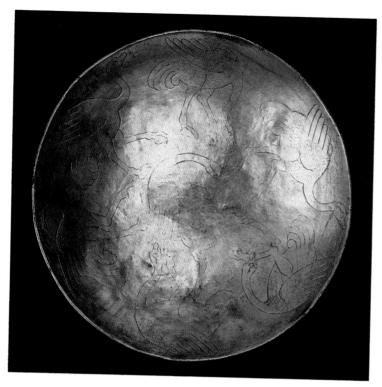

146 鏨刻駝鳥紋銀盤 Silver Tray Engrtaving Ostriches Patterns

147 雙聯金牛頭 Double Golden Heads of Ox

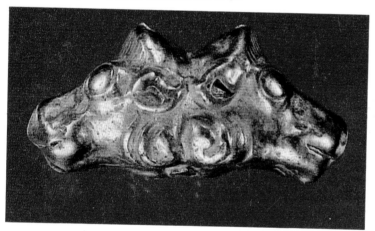

149 金耳環 Golden Earrings

148 銀碗 Silver Bowl

150 察合台汗國金幣　Jagatai Golden Coin

151 東羅馬金幣　Eastern Roman (Byzantine) Empire Golden Coin

152 波斯銀幣　Persian Silver Coins

154 察合台汗國銀幣　Jagatai Silver Coins

153 和闐銀幣　Hotan Silver Coin

岩畫

　　岩畫藝術，起源於遠古的石器時代。新疆岩畫主要分布在阿爾泰山麓、天山、崑崙山，以及三山環抱的準噶爾盆地、塔里木盆地周緣的丘陵山地。上述地區的自然條件優越，有豐盛的牧草，自古以來就是各族人民狩獵、放牧的理想天地。岩畫反映出主人們生產活動和社會生活狀況。如自然界中的飛禽走獸等動物形象，狩獵與放牧的場面，舞蹈、雜耍、格鬥、征戰，以及對人類祖先、圖騰等崇拜的畫面。只有熟悉岩畫分布環境的地理特點，才可能準確認識和理解新疆岩畫藝術產生和發展的軌跡。

　　迄今為止的考古研究表明，新疆岩畫的時代上限可追溯到石器時代，但其延續時間很長，晚的可到公元十二、十三世紀的蒙古時期，而青銅時代則是岩畫藝術蓬勃發展的重要歷史階段，在這個歷史時期中，許多岩畫的附近都有青銅時代或是鐵器時代的遺址或墓地，表明了二者之間的關係。

　　享有盛譽的新疆阿爾泰山麓岩畫數量最多，內容多為奔跑的駿馬、鹿和羊群，其線條簡練、造型生動。數以千幅的岩畫大都以陰刻線的方法雕刻在山體的岩壁或較大的岩石面上，所表現的題材和內容豐富多采。

　　近年在天山中部呼圖壁康家石門子發現的大型岩畫，是表現人類生殖崇拜的岩畫藝術作品。在120平方米左右的巨大畫面上，鑿刻出數百個男女互相交媾和舞蹈的情景，既著重於寫實，表現出人體的自然美，又對性器官採取誇張的表現形式。在岩畫的雕刻技法方面也很有特色，即在傳統的陰刻線的基礎上，按照人體的形象進行局部磨刻「減地」的工藝，使岩畫背景部份岩體表面與人物形象之間產生一種近似淺浮雕的藝術效果，使畫面的主體形象更為突出。康家石門子岩畫以其獨特的雕刻藝術語言，將現實中的形象通過變形處理重新組合，達到內容和形式的完美統一，使雕刻於岩壁上的作品具有永久的藝術魅力。

　　新疆的古代岩畫，還有許多有待於進一步發現和研究，這也是史學家、美術家和考古學家都感興趣的重大課題。

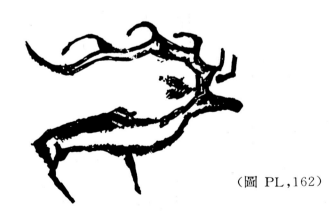

(圖 PL,162)

ROCK CARVING

Rock carving originated in Stone Age. The rock carvings in Xinjiang are mainly distributed in the Altay, Tianshan and Kunlun Mountains, the hilly and mountainous regions around the Junggar and Tarim Basins. These areas all enjoy good natural conditions and are rich in herbage. They are the ideal areas for hunting and herding for all nationalities in Xinjiang. The rock carvings in Xinjiang reflect the productive activites and social conditions of ancient peoples.

Archaeological research has so far revealed that the history of the rock carvings in Xinjiang can be traced back to Stone Age, and covered a long period which lasted until the Mongol Period of 12-13th century A. D. Rock carving art grew vigorously during Bronze Age. Around the rock carvings in Xinjiang there found the sites and tombs of Bronze Age or Iron Age. This marks their relations and the importance of Bronze Age for rock carving.

The rock carvings in the Altay Mountains are very famous. Their themes are mainly animal figures, such as running horse, deer and sheep, Thousands pieces of rock carvings were usually incised on the cliffs and surfaces of large rocks. They are rich in subject and content.

Recently, a large-sized rock carving was found in Kangjiashimenzi, Hutubi,in the middle of the Tianshan Mountains. It is an artistic work of reproduction worshipping. Hundreds male and female figures, in the posture of sexual intercourse and dancing, were incised on a cliff. The whole picture covers an area of over 120 sqm. The human bodies in this picture were depicted realistically so as to display their natural beauty, whereas the sexual organs were exaggerated. The technique of this rock carving has its own characteristic,i.e., on the base of traditional incising method, the figures were rubbed out concavely, so the picture got the artistic effcct of low relief and the figures became prominent. These figures, being rearranged after transformation, attain to perfect unity of content and form. They endow the picture with everlasting artistic charm.

Ancient rock carvings in Xinjiang remain to be discovered and studied still further. They attract historians, artists as well as archaeologists.

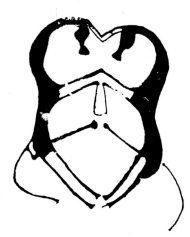

(圖 PL,157)

岩畫 *Rock Carving*

155　生殖崇拜圖（局部）　Reproduction Worship

156　舞蹈圖（局部）　Dancers

157　對馬圖（局部）　Double Horses

158　人虎圖（局部）　Persons and Tigers

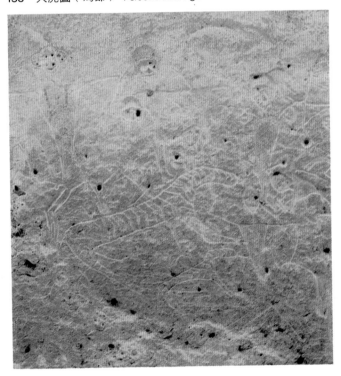

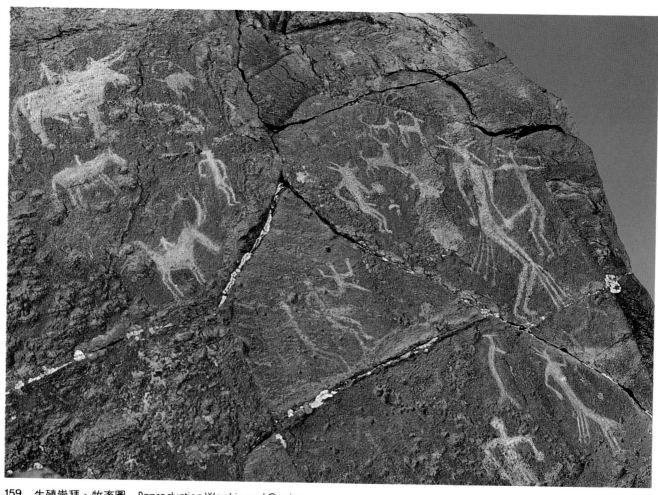

159 生殖崇拜、牧畜圖　Reproduction Worship and Grazing

160 馬羊圖　Two Horses and a Goat

162　馴鹿圖　Reindeers

161　彩繪神靈圖　Celestial Being

163　步牧圖　Herding

164 雜技圖 Acrobatics

165 群羊圖 Goats

166 奔鹿圖 Running Deers

68

167　爭戰圖　Cavalrymen

168　戰騎圖　Cavalrymen and Horses

繪畫

新疆古代繪畫，種類極為豐富。主要有佛教、摩尼教、景教石窟寺壁畫，古墓室中的壁畫，木板畫、紙畫、絹畫等。其中，佛教石窟寺壁畫的數量最多、質量最高，內容最豐富，在新疆繪畫藝術中有突出的地位。

隨著佛教的傳入，鑿窟建寺、塑造佛像、繪製壁畫在塔里木盆地周圍地區蓬勃興起。公元三、四世紀時佛教繪畫已有相當發展，至七、八世紀時達到極盛時期。這種石窟寺壁畫藝術的出現和發展是同當時的政治、經濟和宗教密切相聯繫的。那時的西域不但是著名的佛教地區，也是佛教藝術高度發達的地區，人們從和闐、策勒、于闐、若羌、庫車、拜城等地的石窟寺壁畫中，可窺視到古代各族藝術家們對外來文化藝術的吸收與融匯，並逐漸形成了介於印度、東方與西方之間的古代新疆繪畫藝術風格。

龜茲石窟壁畫的菱形結構佈局，人物造型，以及線條、色彩、暈染等頗具特色。如壁畫的技法有的使用細蘆管等硬筆勾線，線條勻稱而樸拙；有的則是在中原繪畫技法影響下的線描手法，線細而不弱，柔中有剛，圓轉優美，富於彈力。色彩表現方面則多採用原色，如石青、石綠、朱砂、土紅等。早期壁畫常以重色鋪底，用明亮的淺色來表現主題。晚期則用大面積的亮白色做底，主題部份相對著色較深。這些以色彩進行對比的手法，極大地加強了對主題形象的表現。在人物的表現上則採用暈染法，即把人體按照結構劃分成大小長短不同的圓柱體或圓球體，在邊沿染上深一些的赭紅色，逐漸向中間減淡，達到了表現人物立體感的視覺效果。這種人體肌肉的暈染，和部份裸體的形象，是龜茲繪畫藝術的特點。于闐繪畫，無論在內容上還是形式上，也吸收了波斯、印度和中原繪畫的因素，形成兼收並蓄的混合型的于闐畫風。著名的于闐畫家尉遲跋質那和尉遲乙僧父子的繪畫技法和風格，還曾對中原地區的繪畫產了深遠影響。

吐魯番古墓中出土的晉——唐絹畫、紙畫，以及墓室牆壁上繪製的壁畫，其表現形式則是典型的中原漢地繪畫藝術風格。這些繪畫作品均出自墓葬中，有較明確的紀年，對我國繪畫史的研究提供了珍貴的形象資料。

九世紀以來，回鶻民族成為吐魯番等地定居的主體民族，在同其他兄弟民族的文化交流中發展了本民族的文化藝術。這時期的吐魯番已成為新疆摩尼教、佛教、景教並存、文化兼蓄的特殊地區。至今保存於柏孜克里克石窟中屬於回鶻時期的壁畫藝術，舉世矚目，是我國繪畫藝術百花園中的一支絢麗花朵。

(圖 PL，241)

PAINTING

The ancient painting of Xinjiang was rich in types, for instance, the Budhist, Manichean and Zoroastrianist wall paintings in grotto temples, wall paintings in ancient tombs, paintings on wooden boards, paper and silk paintings.　Among them, the wall paintings in Buddhist grotto temples rank lst in numbers, quality and content, and hold a prominent postion.

Along with the spread of Buddhism into Xinjiang, there appeared numerous grottoes, temples, figures of Buddha and wall paintings around the rim of the Tarim Basin.　During the 3rd and 4th century, Buddhist painting developed considerably.　It reached its zenithin the 7-8th century.　The wall paintings preserved in the grotto temples in Hotan, Qira, Yutian, Ruoqiang, Kucha and Baicheng display the absorption and combination of exotic cultures and arts.

The wall paintings in Kucha Grottoes are very special in their rhomboid seperation of the pictures,and their figures, lines, colors, etc.　For example, the wall paintings were usually painted with reed stem in simple but symmetrical lines, some were painted by the method of line drawing of the Central Plains, primary colors were mostly used.　A unique technique was applied when figures were painted, and this gave the figures a three-dimensional effect. The paintings of Khotan, however, absorbed the elements of the paintings in Persia, India and the Central Plains, and fromed its own style.　The painting technique and style of famous Hotan painters Yuchibazhina and his son Yuchiyisen even had a profound influence on the painting in the Central Plains.

The silk paintings, paper paintings and wall paintings of the Jin and Tang Dynasties unearthed from ancient tombs in Turfan bear typical painting style of the Central Plains. These paintings, all found in ancient tombs, have definite dates and provide the study of the painting history of China with valuable materials.

After the 9th century,the Uighurs became the main part of population in Turfan.They developed their own culture and art.　Turfan became a special region with Manicheaism, Buddhism and Zoroastrianism existing side by side.　The wall painting art of the Uighur-domination Age preserved in Bezeklik Grottoes attract worldwide attention.　They are wonderful works of the painting art in China.

（圖 PL，178）

繪畫 *Painting*

169 飛天圖　A Gandharva

170 吉祥慧裸体女像　The Lying Woman

171 佛教故事版畫 Painting from Buddhist Stories

172. 駱駝哺乳圖 Camels

174 佛教木版畫 Painting on Wooden Plank

173 佛教木版畫 Painting on Wooden Plank

175　鬼子母圖　The Goddess Hariti

176　佛像　Head dof Buddha

177　供養菩薩像　Worshipping Bodhisattva

178 有翼天使像 Winged Angel

179 佛陀與比丘像 Portrails of Buddha and Six Bhiksus

180 盧遮那佛像 Vairocana

181 菱格姻緣故事畫　Stories about the Causes

182 托鉢立佛版畫　Standing Buddha

183 樂神善愛圖　Devatas

184 蛤天人因緣故事畫（局部）
The Cowherd Nanda

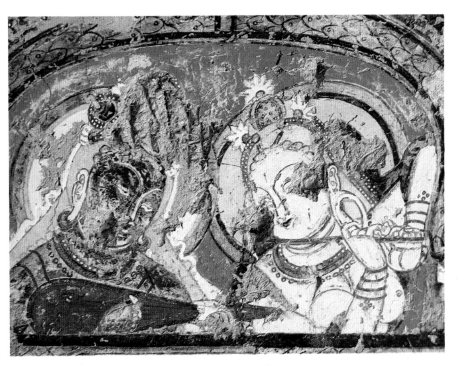

185 天宮伎樂圖　The Bodhisattvas Playing Instruments

186 魔女誘佛圖　Scenes of Buddha Vanquishing the Daughters of Mara

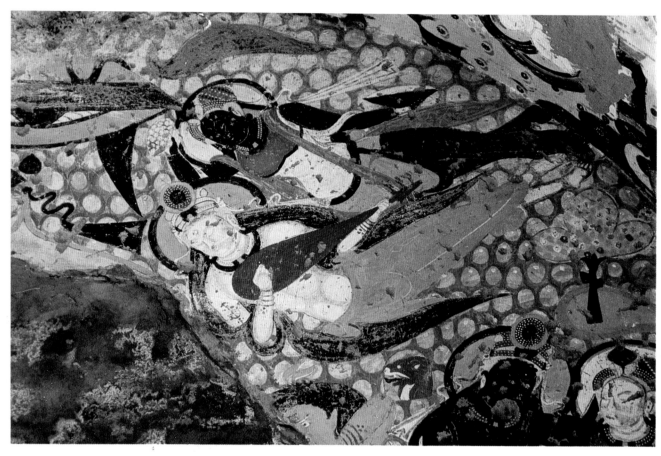

187　伎樂飛天　Gandharvas

188　聽法菩薩像　Bodhisattva

189　樂舞供養天像　Devatas

190　樂舞圖　Dancer and Musician

191　供養菩薩群像（局部）　Group of Bodhisattvas (part)

192　飛天（摹本）　Gandharvas (Facsimile)

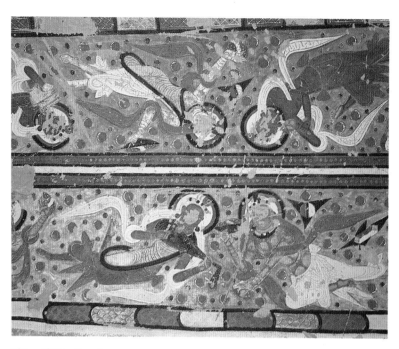

193 飛天 Gandharvas

194 猴王本生故事畫 Jataka Story of the Royal
Monkey

195 阿闍世王夢靈、沐浴圖 Ajatasatru

196 須大拏太子本生故事畫 Scene from the Vishvantara Jataka

197 金剛像 Seated Vajrapani

198 菩薩說法圖 The Bodhisattva Preaching

199　佛傳故事國王王后大臣像　Three Half - Figures

200　龜茲國王及王后供養像
The king and His Wife

201　龜茲貴族供養人像　Two Donors

202　龜茲樂舞舍利盒　Paintings of Dancing and Playing on a Reliquary

203　龜茲樂舞舍利盒局部（摹本）　The Dancers and Players

204 佛体焚化圖 Scenes of Buddha Cremated

205 爭分舍利圖（局部）Scenes of Contending for Buddha's Relics

206 耕作圖 Farming

207 供養人群像 Group of Donors

208 比丘尼像 Bhiksuni

209 比丘受教圖 The Bhiksus in Teaching

210　仕女弈棋圖　A Young Woman Playing Weiqi

211　仕女圖　A Young Woman

212　童子圖　A Boy

213　托盞侍女圖　A Young Maidservant Holding A Tea-Tray

214　舞伎圖　A Female Dancer

215　侍女圖　A Young Maidservant

216　侍馬圖　A Groom Leading a Horse

217 六屏式鑒誡畫 Paintings about Warning

218 莊園生活圖 Scenes of Living in the Manor

219 六屏式花鳥壁畫 Flower - and - Bird Painting

220　墓主人生活圖紙畫　Painting on Paper

222　伏羲女媧絹畫　Silk Painting Portraying *Fuxi* and *Nuwa*

221　伏羲女媧絹畫　Silk Painting Portraying *Fuxi* and *Nuwa*

223 高昌景教壁畫 The Nestorian Wall Painting

224 摩尼教典籍中插圖 Fragments from a Manichaean Book

225 摩尼教壁畫 The Manichaean Wall Painting

226　舉哀圖　Scenes of Grieving for Buddha

227　貴婦禮佛像　Lady Worshopping Buddha

228　天王像　The Vaishrvana and His Attendants

229　回鶻王供養像　Uighurian Prince

230　回鶻王像麻布幡　Uighuri Prince

231　回鶻王侯家族群像　Group of Uighurian Royal Kinsmen

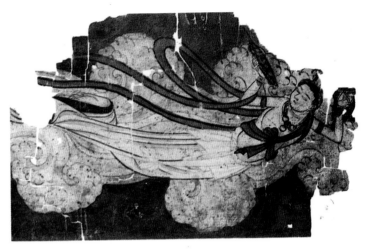

233　飛天絹畫　A Gandharva Steming Flowers

232　龍騰圖　Dragon in a Lake

234　僧統供養像　Three Buddhist Monks

235　回鶻公主供養像　Uighurian Princesses

237 釋迦太子出遊圖 The Excursions of Prince Skayamuni

236 仕女圖 Head of a Young Woman

238 護法神像（局部） Lokapalas

239　樹下人物圖　Figure Painting

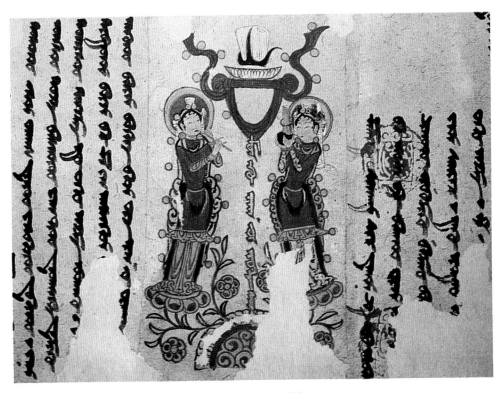

240　摩尼教經卷插圖（局部）　Manichaean Painting on Silk

241　觀世音菩薩像　Avalokiteshvara

242 供養禮佛圖　Scenes of Buddha with Worshippers

243　供養人像（局部）　Donors

244 眾人奏樂圖 Scenes
of Playing Instruments

245 延受命菩薩麻布畫 Bodhisattvas

246 長壽王菩薩絹畫 Silk Painting of a
Bodhisattva (King of Langevity)

247 供養菩薩像 Bodhisattvas

248 王者出行圖 The Procession Scene of a King

編織

　　新疆出土的古代編織物類多、數量大，為全國考古發現之冠。其質地絲、毛、棉、麻、草俱全。論品種，有錦、綺、綾、羅、紗、絹、刺繡、染纈、緙絲等絲織品；有氍、毹、毛繡、毛緯等毛編品；有印花、提花的棉織物，還有毛、絲、麻編結的鞋、帽等。表現出新疆古代社會經濟和科學技術發展的水平，也是「絲綢之路」在服飾文化交流、融匯和繁榮的實物例證。

　　新疆的自然條件，形成了以畜牧業和農業為主的經濟文化。現有考古資料表明，在新疆用動物絨毛捻成紗線製作衣服以抗禦嚴寒的歷史十分久遠，距今至少已有三千八百年，如羅布泊古墓溝出土的隨葬品中就有多種毛織物。

　　新疆各地所見的早期毛織物，主要出土於天山南麓的吐魯番、哈密、塔里木盆地東部羅布泊荒原，以及南緣的且末、民豐、洛浦等地。這些毛織品，在地下雖歷時二、三千年，但出土時依然色澤如新，其種類有粗紗細紗織出的、輕薄的「毛羅」，各種幾何形花紋的氍毹，花紋絢麗的毛繡和編織的毛毯等。繽紛的色彩，平紋和斜紋等、變化組成的紋樣，圖案新穎，組合富於韻律。尤其是彩色織花的毛織品——罽，其織造工藝多樣，紋飾繁縟，色彩鮮艷，頗具濃厚地方文化的特色。值得注意的是，樓蘭和山普拉出土的毛毯、墊毯和緙毛織物，其製作工藝和裝飾紋樣等大部份都具有顯明的西域文化特色，另有兩件緙毛織物，其人首馬身圖案和持矛的人物形象，則明顯具有希臘、羅馬文化風格，代表著新疆毛織物中外來紋樣的藝術色彩。

　　地處「絲綢之路」要隘的新疆地區，出土的輕薄美觀的各類絲綢織物是最為豐富的，時代起自戰國，以至漢唐、宋元各代。其重要的出土地點有：樓蘭、尼雅、托庫孜薩來、阿斯塔那、喀拉和卓等遺址和墓地。新疆各地出土的歷代絲綢圖案，都具有時代的特點。如漢魏時期的絲綢，其花紋布局均成行排列，循環往復。紋飾圖案，多在變幻的雲紋中出現著象徵吉祥的瑞獸，其間穿插種種吉祥用語，如「萬世如意」、「長壽明光」、「延年益壽」等，代表了鮮明的漢文化的特徵。南北朝以後，絲綢紋樣隨著時尚而變，而且由於適應「絲路」外銷的需要而增加了異國紋樣，如獅或佛教藝術題材等。尤以聯珠紋飾為主題圖案的織錦，如「聯珠孔雀」、「貴」字錦、「聯珠對羊」、「對鳥」、「對獸」，以及「聯珠胡王」錦等，具有波斯藝術風格的紋樣。唐代的緙絲、雙面絹，以及出現的印花織物等，文彩紛繁，令人目不暇接，表現了我國古代紡織工藝的高超水平。

（圖 PL,285）

WOVEN WARE

The ancient woven wares rank Xinjiang first in China both in amount and type. Regarding material, they include silk, wool, cotton, hemp and grass, while speaking of vatiety,they include brocade damask, ghatpot, leno, gauze, spun silk, embroidery, painted silk and silk tapestry, etc. They are the material testimony of the communication, combination and flourish of the apparel cultures along the Silk Road and demonstrate the development of ancient Xinjiang's society, ecomomy and technology.

According to archaelolgical finds, the long history of the apparel made of twisted animal hair yarns can be traced back to about 3800 yerars ago, such as the woollen frabrics among the remains from the Gumugou Ancient Tombs, Lopnur.

Early woollen fabrics in Xinjiang are mainly unearthed from the Turfan Basin and Hami Basin, north of the Tianshan Mountains; Lopnur Gobi in the east of the Tarim Basin and Qiemo, Minfeng and Lop in the south. These fabrics, though having a history of two to three thousand years, are as new when being discovered. They range from painted fabrics of woollen yarns, light and thin wool gauzes, woollen blanket with geometrical patterns to colorful wool embroideries and carpets. The woollen blankets, carpets and tapestries unearthed from Loulan and Shanpula merit special attention. Their craftsmanship and patterns are obviously of the Western Regions culture. However, among them there found two pieces of woollen tapestries, having figures of centaurs and persons. They represent the exoticism in the woollen fabrics of Xinjiang with strong cultural styles of Greece and Rome.

But as it is on the strategic pass of the Silk Road, Xinjiang is richest in its remains of various kinds of light and beautiful silk fabrics. Dating from the Warring States Period to the Han, Tang, Song, Yuan Dynasties, they were chiefly unearthed from the sites and tombs of Loulan, Niya, Tokuz-sarai, Astana, Karakhoja, etc. The patterns on the silk fabrics all have unique characteristics of their times. After the Southern and Northern Dynasties, exotic patterns were adopted more and more. The patterns in Persian artistic style, such as granulation, twin-bird and beast, are very popular on brocodes. The silk tapesries, double-faced spun silk and printed fabrics of the Tang Dynasty are variegated in color and dazzling in beauty. All of these various kinds of elegant fabrics found in Xinjiang are valuable for the study of China's ancient history of weaving, dyeing and printing of textiles.

（圖 PL，267）

編織 *Woven Ware*

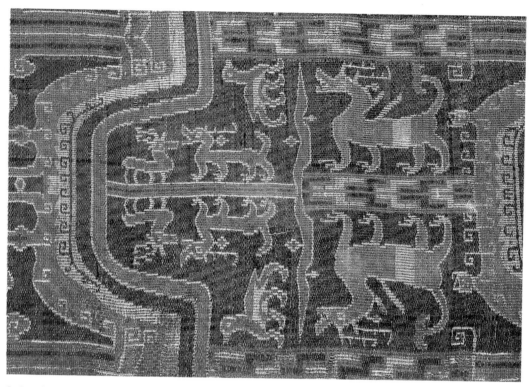

249　禽獸紋錦（局部）　Part of the Brocade with Bird and Beast Designs

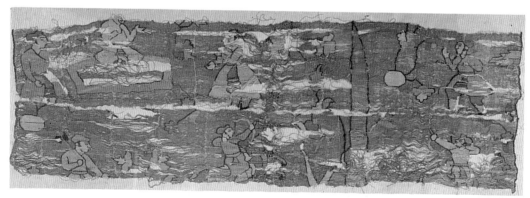

250　織金錦　Satin dorure de Nankin (damaged)

251　毛綉殘片（局部）　Fragment of Woollen Embrodiery

252　草編簍　Grass Woven Basket

254　尖頂毡帽　Felt Cap

253　毛線編織帽毡帽　Wool Knitted Cap and Felt Cap

255 毛織衣 Woollen Coat

256 毛布男褲 Man's Woollen Trousers

257 栽絨毯 Woollen Carpet

104

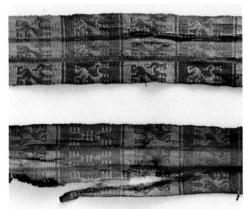

259　龍紋絲織帶（局部）　Brocade Belt with Dragon Design

258　"萬世如意"錦袍　Brocade Coat

260　印花棉布（殘片）　Cotton Cloth with Buddha and Dragon Designs (Fragmentary)

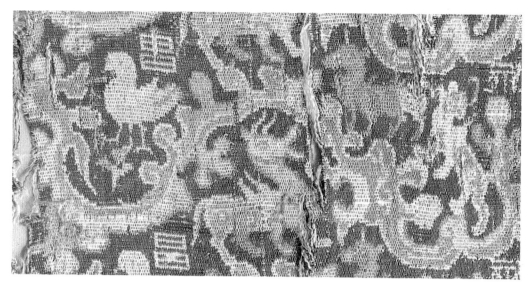

261　"永昌錦"（局部）　Part of "*Perpetual Prosperity*" Brocade

262　"延年益壽大宜子孫"錦（局部）　Part of "*Longvity and Having Most Descentants*"Brocade

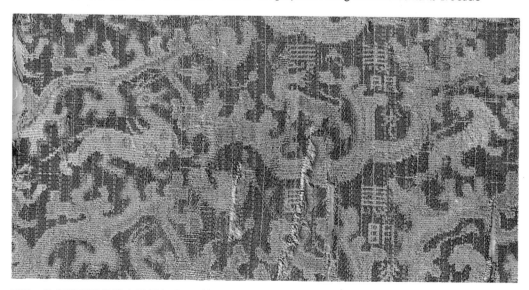

263　"長壽明光"錦（局部）　Part of "*Longvity and Prosperity*"Brocade

264 魚禽紋錦（局部） part of the Brocade with Fish and Bird Designs

265 三葉花絣毛（局部） Part of Woollen Cloth

266 卍字邊幾何紋絣毛（局部） Part of the Woolen Cloth with Wefting Pattern

267 人首馬身毛織·壁挂（部分）Part of the Woollen Tapestry with Centaur Design

268 栽絨鞍毯 Woollen Saddle Blanket

269 武士像 毛織 壁掛（部分） Part of the Woollen Tapestry with Wefting
Warrior Design

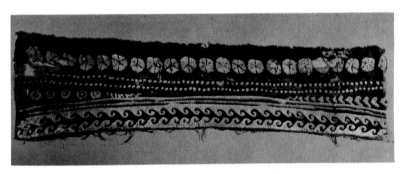

271 藍地白花紋棉布 Blue Cotton Cloth with Printed Patterns

270 人首馬身武士像掛毯復原像 Restored Tapestry with
Centaur and Warrior Designs

272 狩獵紋印花絹片 Silk with Printed Hunting Pattern (Fragmentary)

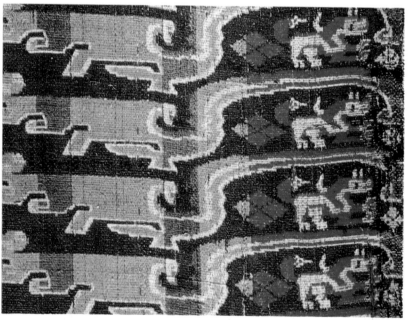

273 "吉"字紋錦（局部） Brocade Decorated with Chinese Character

274 夔紋錦（局部） Brocade with Dragon Design

275 "富且昌宜侯王夫延命長"編織履 Woven Shoes Decorated with Chinese Scripts

276 套環〝貴〝字紋綺（局部） *Qi* (Ancient
Chinese silk fabric)

277 對鳥對羊樹紋錦（局部） Part of the Brocade with Confronting Sheep
and Tree Designs

279 刺繡鎧甲衣片 *Piece of the Cotton Embroidery from an
Armour Suit*

278 母女綉像 Embroidery with Princess and Child Designs

281　紅地對馬紋錦（局部）　The Brocade with the Designs of Double Horses

280　盤絛獅象紋綿　Brocade with Lion and Elephant Designs

282　飛鳳蛺蝶團花錦殘片（局部）　Fragment of A Brocade

283　聯珠對鷄紋錦（局部）　Part of Brocade

284　聯珠鸞鳥紋錦（局部）　Part of the Brocade Decorated with Mythical Bird Design

285　聯珠鹿紋錦（局部）　Part of the Brocade with Garland Circled Deer Design

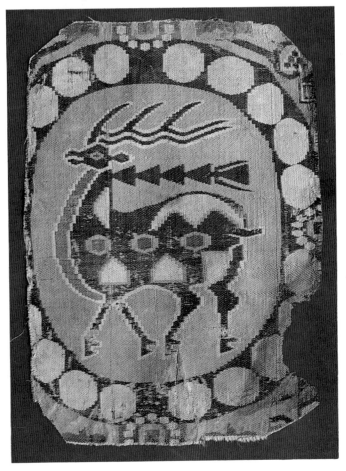

286　聯珠＂胡王＂錦（局部） Brocade

287　狩獵紋印花紗（局部） Part of the Green Gauze with Printed Hunting Patterns

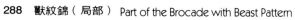

288　獸紋錦（局部） Part of the Brocade with Beast Pattern

289　騎士對獸紋錦 Brocade with Knight and Twin Beast Patterns (Damaged)

290 樹紋錦（局部） Part of the Brocade with Branch Design

291 靈鷲紋錦（局部） Part of the Brocade

293 菱形格絹（局部） Part of the Silk with Printed Rhomboid Design

292 地毯 Carpet with Wefting Pattern

木器

　　木器與石器的歷史同樣久遠，它是人類最早的工具、用具和武器。新疆氣候乾燥，木器輕便耐用又便於攜帶，更為人們所喜愛。在青銅時代，哈密五堡、焉布拉克、羅布泊古墓溝、且末的扎乎魯克等墓地都出土過豐富的木質生活器皿。那時木器加工已出現了砍、削、刻等製作工藝。羅布泊古墓溝出土的半身木雕女俑，用簡潔、粗獷的刀法，削刻出瘦長形的臉龐，頭戴的尖頂帽和長長髮辮，以及顯示女性特徵的乳房和豐碩的臀部等，表現了原始古樸的寫實風格。哈密焉布拉克墓地也出土了多件木刻人像作品，有的僅用簡潔的刀法刻劃出形體，有的削刻出完整的形體，其中對男女性別特徵刻劃都表現得十分明顯。這種對人類自身性器官的誇張表現是新疆早期木雕人體藝術的一個特點。

　　隨著生產技術的進步，木器製作的雕刻等工藝有所提高和發展。漢晉時期，已出現了削、刻、琢、旋、磨等多種工藝，製作的几案、盆、盤、碗、罐、壺等生活器皿，以及浮雕、全雕工藝裝飾的家俱、刻花、鏤空的建築構件、佛教藝術品和隨葬品中的各類冥器。

　　尼雅和樓蘭遺址出土的建築構件中的雕刻裝飾，反映出三——四世紀新疆建築雕飾的藝術水平和濃厚的外來文化的因素。木樑和門楣上均雕刻出多種幾何形圖案、植物和各類花卉等圖案。尼雅遺址出土的木雕桌腿，造型新穎，浮雕的植物花紋、幾何紋瓶花等圖案，刻工精細。其中彩繪的木雕人物椅腿，是人身馬足，造型十分精湛，人物的五官相貌的刻劃富於表情，強調了動態的藝術表現形式，具有濃厚的希臘—羅馬藝術風格的影響。

　　佛教題材的藝術雕刻，以其獨特的風格在新疆古代藝術史上占有重要的一頁。那一尊尊釋迦、菩薩比丘供養人等雕像，造型剛健豐盈，富有表情，衣紋線條流暢清晰，有輕薄欲飄之狀。其藝術風格顯然是受到來自古代犍陀羅地區佛教文化的影響。

　　吐魯番晉—唐墓葬出土的木雕俑像、家畜、家禽以及牛、馬、車等模型，形象生動，比例準確，雕刻細微精美。其中彩繪木雕中的武士、天王、馬夫俑和各具形態的仕女俑等，都是古代木雕藝術精品，也為研究古代造型藝術、舞蹈雜技、埋葬習俗和社會制度，以及當時生活面貌，提供了真實而形象的藝術資料。

（圖 PL，295）

WOODEN ARTICLE

As the earliest tools, implements and weapons of human beings, wooden articles have a history as long as that of stone implements. The dry climate of Xinjiang endowed wooden articles with lightness and durability, so they were widely used in Xinjiang. A great number of wooden articles of everyday use as early as Bronze Age have been found in Wupu and Yanbulake in Hami, the Gumugou Gully in Lopnur, etc. The skills of chopping, cutting and carving appeared then too; the wooden female bust found in the Gumugou Gully in Lopnur displays primitive and simple style with roughly-curved face, pointed hat, long braids, full breasts and buttocks. However, the wooden figures unearthed from the Yanbulak Ancient Tombs in Hami have simply-carved bodies and exaggerated sexual organs. The exaggerated description of sexual organ was one characteristic of the early wooden figure art in Xinjiang.

The skills of wood carving developed along with the progressing of productive technique. During the Han and Jin Dynasties, wooden articles for daily use, such as desks, pots bowls, jars, etc., and furniture, building decorations, Buddhist works and burial objects were made with the skills of chopping, carving, drilling, spinning, etc.

The decorations of the structure members found in Niya and Loulan Sites reflect the artistic level and exotic elements of the building decorations of Xinjiang in the 3rd and 4th centuries. The man-shaped wooden chair legs found in Niya Site were strongly influenced by Greek-Rome artistic style.

The wooden articles of Buddhist subject occupied an important place in the history of Xinjiang art with their unique style. Those figures of Gautama, bodhisattvas, bhiksus and donors were obviously influenced by early Buddhist culture of Gandhara.

The wooden figures, livestocks, poultry and models of wagons unearthed from the ancient tombs of the Jin and Tang Dynasties were all carved proportionally and exquisitely. Among them, the painted wooden figures of warriors, vaishravanas, grooms and beauties are all excellent works of art and provide true and lively material for the study of ancient plastic art, dance, music, acrobatics, burial customs and social systems.

(圖 PL, 326)

木器 *Wooden Article*

294 木雕人物椅腿 Two Painted Wooden Sculptures

295　半身木雕女像　Female Half-Figure

297　男女木雕像　A Man and a Woman

296　鳥柄木碗　The Wooden Bowl with a Bird - Shaped
　　　Handle

298　羊形柄木梳　Wooden Comb in Sheep Shape

299　木耜　Wooden Si

300　木鉢木勺　Wooden Bowl and Ladle

301　蛇形弓、箭　Wooden Bowl and Arrows

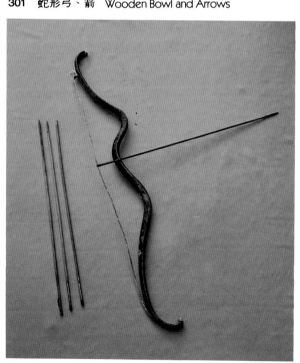

302　漆花木梳　Painted Wooden Comb

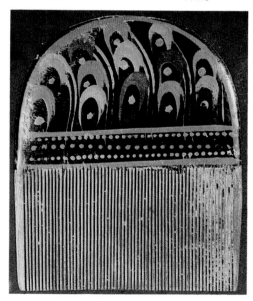

304 佉盧文木牘 Inscribed Wooden Tablet with Kharosthi Scripts

303 木雕飾板 Sculpture on a Wooden Door-Leaf

305 木几 Wooden Table

306 木碗木杯 Bowls and Cups

307　斷頭菩薩立像　Standing Bodhisattva

308　木雕菩薩立像　Standing Bodhisattva

309　坐佛像　Seated Buddha

310　擊腰鼓天人木雕　A Devata Playing Waist—drum

122

312 交腳菩薩像　A Bodhisattva Sitting
Cross-Ankled

311 佛立像　Standing Buddha

313 木雕佛首　Head of a Buddha

314 觀音立像　Standing Avalokitesvara

123

315 力士木雕像 Standing Vajrapani

316 彩繪木雕佛龕 Painted Wooden Niche for Buddha's Statues

317 木雕桌腿 The Wooden Sculptures of Desk's Legs

318　木雕佛像　Seated Buddha

319　塔式彩繪木舍利盒　Reliquary

320　彩繪木舍利盒　Buddha's Reliquary

321　木雕坐佛　Seated Buddha

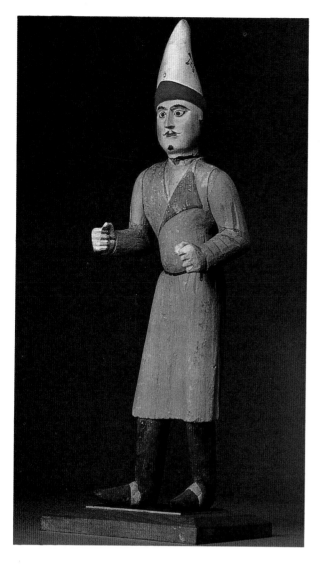

323　彩繪木鴨　Wooden Ducks

322　彩繪馬夫木俑　Wooden Figure of a Groom

324　木牛車　Wooden Ox and Cart

325　彩繪木罐　Painted Wooden Jar

326 彩繪仕女木俑　A Woman　327 彩繪女木俑　A Young Woman

328 彩繪天王踏鬼木俑　The Wooden Figure of a Lokapala
Stepping on a Demon

石雕

　　新疆古代的石雕藝術，在青銅時代及早期鐵器時代裡，出土的人體雕刻中普遍的特徵是對於男女性別特點的著意刻劃。如羅布泊古墓溝出土的木質、石質的半身女雕像，都突出了對女性雙乳的強調雕刻；木壘四道溝出土的「石祖」，則著意刻劃了男性生殖器官。這些著意表現性的雕刻藝術，是原始藝術中常見的，屬於生殖崇拜在藝術方面的反映。阿爾泰地區的鹿石，其淺浮雕具有繪畫的某些特點，系利用明暗對比的手法雕刻出奔跑的鹿群，則是為中亞地區遠古時期以自然崇拜為主題的文化的傑出代表。

　　在新疆石雕藝術中，發現最多、也最有獨特藝術風格和特點的是草原石雕人像。它往往選取一塊近似人體的扁長形石材，雕鑿成人體的全身形像或僅僅刻出五官或頭像。其形像生動、寫實，風格粗獷而古樸，具有長久的藝術魅力。在新疆古代文化中習慣稱之為「草原石人」。

　　新疆石人主要分布在天山北麓，阿爾泰山南麓、准噶爾盆地周緣，伊犁河、額爾濟斯河流域的草原地帶。在南疆地區也有少量的發現。值得注意的是，石雕人像附近都有墓葬或遺址並存，表明了這種藝術品與當時的葬俗和人類活動有著直接關係。結合歷史文獻的記載，這些石人應是公元五至七世紀活動於天山北麓的突厥民族文化遺存。

　　考古調查表明，這些石雕人像的表現風格與造型特點，有著時代的不同，以及文化內涵間的細微變化。主要可有三種形式：即只有簡單的陰刻線，在石人面部僅僅刻出眼鼻口形象；二是按照人體形狀進行整雕和局部刻劃的半圓雕。有許多石雕人像，在正面雕刻出人物面部的容貌。如阿勒泰、昭蘇等地石雕人像中的男性雕像，寬圓型的臉龐顴骨突出，與額際連成直線的鼻樑，深深的雙目，揚起的濃眉，以及微微翹起的鬍鬚，面部表情刻劃生動，流露出內心世界的藝術美。女性雕像，古樸而粗獷的雕刻技法雕出頭部，髮辮，頸部的項鏈裝飾，扁桃形眼睛，嘴角掛著一絲溫雅而恬靜的微笑，豐滿裸露的乳房等，顯示出女性自然美的魅力；三是溫泉石人，高大體壯，右手舉杯狀物，左手持握寶劍，衣著和佩掛物，以及面部的表情等，都注意了人物形象與氣質的統一，表現了古代草原「騎士」的風度。

　　新疆石雕人像，客觀地從不同側面顯示出天山北麓草原民族在藝術的創造與發展等方面所表現的卓越才能，這也是他們自身形象的寫實作品。通過草原石人，使我們可以領略到這個曾經一度稱雄中亞、勇武強悍的游牧民族的風采。

（圖 PL，341）

STONE STATUE

The stone statue art of Xinjing in Bronze Age and early Iron Age concentrated on depicting sexual characteristics of male and female. For example, the stone or wooden female busts unearthed from the Gumugou Gully, Lopnur emphasize the breasts, the stone penis found in the Sidaogou Gully, Mori, painstakingly reflects male sexual organ. This kind of stone statue art, very popular in primitive art, is the characteristic of reproduction worshipping. The stone carvings found in Altay bear certain characteristics of painting.Groupsof running deer were carved in relief. These are theoutstanding representatives of ancient art in Central Asia.

The stone statues found in the prairies of Xinjiang rank first in numbers and artistic style. Usually, an oblong rock was chosen to make the figure of a body, then features were incised out. These vivid statues, known as the prairie stone statues, have everlasting artistic charm.

The stone statues in Xinjiang are mainly distributed in the north of the Tianshan Mountains, the south of the Altay Mountains, areas around the Jungarian Basin, and the grasslands along the Ili River and Ertix River. There are also a few stone statues found in the south of Xinjiang. It's very interesting that tombs and sites were found near stone statues. This reveals the direct relation between these artistic works and human activities. According to historical materials, these stone statues should be regarded as the cultural remains of Turkic people living in the north of Tianshan during 5-7 century A.D.

Archaeoloical investigation revealed that the expressive style and figuring characteristics of these stone statues varied according to their times and cultural content. They include three types, The first, noses, eyes and mouths were simply incised out to show an outline of faces. The second, human bodies were engraved wholly or partially. The third are the stone statues found in Wenquan County. Their strong bodies, gestures and expressions were curved out vividly, reflecting the manner of "cavaliers" in ancient grasslands.

The stone statues in Xinjiang objectively display the outstanding artistic talent of the ancient people in the grasslands, north of the Tianshan Mountains. Indeed, they are the realistic reflections of the real images of ancient peoples.

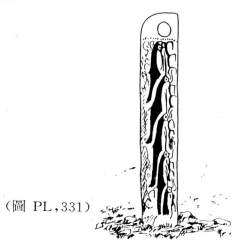

（圖 PL，331）

石雕 *Stone Statue*

329　阿勒泰市阿維灘石人　Stone Statue

330 清河縣什巴爾庫勒鹿石 Lushi (Stone pillar engraved with running deer design)

331 富蘊縣恰爾格爾鹿石 Lushi

332 獸頭柄石杯 Stone Cup with a Beast - head - shaped Handle

333 石雕女像 Stone Female Figure

334 石祖 Stone Penis Model

335 石臼 Stone Mortar

336 踞猴石燈 Macaque - shaped Stone Lamp

337　昭蘇縣1號石人　Stone Statue

338　昭蘇縣2號石人　Stone Statue

340　昭蘇縣小洪那海石人　Stone Statue

339　昭蘇縣3號石人　Stone Statue

342　阿勒泰市汗德尕特石人　Painted Stone Statue

341　溫泉縣阿爾卡特石人　Stone Statue

343　博樂縣蘇里科克石人　Stone Statue

344　額敏縣種羊場石人　Stone Statue

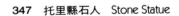

345　烏蘇縣奧瓦特石人　Stone Statue

347　托里縣石人　Stone Statue

346　阿勒泰市布提伊爾敏女石人　Female Stone Statue

348　吉木乃縣森塔斯湖石人　Stone Statue

350　昭蘇縣空古爾布拉克石人
Stone Statue

349　阿合奇縣阿文庫石人
Stone Statue

351　伊吾縣科托果勒石人　Stone Statue

352　高昌石幢　Votive Stone Stupa of Ghaochang

354　九層小石塔　Stone Tower

353　石面具　Stone Mask

泥塑

　　新疆的泥塑歷史源遠流長，與金石或其他材料的雕塑相比，泥塑更能顯示出藝術家得心應手的妙技。由於「絲綢之路」的開通與發展，促使新疆泥塑藝術得到了長足的發展進步，成為新疆古代藝術百花園中色彩豔麗的一支奇葩。

　　迄今為止的考古發現表明，公元三——四世紀，是新疆泥塑發展的重要階段。公元六——九世紀是新疆泥塑藝術的興盛時期。新疆古代的泥塑作品按其性質和作用可分為兩大類：一類是佛教寺廟遺址中發現的佛、菩薩、天人、世俗供養人等塑像。另一類是墓葬中發現的各種用來殉葬的世俗俑像，它們陪伴著死者長眠於墓室。這種以俑殉葬的現象在新疆只限於吐魯番晉——唐時期的墓葬。這種習俗無疑與內地漢人移居新疆有關。他們既帶來了較為先進的科技文化，也帶來了世代相因的千古遺風，均根植於吐魯番這塊綠洲沃土。從而構成了新疆泥塑藝術的一個重要方面。

　　佛教題材的泥塑造像藝術繁榮發展，體現出西域各族藝術家精湛的創作水平。這些泥塑一般採用模製和捏塑方法，以木和草稭為支架，泥塑成型後施彩描繪，有的泥塑經過低溫燒製後，又成為陶塑藝術品。和闐出土的早期佛教塑像，釋迦塑像，形神華肖，身著通肩袈裟，衣紋條理清晰，削瘦的臉型中，清眉閉目的神態，極富於表情。巴楚、庫車、焉耆佛寺的菩薩、天部泥塑，微妙的表情和豐盈的體態，委婉而有彈性的身軀，呈現出曲線型的美，表現出犍陀羅、笈多藝術的直接影響。

　　泥塑的創作與繪畫有機的結合，使其藝術作品更趨富麗堂皇。吐魯番古墓中出土的泥塑都著色鮮豔，如侍奉墓主人的文史、宦者和樂舞俑、仕女俑、身披甲胄、手持兵器的武士，現實生活寫照的勞動群俑、雜耍百戰俑、十二生肖等等，在造型上有的作品完全寫實，也有則進行了誇張變形的藝術創造。樸素無華的駱駝俑、牽馬俑，靜中有神，湛然生動；小彩塑的非洲「崑崙奴」，其神態和動作更為活潑傳神；人首獸身的鎮墓獸則有怪誕中見恐怖的藝術特色。

　　新疆泥塑、俑像的出土，對研究我國古代造型藝術、舞樂、雜戲，乃至社會生產生活，都提供了生動形象的實物資料。

（圖 PL，393）

CLAY　SCULPTURE

The history of the clay sculptures in Xinjiang goes back to ancient times.　The open-up and development of the Silk Road prompted the clay-molding art in Xinjiang to make great progress and become a wonderful work of the ancient art in Xinjiang.

Archaeological findings so far revealed that the period of the 3rd-4th century A.D. was very important for the development of the clay-molding art in Xinjiang, and the time from the 6th century A. D. to 9th century A. D. was the prosperous period of the clay-molding art in Xinjiang.　The clay sculptures in Xinjiang can be divided into two groups: figures of Buddha, bodhisattvas, Nandas and donors found at the sites of Buddhist temples; secular figures unearthed from ancient tombs.　The latter were found only in the tombs of the Jin and Tang Dynasties in Turfan.　This reflects the burial custom brought in to Turfan by the migrants of Han nationality.　They brought in their customs passed on from generation to generation as well as developed technique and culture to Xinjiang.This makes up an important part of the clay sculpture art in Xinjiang.

The flourish of Buddhist clay-molding art showed the excellent creative ability of the ancient artisans in the Western Regions.　Figures of early Buddhism unearthed from Hotan, such as Sakyamuni, are true to life both in figure and expression.　Figures of Bodhsattvas, divine beings found in the Buddhist temples of Bachu, Kuqa and Yanqi reflect the direct influences from Gandhara and Gupta.

When the production of clay sculpture was combined with painting, they became splendid, such as the clay sculptures unearthed from Turfan.　They include officials, eunuches, dancers, beauties, warriors, workers, animals, etc.　Some of them were made realistically, the others were exaggerated.

The clay suclptures of Xinjiang provide rich and lively material testimony for the research of ancient plastic art, music, dance, varideville, social production and activities.

（圖 PL，357）

泥塑 Clay Sculpture

355　泥塑天人像　Devata

356 泥塑小飛天 Gandharva

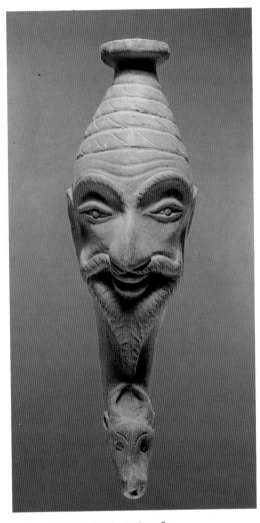

357 人首牛頭陶杯 Pottery Cup

358 伎樂陶殘片 Musicians

359 陶鳥 Pottery Bird

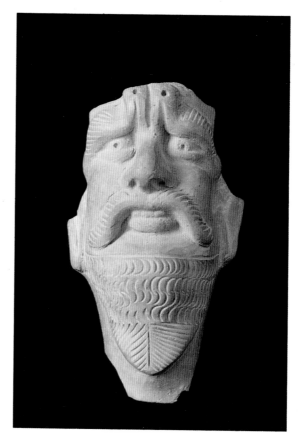

360　人首陶杯　Pottery Cup

361　人頭像　Head of a Man

362　陶製帝王像　Pottery Sculpture of a King

363　佛面範　The Mould of Buddha's Face

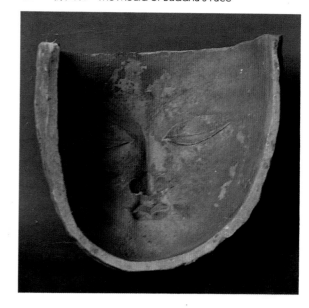

364 蓮花坐佛　Seated Buddha

365 泥塑立佛像 Standing Buddha

367 雄性陶猴　Pottery Monkey

366 陶塑婦人半身像　Half-figure of a Woman

368　坐佛像　Seated Buddha

369　菩薩頭像　Head of a Bodhisattva

370　惡鬼頭像　Head of a Demon

371　菩薩頭像　Head of a Bodhisattva

372　天人半身像　Half-Figure of a Devata

373　天部全身像　Standing Devata

374 泥塑立猴 Standing Clay Monkey

375 菩薩頭像 Head of a Bodhisattva

377 大佛頭像 Head of a Buddha

376 人首象身泥塑 The Clay Sculpture with Human
Head and Elephant's Body

378 彩塑菩薩頭像 Head of a Bodhisattva

381 武士像 Warrior

379 男子頭像 Head of a Man

380 菩薩頭像 Head of a Bodhisattva

382 舞女俑 A Woman

383 男裝仕女頭像
Head of a Woman

384 思維女俑 A Woman
in Meditation

385 彩繪宦者俑 Eunuches

386　青鬼頭像　Blue Demon

388　彩繪文吏俑　A Civil Official

387　武士頭像　Head of a Warrior

389 人物俑　Male Figures

390 單峰駝　One-Humped Camel

391 泥牛俑　An Ox

392　彩繪胡人俑　A Man

393　彩繪打馬球俑　The Polo Game

395　人首豹身鎮墓獸　Animal Guarding the Graves

394　馬形陶燈　Pottery Horse

396 鎮墓獸 The Animal Guarding the Graves

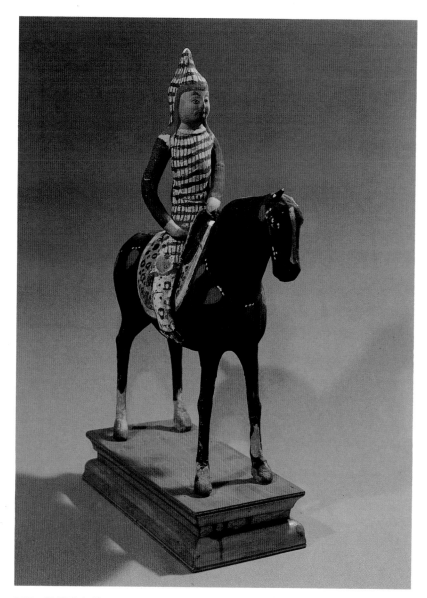

398　女士半身像　Female Half - figure

397　騎馬武士俑　The Warrior Riding a Horse

399　雜技馬舞俑　Acrobatics

400　彩繪馬俑　A Standing Horse

401　騎馬仕女俑　A Young Woman Riding a Horse

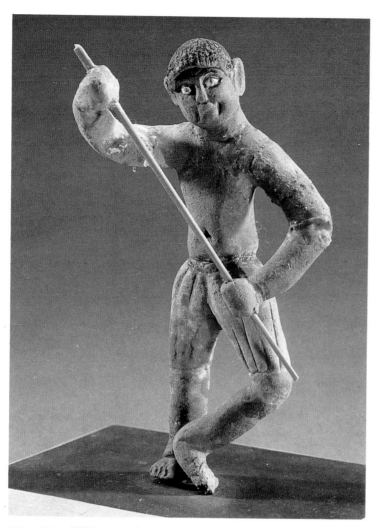

403 舞獅俑 Dancers with Lion's Mask

402 黑人百戲俑 A Black Man

404 彩繪舞蹈泥俑 A Dancer

405　彩繪勞作俑群　Group of Working Women

406　雞首人身俑　Clay Sculpture　　　　**407**　豬首人身俑　Clay Sculpture

玉琢

　　玉器的出現，與新石器時代磨製石器的產生有著密切的關係。我國中原新石器時代的遺址中都有玉璧、玉塊、玉管、玉珠、玉墜、玉斧、玉鏟等玉器出土。

　　新疆以出產美玉著稱於世。新疆玉石的開發和利用源遠流長。據考古發現，早在距今二、三千年的古樓蘭和古尼雅等遺址裡就已有了玉器的出土。先秦時期的漢文史籍已明確記載了崑崙山盛產玉料，或作為商品，或作為貢物而大量輸入中原各地。值得注意的是，河南殷商婦好墓出土了數百件玉石雕刻的藝術品，種類之繁多，雕琢之精美，令人嘆為觀止。這些玉料，經鑑定全是來自新疆和闐出產的子玉，亦即「崑崙之玉」。由此可見，新疆玉石輸入中原的歷史可追溯到公元前十三世紀。

　　新疆迄今發現最早的玉器是孔雀河古墓出土的串珠，其時代為距今3800年前後，玉色為淡黃色，造型為圓柱形或菱形，中鑽孔，為佩帶在人們身上的裝飾品。

　　漢唐以來，與產玉有關的山川、河流的記載更是屢見不鮮。如「玉河」、「白玉河」、「墨玉河」、「玉門關」等名稱都與新疆玉石結下了不解之緣。其中尤以和闐所產的玉石數量多，質量好，享有和闐玉石甲天下的美譽。

　　伴隨「絲綢之路」貿易和文化交流的擴大，在玉石原料輸入中原的同時，內地先進的玉雕工藝也植於新疆的玉石之鄉，使新疆本土的玉器工藝有了長足的發展，能用解玉砂切玉，採用砥、磨、刻、鑽、琢、雕等多種方法攻玉。宋元時期，在喀什、和闐等地已出現大量的專業採玉、琢玉的匠人，玉器制作已成為一種富於民族傳統特色的行業。

　　清代文獻記載，喀什、莎車、和闐等地的維吾爾族工匠，「尤多技藝」、「攻玉鏤雕，色色精巧」。這些出於能工巧匠之手的玉石雕琢品，最大的特點是實用性，並具有鮮明的地方特點和民族特色。如三嘴白玉吊燈、白玉扶手、玉杯、水盂、玉盤、玉硯等，造型美觀、樸素，形象生動，既實用又美觀。這些「雪之白、翠之青、蠟之黃、丹之赤、墨之黑」的溫潤光潔、晶瑩璀璨的西域玉器，豐富了中國玉雕工藝，也為東方玉雕工藝增添了光彩。

（圖 PL，415）

JADE

The appearance of jadeware has a close relation with the origination of polished stone tool. Jadewares such as flat pieces of jade, jade cubes, beads, pendants, oxes and spades, have been found in the sites of Neolithic Age in the Central Plains of China.

Xinjiang is famous for its excellent jades. The exploitation and utilization of the jades in Xinjiang go back to ancient times. According to archaeological finds, there unearthed jadewares from ancient Loulan Site and Niya Site. Chinese historical sources of Pre-Qin Times record clearly that the Kunlun Mountains is rich in jades. They were transported to the Central Plains either as goods or as articles of tribute. This fact merits our attention that hundred spieces of jade articles were excavated from the Tomb of Fuhao. According to examination, they were made out of the jades from Hotan, Xingiang. From this we can see that the transportation of the jades from Xinjang to the Central Plains can be traced back to the 13th century B. C.

The earlist jadeware found in Xinjiang is a string of jade beads from the ancient tombs in the Peacock River about 3800 Years ago. These beads, in the color of pale yellow and shapes of cylinder and rhombohedron were the ornaments of ancijent people.

Since the Han and Tang Dynasties, more and more names of mountains and rivers related to jade had been recorded in historical materials, such as "jade river", "white jade river" and "jade gate", etc. Hotan was especially famous for its jades.

Following the deepening of the cultural communication and trade along the Silk Road, the advanced jade carving craft of inner China was introduced to Xinjiang while the jade materials of Xinjiang were transported to inner China. Xinjiang made considerable development in jade carving, such as the use of whitting, polishing, carving, drilling and grinding skills. During the Song and Yuan Dynasties, large groups of artisans were engaged in professional jade carving and mining. According to the historical materials of the Qing Dynasty, the Uygurian artisans in Kashgar, Shache and Hotan were "versatile", "good at jade carving and chiseling and well versed in various areas". The jade carvings of these artisans are very practical and bear strong local and ethnical characteristics. They enrich the jade carving craft of China as well as oriental jade carving craft.

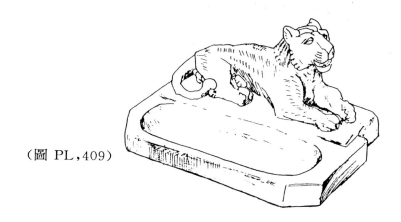

（圖 PL，409）

玉琢 *Jade*

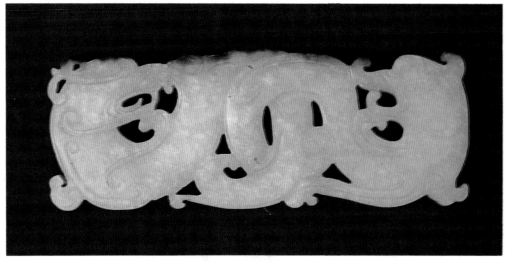

408 雙龍玉牌 Jade Applique Plate with Twin Dragon in Relief

409 臥虎玉硯 Jade Inkslab

410 項珠飾品　Necklaces

411 玉璧　*Bi* (A round flat piece of jade)

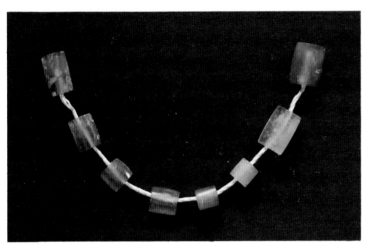

412 串珠　Jade Beads

414 人形花押　Agate Seal with Human
Figure in Relief

413 人形花押　Agate Seal with
Human Figure in Relief

415　雙龍耳玉杯　Jade Cup with Two Dragon-shaped Handles

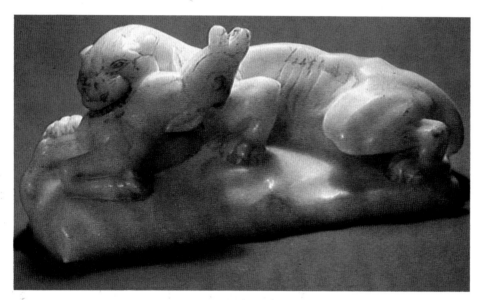

416　虎噬羊鎮子　Jade *Yu* with Tiger Eating Donkey Statuette

417　白玉透雕椅扶手　White-jade Armrest

418　白玉盤　White-Jade Dish

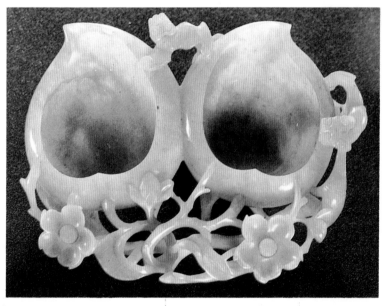

419　桃形雙聯玉洗　Peach-shaped Jade Bowl

420　三嘴白玉吊燈　White-jade 3-opening Lamp

建築

新疆的古代建築，其歷史悠久，形式多樣，具有地方特點和民族特色。最早的古建築可追溯到青銅時代。

由於新疆具有氣候乾燥的自然特點，至今地面上仍保存著豐富的各種類型的生土建築。如位於古代交通要道沿線的漢唐時期的烽火台、戍城堡建築，以及享有盛譽的高昌故城、交河故城、北庭故城等「絲路」名城：在這些千年古城中，顯赫的官宅，塔廟相映的寺院、佈局合理的街巷，井然有序的民宅等建築，至今還歷歷在目，生動地展現了我國傳統建築藝術的風貌。

印度佛教文化的東傳，給新疆古代建築藝術輸入了新的血液，在喀什、和闐、庫車、拜城、吐魯番等地，現在還保存著大量依山傍水開鑿的石窟，以及地面營建的塔廟建築。如著名的克孜爾、庫木吐拉、柏孜克里克石窟，莫爾、熱瓦克、尼雅、米蘭、蘇巴什等塔廟。這些石窟和塔廟建築，因地制宜，既充分利用了我國傳統的建築技法，又吸收和融匯了印度、伊朗等外來文化因素，從而產生了新的建築藝術風格，曾給我國內地的建築藝術以深遠的影響。

伊斯蘭教在新疆的傳播，又產生出具有伊斯蘭教特點的許多建築。如霍城縣的禿黑魯帖木爾汗陵，是新疆早期伊斯蘭建築的代表。陵墓為磚結構，琉璃磚貼面，上覆高約14米的穹窿形墓頂；正面大門兩側鑲有藍、紫、白三色琉璃磚組成的幾何形裝飾圖案和長聯式的阿拉伯文書法藝術。吐魯番的蘇公塔（額敏塔）清真寺，建於1778年。它以形體高大雄偉而美觀的磚塔著稱於世。塔內一螺旋台階可通達頂部。寺院為土坯建築，外面飾有許多壁龕和楞帶等裝飾。此外還有庫車大寺、喀什的艾提朵爾大寺、阿帕霍加墓、哈密回王墳等也都是新疆民族建築藝術中的瑰寶。

清代的磚木建築中，以昭蘇的喇嘛廟、伊寧回族寺及惠遠城鐘樓為代表。三層三檐歇山頂的鐘樓，斗拱飛檐、雕樑畫棟，屋檐頂端排列的瑞獸，檐角倒懸著鐵馬金鐘，與綠色的琉璃瓦當交相輝映，顯示出我國傳統建築藝術的民族風格。那高居烏魯木齊紅山頂端的寶塔，為八角九級樓閣式磚塔，古樸凝重，是清代邊城烏魯木齊城市的勝景之一。

（圖 PL，433）

ARCTECTURE

The ancient architecture of Xinjiang has its own local and national characteristics with a long history and varied styles.   The earliest structure can be traced back to Bronze Age.

Various kinds of ancient clay structures have been remained due to the dry climate in Xinjiang.   Such as the beacon towers, stations along the strategic lines of the Han and Tang Dynasties; the famous ruins of Gaochang, Jiaohe and Beiting along the Silk Road.Greatly distinguished residences of officials, temples have been preserved up to now in these sites. They fully display the style and features of the traditional architecture art of China .

The Buddhist culture of India input new blood into the ancient architecture art of Xinjiang.   Grottoes built on cliffs, temples and towers still can be found in large numbers in Kashgar, Hotan, Kuqa, Baicheng and Turfan, such as well-known Kizil, Kumtura and Bezeklik Grottoes, temples and towers in Mol, Rawak, Niya, Milan and Subashi.   These grottoes, temples and towers, absorbing the exotic cultural elements from India and Iran as well as using the traditional architectural technique   of   China.   , created a new architectural style and strongly influenced the architecture art of inner China.

The spread of Islam in Xinjiang gave rise to Islamic architecture.   The Tuguluk-Temur Mazar in Huocheng County represents the early Islamic architecture in Xinjiang.   The Emin Minaret, built in 1778, is famous for its high and beautiful brick tower.   Besides, the Great Mosque in Kuqa, the Id kah Mosque and Apakhoja Tomb in Kashgar and the Tomb of the kings of Hami are all excellent works of the national architecture art in Xinjiang.

Among the brick-wood structures of the Qing Dynasty, the lamasery in Zhaosu, mosque in Yining and Huiyuan Bell Tower merit attention.   They reflect the national style of the traditional architecture art of China.   However, the octagonal brick pagoda on the top of Hongshan Hill in Urumqi embellished the scenery of Urumqi in the Qing Dynasty.

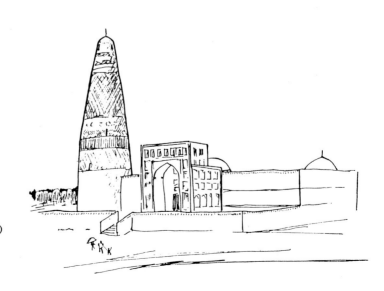

（圖 PL，442）

建築　*Architecture*

421　樓蘭佛塔　Stupa in Loulan Ancient City

422　霍城吐虎魯鐵木耳麻扎　The Tuguluk-Temur Mazar

423 交河故城 *The Ancient City of Jiaohe*

424 交河故城大佛殿佛龕、佛像（殘） *Niches and the Figures of Buddha*

425 交河故城塔林 *A Group of Stupas*

426　高昌故城　The Ancient City of Gaochang

427　高昌故城城牆
City Wall of Gaochang Ancient City

428 高昌故城佛塔
The Stupa of Gaochang

429 拜城克孜爾石窟 The Kizil Caves

430 中心柱窟窟形 The Cave with a Centural Piliar

431 若羌米蘭佛塔 Stupa in Milan

432 民豐尼雅佛塔 Stupa in the Niya Site

433 喀什莫爾佛塔 The Mol Stupas

434 洛浦熱瓦克佛寺 The Rewak Buddhist Temple

436 鄯善烽火台 Beacon Tower

435 庫車昭怙喱佛塔 Stupa

437 庫車克孜爾尕哈佛塔 The Kizil-Kargha
Stupa

171

438 艾提尕爾清真寺 The Id Kah Mosque

439 艾提尕爾禮拜寺敞廊 The Worshipping Hall of Id Kah Mosque

440 阿巴霍加陵墓 The Apakhoja Tomb

441 庫車大寺 The Kuqa Mosque

442 蘇公塔清眞寺 The Emin Minaret and Mosque

443 蘇公塔（額敏塔）身 The Body of the Emin Minaret

444 塔塔爾寺 The Tatar Mosque

446 哈密回王墳 The Tomb of the King of Hami

445 艾買爾太陵墓 Aimaiertai Tomb

447 惠遠新城鐘鼓樓　The Bell and Drum Tower of Huiyuan Town

448 昭蘇聖佑廟大殿　The Main Temple of the Lamasery

449 烏魯木齊紅山寶塔　The Hongshan Pagoda

450 烏魯木齊文廟　The Confucian Temple

後 記

位于古代絲綢之路中段的新疆,是古代東西方文化、經濟相互交匯之地,有着極其豐富的古代文物,許多文物同時也是價值極高的藝術品。藝術品是人類精神文明和物質文明的形象反映,更是文明歷史的見證。為了介紹古代新疆文物藝術瑰寶,編寫了《中國新疆古代藝術》一書。

從上世紀末到本世紀初,外國眾多的"考察隊"到新疆各地"挖寶",將許多精美絕倫的文物運往國外,曾引起世界轟動。從五十年代以來,中國考古學者在新疆各地不間斷地進行考察、發掘,發現了大量罕見的珍貴文物。近年來雖有新疆考古藝術方面的畫冊出版,但是由于選題的角度不同,或是對文物的收集不夠豐富,使外界很難全面、系統地了解新疆的古代文物,從而難以揭示新疆的古代文明。

我們盡可能對國內外各類材料進行搜集、整理,在浩如烟海的文物中,篩選了400余件最具代表性的精品,對其進行分類、編排,對每件文物進行研究對比,編寫文字說明,而且將全部文字譯成英文,直可謂數年心血凝成了此書。我們願以此書奉獻給各國學者和朋友們。

特別要說明的是,新疆美術攝影出版社總編輯祁協玉先生、編審柳用能先生、副編審馮中平女士,對本書的稿件進行了認真負責的審校、潤色,聯系各項出版事宜,為《中國新疆古代藝術》畫冊的出版費盡了心血。在此表示誠摯的感謝。

在編輯《中國新疆古代藝術》畫冊的進程中,遇到各種各樣的困難,曾得到許多學者和朋友們的熱情幫助和支持,他(她)們是賈應逸教授、霍旭初教授、王明哲教授、蔣其祥教授、陳世良教授,及楊萍、邱陵、陳霞、朱一凡、李宇虹、鄭渤秋、胡桂株、岑雲飛、侯世新、劉新、張寶春、趙鵬彬、羊毅勇、趙靜、萬立、許建英、何漢民、李廣寬、胡文康、張玉忠、邢開鼎、常喜恩、薩恆塔伊、郭建國、張鐵男、王毅龍、譚大海、楊富學、郭文清、賀新、梁勇、徐永明、陳德松、宋濤等同志,特表示感謝。

由于時間倉促,學識水平有限,難免存在一些疏漏。竭誠希望專家學者和讀者給予指正。

作　者
一九九三年六月八日

POSTSCRIPT

Xinjiang, located in the middle section of ancient Silk Road, is a placewhere the eastern and western cultures met in ancient times. Numerouscultural relics exist here and some of them are valuable works of art . Thework of art is not only a vivid reflection of the ideological progress andmaterial progress of human beings, but also a telling witness of the historyof civilization. The compilation of this book is to introduce these preciousjewels of art in ancient Xinjiang.

At the end of the nineteenth century and in the early twentieth century,many foreign "expeditions" came to Xinjiang in quest for treasures. Lots ofexquisite and incomparable cultural relics were taken abroad and caused agreat sensation in the world. Since the 1950s, Chinese archaeologists haveengaged in investigation and excavation ceaselessly, and large quantities ofpriceless cultural relics have been found here.

In recent years, there have published several picture albums on thearchaeological art in Xinjiang. But, due to the variation of themes andincompleteness of the collection of cultural relics in these albums, theancient civilization in Xinjiang has not been fully revealed.

We have done our best to collect and arrange various kinds of materialsabout cultural relics and chosen more than 400 pieces of most representativeones. We studied and compared them, and then classified and rearranged them. Entries were written for every picture and translated into English. This bookis the fruit of our painstaking labour. Now, we are glad to present it toscholars and friends all over the world.

Our warmest thanks go to Mr. Qi Xieyu, Chief Editor of The Xinjiang FineArts and Photographing Press, to Mr. Liu Yongneng, Senior Editor, and to MrsFeng Zhongping, Deputy Senior Editor. They went over all manuscriptscarefully and made reasonable revisions, and undertook all matters relatingto the publication of this book. We really appreciate their devotions to thisproject. Acknowledgments are also due to Professor Jia Yingyi, Professor HuoXuchu, Professor Wang Mingzhe, Professor Jiang Qixiang, Professor ChenShiliang, Yang Ping, Chen Xia, Li Yuhong, Qiu Ling, Zheng Boqiu, Hu Guizhu,Hou Shixin, Liu Xin,Zhang Baochun,Zhao Pengbin, Yang Yiyong, Zhao Jing, Wanli, Xu Jianying, He Hanmin, Li Guangkuan, Hu Wenkang, Zhang Yuzhong, XingKaiding, Chang Xien, Sahengtayi, Guo Jianguo, Zhang Tienan, Wang Yilong, TanDahai,Guo Wenqing, He Xin,Liang Yong, Xu Yongming, Cheng Desong, Song Tao. Without their help, the realization of this program is impossible.

The Authors

June 8, 1993

參考資料

(1)《新疆考古三十年》，新疆人民出版社，1983年。

(2)《新疆出土文物》，文物出版社，1957年。

(3)《新疆古代民族文物》，文物出版社，1985年。

(4)《中國美術全集》，繪畫編16新疆石窟壁畫，文物出版社，1989年。

(5)《中國美術全集》，工藝美術編6印染織繡，文物出版社，1989年。

(6)《新疆博物館》，文物出版社講談社合編，1991年。

(7)《西域美術》，第3卷，講談社，1981年。

(8)《絲綢之路・中亞藝術》，美國紐約大都會博物館編，1982年。

(9)《高昌》，大學印刷出版社，格拉茨，1979年。

(10)《中亞美術》，韓國國立中央博物館編，1986年。

REFERENCES

(1)"*30-year Archaeological Work in Xinjiang.*" Xinjiang People's Press Urumqi, 1983.

(2)"*The Cultural Relics Unearthed from Xinjiang.*"The Cultural Relics Press, Beijing, 1985.

(3)"*Ancient National Cultural Relics of Xinjiang.*"TheCultural Relics Press. Beijing, 1985.

(4)"*The Collected Works of Chinese Fine Arts*". Painting 16: *The Wall paintings in the Grottoes of Xinjiang.* The Cultural Relics Press, Beijing, 1989.

(5)"*The Collected works of Chinese Fine Arts*". *Arts and Crafts 6: Printing Dyeing, Weaving and Embroidering.* The Cultural Relics Press, Beijing, 1988.

(6)"*Xinjiang Museum*". The Cultural Relics Press and Kodansha, 1991.

(7)"*The Art of Central Asia*". Vol. 3 , Kodansha, Tokyo, 1981.

(8)"*Along the Silk Road: Central Asian Art from the West Berling State Museums*". The Metro-politan Museum of Art. New York, 1982.

(9)"*CHOTSCHO*". Arademische Druck — u Verlagsanstalt, Graz, 1979.

(10)"*Central Asian Art.*"The National Museum of Korea, Seoul, 1986.

圖版説明

石 器 類

001 石鏃

新石器時代，長2.9—5.5cm，羅布泊出土。5件，為玉髓或燧石質。這5件石鏃均用「壓琢法」製成。形狀各異，鋌部也各不相同。從左到右為：①三角形凹底石鏃，②圓頭石鏃，③帶柄石鏃，④桂葉形尖狀器，⑤凹底投槍頭。現存新疆考古所。

002 桂葉形石矛

新石器時代，通長7.9cm，羅布泊出土。燧石質，造型呈桂葉形。一端加工成尖狀，一端約略加工出鋌部，兩側加工成刃。它的特色在於其獨特的加工技藝，即採用微觀加工的「壓琢」工藝，使矛面通體呈「魚鱗」狀。石矛也可稱為投槍頭。現存新疆考古所。

003 石球

新石器時代，直徑7cm，托克遜縣小草湖遺址出土。砂岩質，黃褐色，採用琢磨技術加工製造而成。呈比較規則的圓球狀，表面打磨得較為光滑、勻稱，有撞擊使用痕跡。器物整體渾圓古樸。現存吐魯番博物館。

004 白玉斧

新石器時代，長11.6、刃寬6cm，羅布泊出土。形體較規則，近似長方形，通體均經琢磨加工。其刃部經兩面磨製而成，至今仍甚鋒利。玉斧質地晶瑩光潔，以珍貴的羊脂玉製成。造型質樸簡潔，表現出一種古樸無華的風格。現存新疆考古所。

005 石核

中石器時代晚期——新石器時代初期，長分別為3.5、6cm，鄯善縣迪坎爾遺址採集。燧石質。兩件石核皆呈柱體狀，是剝取石葉以製作細石器的石料。現存吐魯番博物館。

006 三角形石鋤

青銅時代，寬22、高17cm，塔城衛校遺址出土。呈圓角等腰三角形，表面乳黃色，磨製而成。在「三角形」底邊磨製出刃。中央有一鑽孔，以穿插鋤柄。石鋤造型規整，表現了很成熟的製造工藝。現存新疆考古所。

007 石鋤

青銅時代，長17.5cm。阜康縣三宮鄉出土。利用扁圓形礫石經鑽、磨而成。一端磨成尖圓狀刃，另一端較粗厚，鑽磨出一內徑2.1cm的孔。整體風格厚重古樸，選材獨具匠心，造型拙中藏巧。現存新疆考古所。

008 石鐮

新石器時代，長15.3cm，疏附縣阿克塔那遺址出土。砂岩質，鐮體稍呈弧形，一端較寬，為裝柄之用，一端成尖狀。內側磨成鐮刃，通體造型渾厚樸實。現存新疆博物館。

009 青玉斧

銅石並用時代，長8.8cm，寬4.3cm。和碩縣新塔拉遺址出土。青玉質，磨製而成，器身扁平，弧形刃兩面磨製。製作精細，器形規整。現存新疆考古所。

010 鶴嘴鋤

銅石並用時代，長13.1、厚3cm，哈密天山區板房溝出土。花崗岩質，整體略呈菱形，但一端較長而尖，似鶴嘴狀，係採用琢磨技術加工而成。中間偏上處有一鑽孔，用以裝柄。奇特的是在鋤體周緣又琢磨出一道凹槽。現存哈密博物館。

陶 器 類

011 複彩波浪紋彩陶豆

公元前5世紀，18.2cm，鄯善縣洋海墓地出土。上為鉢狀，下為高圈足。尖唇，斂口，單耳在口沿處。上部塗紅底黑彩，紋飾為一組等距的雙波浪紋及平行斜線紋。造型大方，繪彩精美，為新疆彩陶器之上品。現存吐魯番博物館。

012 敞口帶流束頸圓腹壺

公元前5世紀，高26cm，拜城縣克孜爾水庫墓地出土。造型別緻。方唇，大敞口呈喇叭狀，束頸，長而寬的流外伸稍上翹，長條形單耳由口沿斜延至肩部。鼓腹，平底。頸部有一圈斷續的附加乳釘。現存新疆考古所。

013 幾何紋單耳帶流杯

公元前10—公元前5世紀，高12.5cm，和靜縣察吾呼溝出土。尖唇，侈口，粗頸，鼓腹，平底。單耳在肩部處。紅衣黑彩，上部至口沿施彩繪。圖案由兩部份構成，近耳部為排列十分規整的上下八排倒三角紋，流下為變形迴紋，下部平塗紅彩。是新疆彩陶藝術中的珍品。現存新疆考古所。

014 夾砂灰陶杯

公元前10世紀，左高12、右高2.3cm，塔城衛校墓地出土。造型相似，均方唇，口微斂，下收為平底，左側較大陶杯口沿下飾折線狀點印紋，右側較小者通體飾指印紋。現存塔城博物館。

015 倒三角狀錐刺紋陶杯

公元前15世紀，高9cm，和碩縣新塔那遺址出土。黑陶質，敞口，直腹，平底。上腹部有一圈錐刺紋組成的倒三角紋飾。現存博物館。

016 四口鼓腹罐

公元前10—公元前5世紀，高34cm，塔城市二宮鄉喀浪古爾村採集。夾砂紅陶，手製，鼓腹，四口，腹徑44cm。四口中一大三小，大者位於罐上部正中，口徑17cm，敞口，沿外有2道凸棱。其餘三嘴直徑7.5cm左右，等距勻稱分布於肩部。此罐造型獨特，製作精巧。現存塔城博物館。

017 水波紋環底罐

公元前12—公元前7世紀，高17cm，阿勒泰市克爾木齊出土。斂口，唇略尖，鼓腹，尖環底。整個器物略呈橄欖形。口沿為指印紋，腹部為壓印弧線紋，呈扇面狀，互相疊套。該器物及紋飾與哈薩克斯坦卡拉蘇克文化中的同類器物相似。現存新疆考古所。

018 植物紋彩陶罐

公元前10—公元前5世紀，高35.6cm，和靜縣察吾呼溝出土。方唇略外折，溜肩，鼓腹，平底。通體深紅彩，頸肩部彩繪紋飾，為四組圖案。其中有不規整的網格紋和葡萄藤蔓紋。現存新疆考古所。

019 長流單耳陶杯

公元前10—公元前5世紀，高11.5cm，和靜縣察吾呼溝出土。圓唇，敞口，圓腹，口徑大於腹徑，平底。流長上翹呈鳥喙狀。頸部有一圈附加堆紋。現存巴音郭楞蒙古自治州博物館。

020 臥駝紋單耳帶流彩陶罐

公元前10—公元前5世紀，高21.3cm，和靜縣察吾呼溝出土。夾砂紅陶，手製，方唇，溜肩，平底，白衣紅彩。繞頸一周飾一排峰駝紋，駝跪地，頭和細長的脖頸前伸作臥而欲起狀。描繪生動。為新疆古代的一件藝術珍品。現存新疆考古所。

021 變形鳥紋單耳帶流彩陶杯

公元前10—公元前5世紀，高14.2cm，和靜縣察吾呼溝出土。圓唇，口微敞，粗頸，鼓腹，平底。短流向外平伸。紅衣紅彩，通體繪有等距的豎向折線紋，在折線紋中繪一寬斜帶，帶內繪有排列整齊的變形鳥紋。是新疆古代彩陶藝術中的精品。現存新疆考古所。

022 三葉草紋雙耳彩陶罐

公元前5世紀，高16cm，哈密市林雅墓地出土。泥質紅陶，手製，圓唇，口微敞，斜肩，鼓腹，下收為小平底，雙耳。衣黑紅彩，自口沿向下繪距離相等之平行線條，並於平行線間最大腹徑處，點綴以小三葉草紋。此類器物亦見於甘、青地區。現存哈密博物館。

023 單耳彩陶鉢

公元前5世紀，高6.4cm，哈密馬不拉克出土。泥質紅陶。方唇，大平底，一側有扳狀耳。口沿下飾二周連續平行折線，平行線下為斷續的折線紋。鉢底有一小孔。現存哈密博物館。

024 環帶折線單耳彩陶壺

公元前3世紀，高18cm，巴里坤縣大河鄉出土。夾砂紅陶，手製，方唇，口略敞，頸略長，溜肩，弧腹，平底。腹部有帶狀單耳。紅衣紅彩，在口沿、頸部、腹部各繪一條繞器一周的寬彩帶。寬帶內繪曲折水波紋圖案，耳部也繪同樣紋飾。現存新疆博物館。

025 長頸雙耳彩陶壺

公元前5世紀，高19cm，哈密馬不拉克出土。圓唇，長粗頸，口微侈，鼓腹，平底。口沿內外飾不規整的三角紋，頸部用粗細不等的線條勾勒，腹部大體為豎平行線，有兩小耳，位於腹部。現存哈密博物館。

026 連續波狀紋貫耳壺

公元前5世紀，高16.7cm，哈密林場辦事處古墓出土。圓唇，斂口，腹微鼓，小平底。近口處兩側有橫向扳耳。紅底黑彩，通體為波折紋。現存哈密博物館。

027 高流大彩陶罐

公元前10世紀，高39cm，拜城縣克孜爾水庫墓地出土。圓唇，口微敞，溜肩，鼓腹，環底，流寬長而上翹。頸的上部為平塗的紅彩，下為錯疊的橫三角形紋飾。現存新疆考古所。

028 垂幛紋帶流罐

公元前10世紀，高28cm，拜城縣克孜爾水庫墓地出土。圓唇，粗頸，小平底，短流上翹。口沿至上腹繪折線或折線點紋。現存新疆考古所。

029 山川紋彩陶釜

公元前5世紀，高22.5cm，口徑34cm，拜城縣克孜爾水庫墓地出土。方唇，折沿，鼓腹，環底，單扳耳。頸和下腹底部各繪一周帶狀彩。上為二周交錯的山形紋，下繪三條平行折線。整個圖案既有上下互異的動感，以又左右重複的靜感，極富藝術感染力。現存新疆考古所。

030 直筒單耳彩陶杯

公元前5世紀，高10.2cm，鄯善縣蘇貝希墓地出土。方唇，直壁，平底。紅衣黑彩，口沿內外有倒三角紋。中腹以下為大倒三角紋。上、下三角紋之間以線隔開。現存新疆考古所。

031 條紋單耳彩陶杯

公元前5世紀，高11.3cm，鄯善縣洋海墓地出土。方唇，口略侈，鼓腹環底。單耳，自口沿斜向下，貼於器底。口內沿飾一圈小三角紋。器表自口沿向下為上粗下細的平行線紅彩，構圖簡潔。現存吐魯番博物館。

032 葫蘆形單耳壺

公元前5世紀，高4.2cm，鄯善縣洋海墓地出土。圓唇，高細頸，收為小口，圓腹，環底，形似葫蘆。器身有不規則的斷續繩紋。此器形在新疆罕見。現存吐魯番博物館。

033 長頸壺

公元1世紀，高20cm，鄯善縣蘇巴什墓地採集。方唇，侈口，細長頸，溜肩，鼓腹，小平底，腹部有附加堆紋，呈豎條狀和半圓形。現存新疆博物館。

034 單耳彩陶缽

公元前5世紀，高10cm，鄯善縣洋海墓地出土。方唇，大口，沿微折，弧腹，下收為小平底，一側有橫耳。紅衣紅彩，由口沿向下飾一周細長倒三角紋。現存吐魯番博物館。

035 人頭像單耳帶流彩陶罐

公元前10—公元前5世紀，高23cm，輪台縣群巴克墓地出土。圓唇，直口，鼓腹，平底，流短上翹。通體圖案，上下兩周為平行線三角紋，三角紋之間的菱形空格中繪以不同的小紋樣，其中有一半身側面人像。現存巴音郭楞蒙古自治州博物館。

036 斜帶彩陶杯

公元前5世紀，高18.5cm。輪台縣群巴克墓地出土。尖唇，圓口，粗頸，鼓腹，平底，紅彩。自口沿斜向器底塗兩條白色帶狀紋飾，帶中繪紅色斜方格紋，如同長梯狀。現存巴音郭楞蒙古自治州博物館。

037 單耳彩陶豆

公元前5世紀，高19.6cm，烏魯木齊南山礦區東風廠出土。夾砂紅陶，手製，方唇，口略敞，豆的上部為鉢狀，單耳過器口，下為圈足。通體飾紅陶衣。口沿外飾不規範的豎黑條紋。豆類器物在新疆主要發現於東疆地區。現存新疆考古所。

038 孤形三角紋單耳彩陶罐

公元前5世紀，高12cm，烏魯木齊烏拉泊水庫墓地出土。方唇，直項微外侈，鼓腹，小平底。紅衣黑彩，口沿下為一周小而長的倒三角紋，腹部為上下錯對的豎平行線三角紋，三角的邊線或凹或凸，彩繪線條極為規整、流暢。現存新疆考古所。

039 條網紋單耳彩陶罐

公元前5世紀，高13.6cm，烏魯木齊南山礦區阿拉溝出土。夾砂紅陶，手製，方唇，高頸，口略外敞，溜肩，鼓腹，環底。肩與頸部手製接痕明顯。口頸處繪網紋，腹部飾一周銜連的倒三角紋，三角內滿繪豎平行線。現存新疆博物館。

040 樹叉紋單耳彩陶罐

公元前5世紀，高16.6cm，烏魯木齊南山礦區阿拉溝出土。方唇，高頸，鼓腹，平底。與單耳相對的一側略高。紅衣紅彩，花紋呈不甚規整的樹枝狀。現存新疆博物館。

041 三角紋渦紋單耳彩陶罐

公元前5—公元前4世紀，高11.5cm，烏魯木齊南山礦區魚兒溝出土。夾砂紅陶，手製，尖唇，口略敞，溜肩，平底，一側有扳狀耳，頸部飾兩排連續倒三角紋。腹部飾三組渦紋。現存新疆博物館。

042 折線紋彩陶壺

公元前3—公元前2世紀，高29cm，昭蘇縣夏台土墩墓出土。圓唇，高頸，圓腹，環底。紅衣紅彩，口沿繪倒三角紋，頸部方格紋，腹部為平行折線繪成之倒三角紋。現存新疆博物館。

043 繭形陶壺

公元1世紀，高20cm，昭蘇縣夏台土墩墓出土。器形作蠶繭狀，器口較高，兩側肩部有泥條裝飾，泥條上穿眼。器體一側鼓起，整體造型仿游牧民族的皮鑲壺。類似器物在關中地區秦墓中亦有發現。現存新疆博物館。

044 雙孔陶燭台

公元1世紀，高8.3cm，昭蘇縣夏台土墩墓出土。上部為鉢狀，下為圈足。器底有管狀燭座。現存新疆考古所。

045 連續幾何圖紋鼓腹彩陶壺

公元前2—公元前1世紀，高24cm，昭蘇縣夏台土墩墓出土。方唇，束頸，溜肩，鼓腹，平底。通體赭紅色彩繪。在上腹部隔成的14個長方格內，分別填繪半圓形和網格紋圖案。現存新疆博物館。

046 網紋單耳彩陶杯

公元前3世紀，高12.5cm，新源縣黑山頭墓地出土。手製，方唇，口斂，平底，單耳。通體飾不甚整齊的粗網紋。現存新疆考古所。

047 高腹彩陶壺

公元前5世紀，高35cm，察布查爾縣索墩布拉克古墓出土。方唇，侈口，頸略束，平肩，高腹略鼓，平底。紅衣紅彩，頸肩部為棋盤格紋，腰部分別用直線和弧線繪出菱形、新月形圖案。現存新疆考古所。

048 網格紋短頸彩陶罐

公元前5世紀，高12.5cm，察布查爾縣索墩布拉克古墓出土。方唇，短頸，鼓腹，平底。紅衣紅彩，上部繪網格紋。現存新疆考古所。

049 樹枝紋彩陶缽

公元前5世紀，高12.4cm，察布查爾縣索墩布拉克古墓出土。圓唇，直口，腹微鼓，環底，紅衣紅彩。器身下腹平塗均勻起伏的紅色山狀紋飾，上部飾樹枝紋。現存新疆考古所。

050 黑陶壺

公元2世紀，高22.8cm，民豐縣尼雅出土。方唇，口敞稍呈喇叭狀，唇略外卷，束頸，溜肩，鼓腹，平底。肩部一周上下交錯的三角紋。上排為虛三角，下排為實三角。現存新疆博物館。

051　黑陶杯

公元5—6世紀，高12.3cm，焉耆縣四十里城子出土。方唇，直壁，單耳，平底。口徑略大於底徑。手製，火候較高，造型實用大方。現存巴音郭楞蒙古自治州博物館。

052　桑葉紋陶壺

公元7—9世紀，高23cm，策勒縣達瑪溝出土。泥質紅陶，大折沿，球腹，平底。口沿和頸肩處有曲折線狀劃紋。上腹飾一周桑葉形印紋。葉紋兩兩相對，蒂部向上，葉尖向下。現存和闐博物館。

053　人面紋細嘴單耳壺

公元7—9世紀，高27.5cm，吐魯番出土。紅陶質，侈口，長頸，單耳，肩部塑一細長流嘴，平底。頸部貼塑人面像，臉部豐滿，束高髻，形似菩薩。現存遼寧省旅順博物館。

054　雙系扁陶壺

公元11世紀，高26cm，和闐出土。器體扁平，白陶，小口直頸，兩側有雙系耳，表面有同心圓壓印紋。現存和闐博物館。

055　三耳人物罐

公元6世紀，高45cm，和闐出土。夾砂紅褐陶，範製，喇叭口，頸部三個拱形耳，鼓腹，平底。口沿內飾一周壓印紋和玫瑰形花紋。耳上有簡單的圓圈和線紋。三耳上部各有個印度風格的女頭塑像。頸部三個梯形框內飾有風格獨特的曲線紋飾。腹部飾七組浮雕式圓形圖案，邊緣由兩個同心圓夾一周邊珠紋組成。兩個圓形圖案間填以忍冬卷草紋。圓形圖案內容有三：一為側身而立的女像，左手托著酒杯，右手執壺；一為側身男像，有頭光，左手執杯交腳而坐。另一為雄獅頭像。器物製作精美獨特，飾紋為古印度、希臘羅馬藝術風格。現存柏林。

056　人頭像殘陶片

公元3—5世紀，殘寬28cm，疏附縣烏帕爾出土。陶器腹部殘片，模壓淺浮雕式花紋。上部殘存兩組圓形圖案，其邊緣由三同心圓圈夾一周聯珠紋組成，中飾婆羅門頭像，臉略左側作正視前方狀。頭戴寶冠，身著圓領服裝，圖案間配置忍冬卷草紋。中部為龍尾團花圖案。下部飾葡萄葉紋。紋飾精美，製作水平較高。現存疏附縣文化館。

057　敞口陶薰爐

公元7世紀，高25.7cm，拜城克孜爾石窟第60窟出土。夾細砂紅陶，輪製，由內外兩部份組成。外部：敞口，平沿，斜方唇，直壁外敞，小平底。內部：侈口，束頸，有5個橢圓形熏孔。外壁施淺綠色釉彩。這種形製的香爐與克孜爾石窟壁畫所繪者相同。現存新疆考古所。

058　貼花雙耳瓶

公元3—5世紀，高14cm，和闐出土。方唇，外侈，長頸，溜肩，鼓腹，圈足。雙耳上下各貼一花瓣形附加堆紋。沿內和頸肩處均有一周圈點紋。頸部和腹部一周為貼加圓形花瓣。腹肩間有二道陰刻弦紋。現存韓國漢城。

059　猴耳條紋壺

公元1世紀，高10.6cm，和闐縣約特干遺址出土。口殘，溜肩，鼓腹，平底。耳上有泥塑臥猴一隻，猴杯中抱有一物。通體為被等距分開細泥條狀紋。造型奇特。現存英國倫敦。

060　單耳壺

公元7—8世紀，高14.3cm，和碩縣馬蘭古城出土。方唇，口微敞，頸略束，鼓腹，頸部刻二周陽弦紋。現存巴音郭楞蒙古自治州博物館。

061　單耳彩繪陶罐

公元7世紀，高24.5cm，吐魯番阿斯塔那出土。侈口，束頸，鼓腹，平底。圖案由5部分組成，口沿上為一周綠色點紋；肩部為一圈雲紋圖案，中腹為倒蓮瓣紋，下為弧線、點。現存新疆博物館。

062　陶虎子

公元7—8世紀，高9cm，哈密五堡採集。又名夜壺，整體似龜狀。器口前伸上翹，頸兩側有雙提耳，背上部有圓形鈕。周邊為連續圓珠扣壓紋。現存哈密博物館。

063　陶博山爐

公元3—4世紀，高14cm，若羌縣出土。黑陶。器物由底盤和爐體由二部分組成。爐體略作倒圓錐形，上部為錐狀蓋，蓋上均分佈圓形透孔，是出煙的通道。現存韓國漢城。

064　雙耳黑陶罐

公元7—8世紀，高30cm，巴里坤縣大河古城出土。方唇，侈口，束頸，溜肩，深腹，小平底，雙系耳。現存哈密博物館。

065　喙形嘴單耳壺

公元7—8世紀，高27cm，吐魯番出土。通體橙黃色，上作鳥首狀，長頸起脊，脊兩側有傾斜平行壓劃紋。下綴刻一蓮花。鼓腹，大平底。這是一件既實用又美觀的器物，鳥首可能受古波斯金銀器中鳥首壺的影響。現存韓國漢城。

066　人面花瓣貼塑舍利罐

公元1—2世紀，高20cm，和闐縣約特干出土。斂口，鼓腹，斜肩，下收為圈足。口沿下一周壓印圓圈紋。下為豎線，豎線兩旁為錐刺點紋。腹部有陰弦紋二道，弦紋之間有圓形貼花一周。弦紋之上貼有月牙形裝飾。器腹附加有對稱的人頭圖像。現存英國倫敦。

067　斂口舍利罐

公元7—8世紀，高30cm，庫車縣阿克謝古城出土。斂口，鼓腹，大平底，有蓋，最大腹徑偏上。現存新疆博物館。

068 筒形陶棺

公元5—7世紀，長66cm、直徑30cm，鄯善縣吐峪溝麻扎出土。筒形。上有長方形棺口及從棺體上切下的瓦狀棺蓋。棺體及棺蓋均以泥條裝飾。成人骨骸一具。現存吐魯番博物館。

069 彩繪舍利罐

公元4—5世紀，高24cm，柯坪縣出土。主體圓筒形，上為錐形蓋，蓋頂部有直徑10cm的小口，平底。器蓋在紅褐色底上描白色倒蓮瓣。罐身為黑底，上繪白色菱形紋，並在白線的交叉點上飾以紅色圓點。現存新疆博物館。

070 龍紋青瓷盤

公元13—14世紀，直徑34cm，霍城縣阿力麻里古城出土。淺沿，低圈足，周邊飾雲紋，盤中為貼花雙龍紋圖案。釉色青碧晶瑩。為元代龍泉瓷精品。現存新疆博物館。

071 龍泉青瓷碗

公元13—14世紀，口徑34cm，霍城縣阿力麻里古城出土。圓唇，侈口，深腹，高圈足，器體呈黃綠色，釉質晶瑩。現存新疆博物館。

072 山鳥紋黃褐釉陶壺

公元13—14世紀，高30cm，和闐縣出土。方唇，束頸，鼓腹，高圈足，腹部上下有二周陰刻弦紋，弦紋間繪5隻展翅飛翔的大鳥。頸部用粗細不同的線條繪山紋3組。現存新疆博物館。

073 山水畫青花瓷瓶

公元18—19世紀，高46cm，新疆收集。圓唇，直頸，溜肩，高腹，平底。肩部有兩系耳。頸和腹部繪山水畫。現存新疆博物館。

銅 器 類

074 銅武士俑

公元前5—公元前4世紀，高40cm，新源縣築乃斯河南岸出土。紅銅質，合範鑄造，空心。頭戴高彎鈎寬沿帽，臉部豐腴，雙目前視。上身赤裸，腰系短裙，左腿蹲屈，右腿跪地，赤足。雙手握物（已失）置於腿上。肌肉發達，造型生動，神態栩栩如生，為勇猛的武士形象。現存新疆博物館。

075 高方座承獸銅盤

公元前5—公元前1世紀，高32cm，烏魯木齊南山阿拉溝古墓出土。青銅鑄造。上為方盤，寬平折沿，中央立雙獸，形似獅子。下為方體喇叭狀高圈足。上下焊接而成。現存新疆博物館。

076 對虎銅頸圈

公元前5—公元前4世紀，直徑38cm，新源縣築乃斯河南岸出土。青銅鑄造。虎首相對吻合踞伏，虎身連續起凸棱構成連體銅圈。圈面橢圓，中空，內開口。現存新疆博物館。

077 對翼獸銅項圈

公元前5—公元前4世紀，直徑42.5cm，新源縣築乃斯河南岸出土。青銅鑄造。翼獸相對而臥，獸首似虎，立耳，短鬃，雙角後翹，背側有雙翼。獸體連續起凸棱，後彎曲成圈，圈中空，內開口。現存新疆博物館。

078 三足銅鼎

公元前5—公元前4世紀，高44cm，新源縣築乃斯河南岸出土。紅銅質。合範鑄造，鼓腹，環底。腹部飾三道凸弦紋，並有兩組對稱的橫耳和豎耳。底部三只空心折足，折足上段飾弧形凹紋，下段呈蹄狀。造型古樸渾厚，為古代游牧民族實用器物。現存新疆博物館。

079 雙耳高足銅鍑

公元前5—公元前1世紀，高57cm，烏魯木齊南山林場出土。青銅鑄造，直口，深腹，環底，喇叭形高圈足。口沿對立兩豎耳，耳呈方形，上附三個蘑菇形裝飾。耳雙側口沿上亦各有一蘑菇形裝飾。器腹飾凸線幾何形紋，口沿外飾折線和豎線紋。現存新疆博物館。

080 雙耳高足銅鍑

公元前5—公元前1世紀，高50cm，巴里坤縣蘭州灣子遺址出土。銅質，鑄造，深腹，環底。口沿豎立兩環形直耳，耳上有乳釘。底部焊接喇叭形高圈足。現存新疆博物館。

081 雙耳高足銅鍑

公元前5—公元前1世紀，高76cm，新源縣出土。青銅鑄造。斂口，深腹，下焊接喇叭高圈足，口沿上有相對兩直耳。耳呈環狀，上有小凸飾。現存伊犁博物館。

082 獸首吞蹄式足雙耳銅方盤

公元前5—公元前1世紀，高23cm，長寬76cm，察布查爾縣索布拉克出土。青銅鑄造。方盤，平底，口沿平折，兩側有雙環狀橫耳。四條駝蹄形足上部以人面為飾，其口、眼、鼻清晰可辨。現存新疆博物館。

083 野豬博馬紋銅飾牌

公元前5—公元前1世紀，長13cm，木壘縣東城鎮出土。鑄製，呈透雕狀，長方形。樞內左側鑄有一馬，縮身貼耳，張口咬住野豬頸部。野豬曲腿低頭，咬著馬的前腿，邊框鑄有菱形植物紋。現存木壘縣民族博物館。

084 雙鳥形銅扣

公元前8—公元前5世紀，寬6.4cm，和靜縣察吾呼溝古墓出土。青銅質，鑄製，弓形，兩端各一鳥首，圓目豎冠，短粗喙，扣弓部有繫帶的磨損痕跡。鳥首背面各有一個固定皮帶的圓鉚。現存巴音郭楞蒙古自治州博物館。

085 虎噬羊銅牌

公元前2—公元前1世紀，高5.5cm，吐魯番艾丁湖古墓出土。青銅質。鑄造透雕虎一隻。虎呈行走狀，尾下垂曲卷，身軀強健有力，睜目豎耳，張口叼著一隻羊。羊圓目曲角，軀體反轉卷曲呈圓形，背面有三個環鈕。現存新疆博物館。

086　雙羊銅飾牌

公元前2世紀，寬6cm，烏魯木齊烏拉泊出土。青銅鑄造，透雕，平面略呈梯形。上下邊框刻凹槽數道。中心圖案為兩羊相對而立，昂首，大角後彎至尾部，羊嘴下垂一環狀物。是一件頗具藝術性的裝飾物。現存烏魯木齊博物館。

087　包金虎形銅牌、金箔

公元前6—公元前5世紀，銅牌長4.7cm，金箔長6cm。鄯善縣蘇巴什古墓出土。長方形虎形銅牌上模壓一層金箔，邊緣包折至銅牌背面。銅牌正中鏤空雕刻一虎，後足蜷踞，躬身，尾上翹，右前足上揚，回首張口，形象生動，工藝精湛。銅牌邊框飾圓圈紋，背面有橋鈕。現存吐魯番博物館。

088　野豬紋透雕團形銅飾牌

公元前5—公元前1世紀，直徑7.3cm，木壘縣東城鎮出土。鑄造，呈透雕狀。圓形，中心一野豬，身軀體捲曲呈環形，其外環列五隻野豬，均作覓食狀。造型新穎別緻，工藝水平較高。現存新疆考古所。

089　銅斧

公元前10—公元前8世紀，長24cm，托里縣徵集。青銅質，鑄造。柄部較寬厚，弧頂，上飾杉葉紋，中有橢圓形鑿孔，寬弧刃。現存塔城博物館。

090　銅斧

公元前5世紀，長17cm，拜城縣克孜爾水庫墓地出土。青銅質，鑄造。橢圓形鑿孔，雙面直刃。刃部較闊，斧柄部呈方形，下略收與鑿連。現存新疆考古所。

091　銅斧

公元前10—公元前8世紀，長21cm。巴里坤縣奎蘇疙瘩出土。青銅質，鑄造。整體較厚重，斧身截面呈六面體。圓形鑿孔，窄弧刃。現存哈密博物館。

092　銅鏟

青銅時代，長4.5cm，塔城市徵集。三件，青銅鍛製，均作窄長柄，有檔寬弧刃，較鋒利，係複合工具。現存塔城博物館。

093　銅刀

公元前8—公元前5世紀，長13.5—17.5cm，和靜察吾呼溝出土。三件，青銅鍛製，上：直柄，柄端有孔，近刃處內收，雙面刃，刃部較銳。中：弧柄，環首有孔，內弧刃，尖部已殘。下：直柄，內弧刃，鈍尖微上翹。現存巴音郭楞蒙古自治州博物館。

094　銅馬銜

公元前8—公元前5世紀，長17.5cm，和靜縣察吾呼溝出土。銅質，模製，中間兩環相套，兩端呈馬蹄形，上有

2長方形孔，供連接彎頭、韁繩用。現存新疆考古所。

095　豎鑿銅斧

公元前8—公元前5世紀，長10cm，和靜縣察吾呼溝出土。青銅鑄製，長方形，豎圓鑿，出土時鑿孔內尚存殘斷木柄。鑿沿起棱，沿下有一直系。刃部略寬，兩面加工，呈圓弧狀。現存新疆考古所。

096　銅鐮

青銅時代，長24、23.5、22cm（從上至下），塔城徵集。三件，青銅打製，圓背弧刃，前端收縮成尖狀，鐮柄有小孔，有使有痕跡。現存塔城博物館。

097　銅戈

公元前5—公元前1世紀，長16.1，15.1cm，鄯善縣洋海古墓出土。銅質，合範鑄成。欄為中空的橢圓形鑿孔，上有一孔，內上穿一孔。直援，尖鋒，援中起脊，兩側各有一條凸棱。是新疆地區少見的兵器。現存吐魯番博物館。

098　折背羊首柄銅刀

公元前5—公元前1世紀，長23cm，新源縣查布哈渠出土。青銅鑄造，直柄析背，柄首鑄一瓣有盤角的羊頭。刀身弧刃，較寬，斜接刀柄，刀尖上翹。刀柄上飾有連續交叉紋和半環裝邊珠紋。銅刀整體造型奇特，以動物紋為裝飾，顯示出北方草原游牧民族的藝術風格。現存新疆博物館。

099　熊首青銅刀

公元前8—公元前5世紀，長12.2cm，和靜縣察吾呼溝出土。青銅質，鑄鍛而成。直背、弧刃、扁柄、柄首飾一獸，似熊。大頭圓目，弓背，全身站立。現存新疆考古所。

100　弧背鹿首銅刀

公元前8—公元前5世紀，長36cm哈密市花園村出土。弧背凹刃，刀柄與刀身之間有一舌狀突。刀柄裝飾作鹿形。鹿面額較長眼鼓突，小耳直立，長角向後彎曲成環。現存哈密博物館。

101　環首銅刀

公元前1世紀，長41cm，托克遜縣出土。青銅鑄製，弧柄，環首，下緣有格。背略弧，刃內弧，前收成尖，較鈍。現存新疆博物館。

102　銅弩機

公元1—4世紀，長12cm，高17.7cm，若羌縣阿拉干出土。青銅質，各部件分別製成後鉚合為一整體。上有鉤牙，下有長柄懸刀，外部鉚合有廓，廓頂面有箭槽。這種兵器來自中原。現存新疆博物館。

103　野豬柄短劍

公元13—14世紀，長30cm，察布查爾縣海努克古城出土。銅質，打製。扁柄，柄上刻6道並列豎槽。劍首頂為立式野豬形。鋒尖銳，兩面鋒刃，劍身起三脊。現存伊犁博物館。

104 小銅矛

公元1—3世紀，長11cm，若羌縣樓蘭遺址附近採集。紅銅鑄製，柳葉形，尖鋒，鍛面起脊，鋌呈圓鑿狀，現存新疆考古所。

105 銅矛

公元前8—公元前5世紀，長17cm，和靜縣察吾呼溝出土。青銅鑄製，尖鋒，柳葉形，兩面起刃，中起脊。矛柄圓形鑿孔，孔內尚存殘斷木柄。現存巴音郭楞蒙古自治州博物館。

106 銅鏃

公元前5—公元前1世紀，長4.8，5.9cm，鄯善縣洋海古墓出土。兩件，銅鑄製，鏃鋌部作圓鑿狀，鏃呈翼葉形，脊上起棱。鋒尖，製作精緻。現存吐魯番博物館。

107 蜷獸紋銅鏡

公元前8—公元前5世紀，直徑9cm，和靜縣察吾呼溝出土。圓形，橋鈕，窄緣。中心繞鈕飾一條蜷曲的獸紋，圓目，巨口咧牙，並列短線紋飾於體上尾卷曲，內側有肥碩的後腿，形態凶猛。線條簡煉，為目前在新疆地區僅見的時代最早的銅鏡。現存新疆考古所。

108 直柄銅鏡

公元前8—公元前5世紀，高17cm，和靜縣察吾呼溝出土。素面。鏡面呈圓形，較平整，直徑約10cm，直柄，柄端有一弧形孔。現存巴音郭楞蒙古自治州博物館。

109 羊飾柄銅鏡

公元1世紀，高16cm，巴里坤縣出土。銅質。鏡呈圓餅狀，直徑7.7cm。上方焊接一雙大角羊（鑄造），並足，聳身，昂首，角呈波狀後卷。現存新疆博物館。

110 厚緣銅鏡

公元前5—1世紀，直徑12,5cm，拜城縣克孜爾水庫墓地出土。圓形。鏡面較平直，背面呈淺盤狀，邊緣起棱。橋鈕。現存新疆考古所。

111 四神規矩鏡

公元1世紀，直徑10cm，和靜縣223團機務連出土。鏡中部圓鈕座，座外方框，框內列12地支銘文。12小乳釘，框外四邊還有8枚大乳釘。其間青龍、白虎、朱雀、玄武各佔一方。外區一圈環繞銘文帶為：尚方作鏡真大巧，上有仙人不知老，渴飲玉泉飢食棗，浮游天下漱四海，28個隸書字樣。邊緣飾以三角紋和流雲紋。整個紋飾端莊秀麗，內容豐富，鑄製精良，確為中原漢代銅鏡之精品。現存新疆和靜縣博物館。

112 許由繰父故事鏡

公元7—9世紀，直徑15cm，吐魯番出土。周邊作八瓣菱花形，邊緣高突，圓鈕。鈕左為一枝葉繁茂的大樹。鈕下河邊樹下坐著一人繰絲：鈕右側一人左手牽牛，右手前舉，身後峰巒起伏。傳說堯讓天下與許由，由逃之。繰父聞而洗耳於池濱。樊豎字仲父牽牛飲之，見繰父洗耳，乃驅牛而還，恥令其牛飲下流。此鏡現存韓國漢城。

113 柳毅傳書故事鏡

公元10—12世紀，直徑10cm，阜康縣三宮鄉出土。圓形，寬緣，橋鈕。鈕上方向下伸出一株大樹，枝葉茂密。左側有水，水上站立二女，面向右方。右側一男拱手向左而立，三人隔鈕相對，鈕下一人牽馬而行。鏡上紋飾取材於柳毅傳書的故事。現存新疆考古所。

114 草獸紋銅鏡

公元7—9世紀，直徑9.7cm，烏魯木齊縣烏拉泊古城出土。圓形，圓鈕，邊緣起棱。沿邊飾兩道同心圓圈。圈內飾卷草紋和禽獸紋。具有明顯的中原風格。現存烏魯木齊市博物館。

115 仙騎鏡

公元7—9世紀，直徑11cm，庫爾勒市出土。圓周邊呈八瓣菱花形，邊緣突起，圓鈕。紋飾分區佈置，內區飾四仙人騎獸騎鶴，同向繞鈕，騰空飛翔，仙人背後飄帶翻卷飛揚，獸鶴之間配置祥雲。外區設置蜂蝶花草紋。現存巴音郭楞蒙古自治州博物館。

116 瑞獸鸞鳥鏡

公元7—9世紀，直徑23cm，吉木薩爾縣北庭故城出土。周邊呈八瓣菱花形，圓鈕。內區紋飾為2獅形獸、2鸞鳥相對排列，鳥獸間配置忍冬卷草紋。外區飾以蜂蝶，小鳥和花卉紋，具有明顯的中原地區漢式風格。現存新疆博物館。

117 銅坐佛像

公元7—8世紀，高42cm，策勒縣達瑪溝出土。紅銅鑄製。螺髮高髻，彎眉細眼，鼻樑挺直，口唇微啟，面如滿月。結跏趺坐於覆蓮須彌座上，雙手姆指食指相對作手印，神情端莊安祥。座壁書梵文三行。現存和闐博物館。

118 鍍金銅佛頭

公元3—4世紀，高17cm，和闐縣出土。高肉髻，髻底有雙鈕。前額平闊，上鑲花鈿，端鼻大眼，雙唇緊閉，神態凝重深沈，造型粗放古樸。佛頭表面鍍金，多已剝落。現存日本東京。

119 銅摩尼神像

公元7—9世紀，高8cm，吐魯番出土。黃銅鑄製。空心。為摩尼教創始人摩尼之像。頭戴寶冠，面相清瘦，額下一撮長髯，身著袈裟（雙手已失），呈結跏趺坐於蓮花座上。作工精巧，造型別緻。現為烏魯木齊市個人收藏。

120 鎏金金剛騎馬像

公元15—18世紀，高16cm，烏蘇縣徵集。金剛身軀赤裸，橫騎寶馬，右手上舉，食指翹起，左手托頭器，神情威猛可怖。頭戴骷髏冠，冠後光焰升騰，胸掛瓔珞，胯垂骷髏。坐騎鞍韉齊備，舉步穩健有力。這種離奇古怪、誇張變形的人物形貌，具有鮮明的密教藝術特徵。像內發現有紙質藏文經卷。現存塔城博物館。

121 鎏金銅菩薩坐像

公元12世紀，高17cm，哈密西山鄉徵集。菩薩頭戴寶冠，上身袒裸，半結跏趺坐於單瓣仰覆蓮座上。左手屈指成環形，作「說法印」，右手直伸下垂，作「觸地印」。頸、胸、腰、臂腕、腿各部位裝飾瓔珞、釧鐲等物，上嵌藍、翠、紅各色寶珠，肩部飾梵器。此像彎眉直鼻，秀目薄眉，肌豐腰圓，身形勻稱柔美。具有濃郁的藏傳佛教造像風格。現存哈密博物館。

122 銅立佛像

公元6—7世紀，高9.5cm，吐魯番高昌故城出土。青銅鑄造。高肉髻，面部較圓，有頭光。著袈裟，左手托鉢置胸前，右手垂於體側。手作反扣狀。赤足。下有一方形支釘。姿態凝重古樸。現存德國柏林。

123 鎏金銅菩薩立像

公元7—8世紀，高8.8cm，吐魯番高昌故城出土。銅鑄刻成，鎏金。頭戴寶冠，面相豐腴，雙目低垂。上身袒裸，戴頂鏈，肩披授帶。下身著貼身小裙。右臂上舉，手握拂塵狀物，左手拎淨瓶。赤足立於五級蓮座上。造型輕盈飄逸，動感較強。現存德國柏林。

124 鎏金銅菩薩

公元7—9世紀，高9cm，庫車縣蘇巴什出土。青銅鑄造，鎏金，頭戴寶冠。上身著通肩小衣。右手上舉，衣袖下垂；左手垂於身側。身後衣帶飄逸。下身著貼身小裙，赤足立於蓮台上。蓮台下有兩層空心圓座，座下和腦後有支釘，供附著於其他物上之用。現存新疆考古所。

125 銅香爐

公元16—17世紀，高15.4cm，哈密徵集。長方形口，束頸，腹微鼓，平底。高雙耳外侈，四蹄狀足，足根部圓形。腹部兩側鑄有讚頌安拉的阿拉伯文字。現存哈密博物館。

126 銅獅

公元7—9世紀，長9.7cm，吉木薩爾縣北庭故城出土。銅質，鑄造。銅獅昂首，張口，前腿前屈，後腿後蹬，作急劇昂起撲擊狀。尾粗大健壯，且尾端與兩腳相連。製作精緻，造型生動很有力度感。現存新疆博物館。

127 阿拉伯文宣德爐

公元15世紀，口徑13、高9cm，吐魯番徵集。紅銅鑄製，侈口，扁鼓腹，環底有三足，腹部鑄有三組阿拉伯文，意為「穆罕默德是真主的使者」等吉祥語，爐底中部有「大明宣德年製」字。現為烏魯木齊個人收藏。

128 刻花銅碗

公元13—14世紀，直徑21.5、高13cm，和闐徵集。紅銅質，錘擊成型。敞口、深腹、圈足。腹外有兩組板，上套圓環耳。外壁平鏨紋飾和察合台文，分帶佈置，主要有連環花草紋、變形網格狀四瓣花枝紋、變形蓮瓣紋等。裝飾風格帶有宗教色彩。現存和闐博物館。

129 銅獅鎮子

公元7—9世紀，高7cm，吉木薩爾縣北庭故城出土。紅銅鑄造，鏨刻鎏金，呈蹲踞狀。巨口獠牙、雙目圓睜、

鬃毛卷曲呈渦狀。為雄獅。前足間夾一大圓球。頷球相連成一系孔。是一件具有實用價值的工藝品。現存新疆博物館。

130 銅洗手壺和銅盆

公元17—18世紀，壺高40、盆口徑32cm，喀什徵集。紅銅質，模壓、鍛打、鏤刻、鉚釘成型。壺細頸，扁圓鼓腹，喇叭足，長曲嘴，曲把手。壺蓋與把手上部有活梢相連，通體平鏨和透雕花紋及維吾爾文。盆中心有一圓盤蓋，盆體外有透雕紋飾的套。為維吾爾人日常活用具。現存新疆博物館。

131 黑汗朝錢幣

公元10—13世紀，直徑2.3—3.2cm，阿圖什市出土。圓形薄餅狀，銅質，打壓法製造，不甚規整。錢幣外緣有兩道凸棱紋圓圈，內夾一圈小乳釘。在內側凸棱以內有阿拉伯文科斐體銘文。正面銘文為一句伊斯蘭教用語，一般為「除了安拉別無真神，安拉是唯一的」。背面是錢幣製造者的王號和名字。黑汗朝錢幣採用「打壓法」的製造技藝，與圓形方孔錢的漢文化錢幣體系不同，屬希臘貨幣體系。現存新疆考古所。

132 漢佉二體錢

公元3—4世紀，直徑1.8cm，和闐徵集。紅銅質，打壓法製成。圓形無孔，無周廓。正面中心為立馬像，周圍有佉盧文。背面為漢文「六銖錢」。亦稱「和闐馬錢」，現存中國人民銀行新疆分行金融研究所。

133 貴霜錢

公元2—3世紀，直徑2.7cm，樓蘭古城出土。正面為國王立像（左），周緣有希臘文字，為「貴霜王閻膏珍」錢幣。背為一騎駱駝神像，手持三叉槍。現存中國歷史博物館。

134 高昌吉利錢

公元5—7世紀，直徑2.6cm，吐魯番阿斯塔那古墓出土。紅銅質，圓形方孔，有內外廓。正面鑄「高昌吉利」四字，楷書環讀，背素面。現存吐魯番博物館。

135 龜茲五銖錢

公元4—7世紀，庫車縣出土。八枚，銅質，又稱漢龜二體錢。圓形方孔，鑄造，內外有廓。正面銘文為漢文篆字「五銖（朱）」，背面銘文為龜茲文「ＯＯ」。這種錢幣規格和重量大小不同，多達10餘種。是龜茲國仿漢式五銖錢生產和使用的錢幣。現存新疆考古所。

136 突騎施錢

公元8世紀，直徑2.3cm，木壘縣出土。青銅質，鑄造。圓形方孔，有內外廓。正面有一圈粟特文，為「天、神的突騎施可汗錢幣」，或譯作「天可汗突騎施錢」。背面有印戳符號標誌，形似彎月。現存木壘縣博物館。

137 金馬飾、金鷹鹿飾

公元前8—公元前5世紀，馬飾長5、鷹鹿飾高3cm，阿合奇縣庫蘭薩日克古墓出土。金片打壓製成，馬昂首豎

耳短鬃，雙前足呈奔馳狀，細腰，後部反轉向前至頸，尾翻卷著左前蹄，整體呈圓形。鷹鹿飾為鑄製，立鹿，四足微曲，昂首，角向後伸，背站一鷹，展翅俯視鹿首，造型栩栩如生，製作精緻。現存阿合奇縣銀行。

138 嵌寶石金戒指

公元1世紀，直徑2.2cm，昭蘇縣夏台烏孫墓出土。黃金打製，戒面嵌紅寶石，周圍焊接以用細金珠組成的三角形和弧圈紋。現存新疆博物館。

139 八龍紋金帶扣

公元前1世紀，長9.8cm，寬6cm，焉耆縣永寧鄉出土。金片打製，長方圓角芭蕉葉形，邊緣焊接有以金絲彎曲成的正反「几」形紋。正面打壓八龍輪廓，上焊金絲和細金珠編織的龍紋，並嵌以紅綠寶石。做工精美，裝飾華麗，展現了古代工匠的高超技藝和創造才能。現存新疆博物館。

140 葡萄墜金耳環

公元前5—公元前1世紀，環徑1.3cm，特克斯縣一牧場古墓出土。上端為圓金絲彎曲成的不閉合圓環，環下兩小鈎圈相套下連一墜，墜由8個空心金光焊接而成，形似葡萄，造型小巧，工藝水平較高。現存新疆考古所。

141 六菱形金花飾片

公元前5—公元前4世紀，長5.9cm，鄯善縣洋海古墓出土。金箔模壓花紋，中心一朵團花，周飾長短相同的六角花瓣。花瓣上打壓麥穗紋，中心有小孔。現存吐魯番博物館。

142 金耳環

公元前5—公元前1世紀，長2.5cm，烏魯木齊烏拉泊水庫古墓出土。上端焊接空心塔形墜。墜上端粘密集的小金珠。現存新疆考古所。

143 虎紋圓金牌、金飾帶

公元前5世紀，牌徑6、帶長26cm，烏魯木齊阿拉溝古墓出土。金牌2件，模壓成型。虎作前躍狀，軀體卷曲成圓形，頭一向左一向右。金飾帶模壓而成，兩虎頭張口相對，前腿伸，後腿蹬，尾卷曲。相向作爭鬥狀。製造工藝高超。現存新疆博物館。

144 金鏈飾

公元前5世紀，長25.4cm，烏魯木齊阿拉溝古墓出土。金絲編織成鏈，每隔一定距離在鏈上掛一個由粟特石或白玉與圓錐形金泡串在一起的墜子。做工精細，現存新疆博物館。

145 獅形金牌飾

公元前5—公元前1世紀，長20cm，烏魯木齊南山阿拉溝古墓出土。金箔打壓製成，呈淺浮雕狀。獅張口睜目，豎耳，雙前足上舉作樸食狀，鬃毛卷曲，細腰，後部反轉上卷，尾與鬃相連。身飾弧線條紋和圓渦紋。整體作奔躍咬噬狀。現存新疆博物館。

146 鏨刻駝鳥紋銀盤

公元4—7世紀，口徑21cm，焉耆縣七個星鄉老城村出土。打製成形，大口淺盤，環底。盤中心鏨刻駝鳥1隻，周圍環繞駝鳥6隻。或低頭覓食，或昂首奔走，造型生動逼真，是一件精美的工藝品。現存巴音郭楞蒙古自治州博物館。

147 雙聯金牛頭

公元前5—公元前1世紀，長3.5cm，吐魯番艾丁湖古墓出土。金箔模壓製成，中空。兩牛頭頸部相連，圓目，口微張。造型精巧別緻。現存新疆考古所。

148 銀碗

公元4—7世紀，口徑20.5cm，高7.4cm，焉耆縣七個星鄉老城村出土。打製成形，平口、淺斜腹，圈足。碗壁遍佈放射狀凸線。圈足為焊接，碗邊鏨刻粟特文字。現存巴音郭楞蒙古自治州博物館。

149 金耳環

公元前5—公元前1世紀，外徑2.6cm，哈密林雅古墓出土。由圓柱形金條彎曲成圓杯，未合縫。現存新疆考古所。

150 察合台汗國金幣

公元13—14世紀，直徑3.2cm，博樂市出土。用打壓法製造，圓形無孔。正面銘文意為「感讚安拉，穆罕默德是安拉使者」。背面銘文為：「是最大伊瑪目，除安拉以外別無他神……。安拉是宗教的保衛者，眾信士的首領」。現存博爾塔那蒙古自治州博物館。

151 東羅馬金幣

公元7—8世紀，徑2.2cm，吐魯番阿斯塔那古墓出土。圓形無孔，打壓製成。正面為東羅馬國王頭像，戴王冠，王冠和頸部均有寶珠裝飾。背面為女神立像，有翅，右手持長杖形十字架。圖像周緣均有拉丁字母。現存新疆博物館。

152 波斯銀幣

公元3—4世紀，直徑2.6、3cm，吐魯番高昌故城出土。打壓製成，圓形無孔。正面中部為國王半身像，頭戴聯珠紋等組成的王冠；右側邊緣有銘文。左為波斯阿爾達希二世銀幣，右為波斯沙卜爾二世銀幣。現存新疆博物館。

153 和闐銀幣

公元18世紀，直徑1.6cm，和闐出土。哈比不拉一錢小天罡，打壓法製造。圓形無孔，正反面有銘文。正面銘文為阿拉伯文，意為「真主是唯一的，穆罕默德是真主的使者。回歷1283」。背面銘文為察合台文，意為「和闐精鑄。作價白銀一錢」。現存自治區人民銀行。

154 察合台汗國銀幣

公元13—14世紀，直徑1.8—2.0cm，昌吉古城出土。打壓法製造，圓形無孔，兩面均有銘文。正面中心圈內銘文為鑄造地點或幣戳符號，邊緣周圍內鏨文為「除了阿拉別無他神……」。背面中心部位兩行銘文：「公正的最大的」。周圍小字為回歷年代。現存新疆考古所。

岩　畫　類

155　生殖崇拜圖（局部）

公元前10世紀，呼圖壁縣康家石門子天山崖壁。岩刻，位於縣南天山北麓康家石門子山岩峭壁的下部，總面積100餘平方米。此圖中部為一雙頭同體人像（高170厘米）。其腰右側有一勃起的男性生殖器和兩條斜伸的腿，左側為一男性，腰下左側有一勃起的男性生殖器。胸部刻一人頭像。右側女性腿根處刻有男性生殖器。雙頭同體人像的右下方有一排密集的小人，表示生殖繁衍子女眾多。這是一組男女媾合繁衍子孫的畫面。

156　舞蹈圖（局部）

公元前10世紀，呼圖壁縣康家石門子天山崖壁。岩刻。圖中主題7位女性。人物面型清瘦，濃眉深目，高鼻小口，頭戴高帽上飾有兩枝翎羽。頸細長，兩臂平伸，一肘上曲，一肘下垂，五指張開，寬胸窄腰，兩腿修長。小腿微彎曲作舞蹈狀。這種具有歐羅巴人種特徵的人物，為古代曾生活於新疆之「塞種」。

157　對馬圖（局部）

公元前10世紀，呼圖壁縣康家石門子天山崖壁。岩刻。峭壁上刻有兩組對馬圖，一雄一雌。此圖為雄性對馬圖。兩馬相對，頭及前後腿相聯接。馬頸長伸，身軀細瘦彎曲，馬尾下垂，二馬生殖器挺直、誇張。

158　人虎圖（局部）

公元前10世紀，呼圖壁縣康家石門子天山崖壁。岩刻。圖下部刻雄性立虎兩隻。虎雙耳直立，通體刻有折線斑紋，尾下垂，後腿根部勃起的虎鞭粗長，睾丸下垂。大虎尾後刻有三張搭箭欲發的弓箭。左側男性身材高大，圓目，頭生雙角。女性體型較小，一人雙腿並攏而立，一人張開雙腿露出陰部。畫面較雜亂、重疊。

159　生殖崇拜、牧畜圖

公元前5世紀，塔城巴爾達庫爾。岩刻。畫面上有男女人物、牦牛、馬、狼、北山羊、羚羊等。其重要畫面是右邊的一男女媾合圖：左側男性身材高大，頭戴多角狀冠飾，腰、膝部有帶狀飾，生殖器刻劃得極誇張；右側女性身體比男性小一半，雙手張開，雙腿微彎曲，頭上亦帶有冠飾。二人作性交姿勢。右下方一人頭戴角狀冠，形象下媾合圖中的男子相同。左上方畜群臕肥體壯。牦牛和兩馬背各有一騎者。牦牛生殖器刻劃得極粗壯。兩馬前有一人右手後伸作牽狀。中部是一組男女小孩，均作舞蹈狀。整個畫面的形象刻劃得十分生動逼真。反映了古代人對於生殖的崇拜。

160　馬羊圖

公元前8世紀，阿勒泰市多阿特溝。岩刻。兩馬一羊，均作奔跑狀。馬骨壯肌豐，羊大角後彎，尾上翹，軀體矯健。

161　彩繪神靈圖

史前時期，發現於富蘊縣唐巴楞的一山洞裡。洞壁繪有許多各類宗教彩繪圖案和符號。這是其中的一幅，似與薩滿教有關。

162　馴鹿圖

公元前18世紀。富蘊縣布拉克特牧場。岩刻。圖中立鹿多枝巨形花角後彎，耳直立，臕肥體壯，形象較生動。

163　步牧圖

公元前18世紀。阿勒泰市多阿特溝。岩刻。畫面上有人物、牛、羊、驢、狗和象。動物群右前方的牧人雙手作驅趕狀。各種動物鑿刻生動，畫面意趣盎然，充滿牧區生活的氣息，是一幅反映當時游牧民族生活的寫實作品。

164　雜技圖

公元前5世紀，阿勒泰市喇嘛昭鄉雀兒溝。畫面下部一隻北山羊，大角後彎，尾上翹，在角弓上站立一形體高大的變形人物，其左右長手各提一個一手叉腰的兒童，頭上還騎坐著一個雙手叉腰的成年人。岩畫線條清晰。是一幅不可多得的藝術作品。

165　群羊圖

公元前後，阿勒泰市多阿特溝。均為北山羊，角彎向後，四足直立。造型簡單，形象古拙。一隻羊僅用6根線條勾勒而成。

166　奔鹿圖

公元前5世紀，阿勒泰市喇嘛昭鄉雀兒溝。岩刻。群鹿大小基本同。均昂首前奔，多枝巨角上挺。神態驚慌，似被捕獵情景。

167　爭戰圖

公元9世紀，哈密市泌城鄉頭工村。一巨石上刻8個手執長兵器的騎士圍攻中央一位挺槍迎戰的騎士。騎士形態各異，或躍起而鬥，或俯衝而戰，或伺機沖殺，有的挺矛，有的舉棒。畫面經過磨製，線條流暢，形象生動栩栩如生。

168　戰騎圖

公元7—8世紀，巴里坤縣東北38公里八牆子村。三匹駿馬，二位騎士。騎士執兵器，駿馬臀部渾圓，形體健壯。

繪　畫　類

169　飛天圖

公元7世紀，出自拜城縣克孜爾石窟新1窟。於1973年發現。壁畫。飛天長髮披肩，頭戴單珠寶冠，冠後寶繒飛

189

揚。上身袒裸，頸戴項圈，臂腕戴釧，燕尾式帔帛纏繞於身，腰下著綠色裙褲，兩側帛帶末端挽結。飛天右手握帔帛，左手散花。此畫色澤如新，飛天頸、腹、臂等部位都以赭色暈染，顯得體態碩壯、健美。與印度飛天豐乳圓腰的風格迥然有別。

170　吉祥慧女裸體像

公元5世紀，出自拜城縣克孜爾石窟第84窟。壁畫。吉祥慧女赤身裸體，閉目鎖眉，睡臥姿態安祥平靜。體形勻稱健美，肌膚細膩潤澤，雙乳豐腴健碩，頸、腹、臂、腕裝飾典雅優美，堪稱身心完美統一的佳作。畫面用線纖細纏綿，色調溫馨含蓄，是龜茲裸體藝術的代表。現存德國柏林。

171　佛教故事版畫

公元6世紀，長46cm，策勒縣丹丹烏里克寺院出土。畫面從左至右第一人著菩薩裝，有項光，左手作指示態；第二人頭有項光，髮髻冠式為盛唐典型的菩薩裝束；第三人一頭四臂，右上手持金剛杵，足蹬長韌靴，結跏趺坐於蓮座上，似為護法人（也可能是明王）像；第四人與第一人裝束相同，兩手捧持，似供養天人。現存英國倫敦。

172　駱駝哺乳圖

公元7—8世紀，長14cm，民豐縣安迪爾採集。紙質。這是一幅運筆稚樸的素描圖。圖中母駱駝腹下小駱駝正專心吃奶。母駱駝後腿上有駝主的烙印。現存英國倫敦。

173、174　佛教木版畫

公元7世紀，長33cm，策勒縣丹丹烏里克寺院出土。木板正反兩面分別繪有波斯和印度式兩種不同風格的藝術形像。正面（右）繪一四臂菩薩，高鼻、黑鬚、頭戴波斯王冠，身著綠袍，腰束腰帶，足蹬長韌靴。反面（左）繪一具有印度形貌的三頭四臂神，交腿坐在兩頭臥牛支撐的花格墊上，神的身體肌膚呈暗藍色，右側頭為女性面孔，左側頭呈暗黃色，一副惡魔嘴臉。中頭頂冠裝飾富麗，腰間圍虎皮裙，四隻手都握有法器。現存英國倫敦。

175　鬼子母圖

公元8世紀，出自于闐縣牙依拉克佛寺。壁畫。鬼子母是佛教故事中的食中女魔，因受感化，成為賜福神。圖正中為身著天衣、兩足下垂、坐於宣台上的鬼子母。其左手抱一小兒右，手持吉祥果，肩頭、足邊各坐兩個小兒。此壁畫屬古和闐風格的作品，同時也受到波斯繪畫的影響。現存印度新德里。

176　佛像

公元7—8世紀，出自策勒縣達瑪溝。壁畫。佛臉微側，高肉髻，彎眉細眼，大耳垂輪。頸上有項圈，兩肩繪日、月。圖中對人物鼻子的畫法引人注目，它是用一根線條沿鼻樑而下，而後巧妙地完成鼻槽和上唇的造型，它應是古代和闐藝術家們的獨創。現存印度新德里。

177　供養菩薩像

公元7—8世紀，出自策勒縣達瑪溝。壁畫。菩薩上身袒露，頭戴花冠，耳環下垂，頸、臂、腕部戴有圈、釧、鐲等裝飾品。雙手合掌，臉微揚，跪於佛右供養。本圖人物無論線描、敷彩還是造型均具和闐畫風格。現存印度新德里。

178　有翼天使像

公元4—5世紀，若羌縣米蘭佛塔出土。此畫繪於米蘭佛塔回廊內壁。人物臉型長圓。兩眼大而微凹。炯炯有神，鼻尖略勾，身著圓領通肩衣，背後長雙翅，其形象即希臘神話中的有翼天使。現存英國倫敦。

179　佛陀與比丘像

公元4—5世紀，出自若羌縣，壁畫。前繪身著圓領通肩袈裟的佛陀，彎眉大眼，大耳垂幹，留八字小鬍。前額髮際呈弧線形，髮式獨特，神情莊嚴和善。其身後繪6身比丘，面貌、神情基本相同，其中一比丘手執團扇。本圖與著名的「有翼天使」像畫風相仿。現存印度新德里。

180　盧遮那佛像

公元7—8世紀，出自策勒縣達瑪溝。有背項光，光輪多重。佛像圓臉，五官小而集中。佛經規定此佛全身有表現世間生死輪回的「五道」，故圖中佛像在裸露的上身分別繪有日、月、梵夾、金剛杵、寶珠、牲畜（馬）等。整個畫面著色沈著、淡雅，充滿了神秘的宗教色彩。現存印度新德里。

181　菱格因緣故事畫

公元4—5世紀，拜城縣克孜爾石窟171窟。壁畫。位於該窟（中心柱窟）主室券頂。中脊部位繪一列縱向的天象圖（月天、金翅鳥、立佛、日天），兩側繪數列菱形山巒，內繪各種因緣故事。這種利用有限壁面容納眾多題材的藝術形式，是龜茲畫家獨創的結果，其用意在於在一個特定的空間內給觀者完整地描繪出佛與眾生共居的世界，這個世界天穹高遠，日月朗照，佛法無邊普照眾生。整個券頂高大開闊，構圖疏朗灑脫，色彩斑斕奪目。

182　托缽立佛版畫

公元6世紀，高46cm，拜城縣克孜爾石窟出土。佛立於橢圓形蓮座上，身著袒右肩袈裟，左手舉至肩部，食指與中指間繪出縵網，右手托缽。畫面線條挺秀圓渾，人物表情愉悅安詳，為木板繪畫之上品。畫上端書寫一行婆羅謎文字。現存德國柏林。

183　樂神善愛圖

公元4世紀，拜城縣克孜爾石窟。菩提樹下繪一對情人般相依並行的交足立像，左側裸上身、白膚、戴寶冠、佩瓔珞、披帛帶者為佛化身的樂神，右側彈箜篌者為善愛。這是一幅佛度化善愛的因緣故事畫。畫面運筆如流水行雲，人物眼神互相呼應，生動傳神，引人入勝。現存德國柏林。

184　蛤天人因緣故事畫（局部）

公元4—5世紀，出自拜城縣克孜爾第47窟。畫中人物裸上身，下穿短裙，肩披長帛，手柱木棒，面微側，神情專注。身邊俯臥二牛。這則因緣故事說牧牛人因專心聽法，不意傷害了牧牛棒下的一只蛤蟆，這只蛤蟆因而升天。此畫現存德國柏林。

185　天宮伎樂圖
公元4世紀，拜城縣克孜爾石窟第38窟。壁畫。圖中兩伎樂菩薩在一圓拱形龕內，臉部相向，彼此呼應。右側者吹笛，左側者彈琵琶。人物乳房豐滿，臂部圓潤，造型秀美，栩栩如生。

186　魔女誘佛圖
公元4—5世紀前後，出自拜城縣克孜爾石窟第76窟。釋迦粉碎了魔王波旬的千軍萬馬之後，魔王之女前來誘惑。圖中釋迦結跏趺坐，瘦骨嶙峋。左側立有三身秀麗少女，前端裸體者形態妖艷，左手呈劍指指向佛身，右手叉腰，雙腳蹉步，臀部肥碩，肌體豐腴。右側立有三身白髮老嫗，為釋迦用神力將魔女變成者。本圖人物形象對比鮮明，藝術效果十分強烈，堪稱西域佛教美術的精品。現存德國柏林。

187　伎樂飛天
公元6—7世紀，拜城縣克孜爾石窟第8窟。圖中繪兩身凌空飛舞的伎樂飛天。在上者手持花盤，在下者彈奏琵琶。背景繪菱形山、水池、樹木等。畫面色彩深厚、穩重，線條粗獷、飽滿。

188　聽法菩薩像
公元4世紀，拜城縣克孜爾石窟第38窟。菩薩交腳坐於方座之上，上身袒露，滿披精緻項鏈、釧環、帛帶、胸飾等物，下身穿藍色裙褲，頭戴三珠冠，雙掌相合，神情恬靜，風韻嫣然。在神秘的宗教氛圍中，漾溢出一種人性的溫馨，極富感染力。

189　樂舞供養天像
公元4—5世紀，出自拜城縣克孜爾石窟第76窟。兩身天人均有頭光。左側的著緊身束腰長裙，單手舉蓮花；右側的裸上身、穿裙褲，雙手擊掌。畫面用線圓潤嫻熟，人物黛眉秀目，直鼻薄唇，其形象具有鮮明的印度壁畫特徵。現存德國柏林。

190　樂舞圖
公元10世紀左右，出自庫車縣庫木吐拉石窟第73窟。右側舞蹈者足踏蓮花，揮巾旋轉；左側吹笙者鼓腮奏樂，神情專注。旁邊殘存一繪滿紋飾的箜篌共鳴箱，但樂器的其他部份及演奏者均已殘失。現存德國柏林。

191　供養菩薩群像（局部）
公元4—5世紀，庫車縣庫木吐拉石窟第21窟。此窟發現於1977年，其穹窿頂部壁畫色彩鮮豔，形象完整，引人注目。頂部中心繪大朵蓮花。向外分繪一周鱗紋，五層蓮瓣，一周六瓣蓮，向外是十三條呈放射狀的梯形條幅，每一條幅內各繪一供養菩薩。頭戴各式寶冠、裸上身、著長裙，或托缽，或執華繩，或合十，風姿綽約，神態生動。

本圖是一幅供養菩薩特寫，手執華繩，腰略扭曲。該圖運筆細膩、用色沈著，是一幅原貌保存極好的壁畫佳作。

192　飛天（摹本）
公元8世紀，庫車縣庫木吐拉石窟第16窟。圖中繪兩身飄然而降的散花飛天，上身裸露，下著長裙，露腳，披帛飛揚。身下浮雲飄動，周圍蓮花開放。整個畫面色彩絢爛，精細繁密，給人以滿壁風動之感。此畫繪畫水平之高，足以和同時代中原壁畫媲美。

193　飛天
公元7世紀，庫車縣克孜尕哈石窟第30窟。本窟後室券頂繪有兩列八身由兩側向中心飛翔的飛天，或奏樂舞蹈，或撒放香花，背景有香花和寶物。本圖為其局部，上幅是舞蹈飛天與散花飛天；下幅右側者散花，左側者奏琵琶。飛天體態輕盈靈活，舞帶長裙飄動如雲。

194　猴王本生故事畫
公元4世紀，拜城縣克孜爾石窟第38窟。壁畫正中由上而下繪一條蜿蜒小河，猴王雙足用藤蔓纏繞，雙手抱住對岸的樹，橫身河上並回首環顧，兩小猴正踏身而過。畫面下部還有一張弓射箭之人。這是一幅菱格本生故事畫，說猴王率眾猴入園食果，遭國王追捕，受阻河邊，猴王以身作橋，讓同類逃生，自己墜水而死。

195　阿闍世王夢靈、沐浴圖
公元6世紀，克孜爾石窟第205窟。古印度國王阿闍世曾夢見釋迦已死，痛不欲生。其近臣用一幅繪有佛陀一生化跡的帛畫，向國王暗示佛已涅槃。圖中右側繪阿闍世王哀傷悶絕後被置於澡罐中沐浴、甦醒；左側為阿闍世王及其夫人、侍者聆聽大臣講說；下方畫出佛涅槃後城牆崩塌，日月滾落，傘杆摧折的景象。表現這一內容的壁畫在全國各石窟中僅見於克孜爾一地。整幅壁畫構圖完整，主題鮮明，畫技精湛，堪稱絕世珍品。原存德國柏林，後毀於戰火中。

196　須大拏太子本生故事畫
公元4世紀，拜城縣克孜爾石窟第38窟。葉波國太子須大拏慷慨大度，自幼喜好佈施。當把自己所有財物都施侔舍淨盡之後，又將子女和妻子施與婆羅門為奴。本圖著重表現須大拏施子為奴的情節：著菩薩裝的須大拏正用繩綑住兩個兒，交與瘦弱的婆羅門。畫中將小兒驚恐、依戀的神情刻劃得十分真切、生動。現存德國柏林。

197　金剛像
公元4世紀，拜城縣克孜爾石窟第77窟。圖中金剛左腿下垂、右腿上盤、左手持金剛杵，右手舉拂塵，側首坐於方座上。頭戴珠冠，辮髮垂肩。上身袒裸，各部位分飾珠串、釧環、帔帛等物。下著花邊短裙。彎眉、大眼、長鼻、八字鬍，具印度人特徵。現存德國柏林。

198　菩薩說法圖
公元4—5世紀，拜城縣克孜爾石窟第17窟。壁畫上端為洞窟主室券頂中脊之大象和東西側壁上的菱格本生壁畫。說法圖繪在其下的圓拱形壁面上。正中為一交腳坐於高方座上的菩薩，作說法狀。兩側分別繪兩列五身聽法菩薩像。菩薩皆祖上身，頭戴寶冠，身佩飾物，亦交腳而坐。整個畫面以說法菩薩為中心，左右對稱。圖中的紅色顏料因氧化而變成黑色，意外產生了線條粗獷的效果。本圖是克孜爾現存說法圖中保存最好的一幅。

199　佛傳故事國王王后大臣像

公元4—5世紀，拜城縣克孜爾石窟第22窟。壁畫左側人物頭戴三珠冠，有頭光，後部有華蓋，為古印度國王阿闍世，初肆行暴戾，最終皈依佛教。正中為王后，束高髻，上插三朵花，有頭光，身後背景為宮殿，右側為行雨大臣，祖右肩，肩下裹白布並在左肩處打結，背景為宮殿。現存德國柏林。

200　龜茲國王及王后供養像

公元6世紀，拜城縣克孜爾石窟第205窟。畫面正中為龜茲國王，右側是兩個引薦僧，左側是王后。國王上穿翻領對襟長大衣，下穿緊腿褲和尖頭靴。右手握寶劍，左手持香爐，身後佩長劍。王后穿翻領束腰短袖外套，雙手持花珠鏈。國王、王后頭後都有頭光。本圖所繪龜茲國王、王后虔誠禮佛，正是當時西域統治者崇奉佛教的寫照。現存德國柏林。

201　龜茲貴族供養人像

公元6—7世紀，拜城縣克孜爾石窟第189窟。兩供養人身穿大翻領、鑲寬邊長大衣（左灰底小白花，右白底紅方格），雙手持細長莖蓮花，腰部束帶，上掛短刀。兩人似為龜茲貴族，本圖人物面部描繪彩採用高反差對比色，在白臉上畫粗壯的紅色陰影。現存德國柏林。

202　龜茲樂舞舍利盒

公元7世紀，高31.2cm，庫車縣昭怙厘寺出土。木製。盒身圓筒形，蓋呈尖頂形。盒蓋上繪四身演奏樂器的裸體童子，盒身周繪一隊由21人組成的樂舞圖。整個畫面極富生活氣息，生動反映了古代普遍流行西域的假面舞，那喧鬧的場面，多采的舞姿，絢麗的服飾，各異的樂器，以及人物興奮風趣的表情，都仿佛使人身臨其境。圖中人物多以剛健有力、生動簡潔、圓轉優美的線條塑造，形象鮮明、色彩艷麗、內容豐富，是研究龜茲音樂、舞蹈、服飾的珍貴資料。現存日本東京。

203　龜茲樂舞舍利盒局部（摹本）

繪於盒身，系圖中樂隊的一部份。前面是兩個兒童抬著一面鼓，一鼓手持槌擊打，其後兩人，一個彈豎箜篌、一個彈鳳首箜篌。樂手們身穿翻領緊袖花邊長袍，腰扎聯珠紋式腰帶，下穿長褲，足登高筒皮靴，腰掛短劍，為龜茲世俗男子的裝束。人物形象十分生動，那種邊演奏邊做情意交流的神態刻劃尤為逼真。（李堯天摹）

204　佛體焚化圖

公元6世紀，拜城縣克孜爾石窟第205窟。本圖描繪的是佛涅槃後佛體焚化的情景。畫面正中佛右側臥於龍棺內

，袈裟裹體，神態安詳。棺下堆放數十個牛頭，已燃起火焰。大弟子阿難站在棺頭，雙手托棺蓋。周圍僧徒天人，或合掌敬禮默哀，或跪地嚎啕大哭，或虔誠撒放香花。情景感人，畫面氣氛莊嚴肅穆。現存德國柏林。

205　爭分舍利圖（局部）

公元6世紀拜城縣克孜爾石窟第205窟。佛涅槃並火化後，印度地區八個國家派兵前來索取佛舍利，八國兵將耀武揚威來到佛涅槃的拘尸城下。圖中繪三身著盔甲騎戰馬的武將，腰掛弓箭，手執長矛、馬鞭。坐騎肌豐骨健，舉步有力。前兩身武獎頭後繪有項光。現存德國柏林。

206　耕作圖

公元7世紀，拜城縣克孜爾石窟第175窟。本圖用寫實手法繪身頭頂小帽、身穿短褲的農夫，手持「坎土鏝」農具，作向下用力刨土的姿式。用坎土鏝耕作這種極富地方特色的生產方式，至今在新疆農村仍可見到。該圖為五趣輪回圖局部，表現農民耕作受苦的情景。圖中右下角繪一立佛為五趣的另一內容。

207　供養人群像

公元8—9世紀，出自焉耆縣七個星遺址。壁畫，現存四個人物。最左為一男性，從其臉部線條及其彎曲的背部看，是一老年人，頭戴一頂不常見的高而黑的帽子。老人左側是一高個子婦人，眉目修長，面部豐滿，著長衫。第三人又是老年男子，其帽似為王冠。第四位為婦人，形象上與另一婦人大致相同。現存德國柏林。

208　比丘尼像

公元8—9世紀，出自焉耆縣七個星遺址。畫中比丘上身祖裸，披帛纏繞。束高髻，前髮中分，後髮披肩。有項光。雙手合十，虔誠跪拜。現存英國倫敦。

209　比丘受教圖

公元8—9世紀，出自焉耆縣七個星遺址。這是一幅完整壁畫的殘片。畫中繪一年長比丘斜披印花袈裟，坐在方形床几上，面前跪坐四弟子。大比丘和三弟子一手持長冊，一手握筆；另一弟子雙手合十。天上一散花飛天。此圖繪在內室下壁不顯眼的位置上，題材，敷彩十分簡淡。現存英國倫敦。

210　仕女弈棋圖

公元7—9世紀，吐魯番阿斯塔那古墓出土。絹本，設色。貴婦髮束高髻。闊眉，額間描心形花鈿，身著緋衣綠裙，披帛。其表情凝重，正苦思冥想，舉棋不定。此圖反映出當時貴族婦女閑逸的生活景像。繪畫技法、風格與中原一脈相承。現存新疆博物館。

211　仕女圖

公元7世紀，吐魯番出土。絹畫。圖中仕女束髮平髻。彎眉細眼，兩頰塗朱，雙唇微抿。頸部繪出弧線，顯得肌豐膚潤，身著寬袖大袍，袖手站立。左邊墨書一列漢文。現存瑞典斯德哥爾摩。

212　童子圖

公元7—9世紀，吐魯番阿斯塔那古墓出土。絹本，設色。圖中兒童身著暈裥背帶長褲，左手抱一拂林狗，右手上舉。臉型豐圓，五官端秀，肌膚圓潤，生動可愛。懷中小狗全身絨毛微卷，黑白相間，馴服溫順。整個畫面人物、動物形象惟妙惟肖，意趣盎然，是一幅珍貴的古代風俗畫。現存新疆博物館。

213　托盞侍女圖

公元7—9世紀，高81cm，吐魯番阿斯塔那古墓出土。絹本，設色。束髮平髻，闊眉，描花鈿，身著圓領印花長袍，腰間繫帶，腳穿絲幫麻底鞋，雙手托茶盞。侍女形象肥美而不失靈巧，全身造型適中，神態安詳慈善。現存新疆博物館。

214　舞伎圖

公元7—9世紀，高47cm，吐魯番阿斯塔那古墓出土。絹本，設色。髮挽高髻，額描雉形花鈿，上身著白地黃藍花卷草紋半臂，窄袖，紅裙曳地，足穿重台履，左手輕拈帔帛，臉形清俊，體態修長。現存新疆博物館。

215　侍女圖

公元7—9世紀，高61cm，吐魯番阿斯塔那古墓出土。絹本，設色。頭梳低髻，扎十字紅頭繩，額間描花鈿，身穿圓領紫色長袍。人物神色肅敬，虔誠文靜。透示出侍女忠謹的性格。現存新疆博物館。

216　侍馬圖

公元7—9世紀，吐魯番阿斯塔那古墓出土。絹本，設色，侍馬人頭戴幞頭，身穿白色圓領長袍，足蹬黑靴。左手執鞭，右手牽馬，雙眉緊鎖，步履匆匆。鞍馬骨壯筋豐，舉步穩健。此畫線條起伏流暢，人馬比例適中，神形畢備，是一幅難得的藝術珍品。現存新疆博物館。

217　六屏式鑒誡畫

公元7—9世紀，長400cm，出自吐魯番阿斯塔古墓。這是一幅將倫理說教融於畫圖的六條掛屏式墓室壁畫，繪於阿斯塔那216號墓後壁。左端的一幅繪欹器，形如倒鐘，橫貫一柱，器空時或盛滿水時，器體便會傾斜或翻倒，只有裝水適中方可保持端正平衡。古人以此勸諭人們要謙虛，勿自滿。右端的一幅繪生芻，素絲和撲滿，告誡人們為人端正質樸，為事由微至著，為官清正廉明。中間四幅繪人物，其前胸或後背分別題有「金人」、「石人」、「玉人」等字樣，都是將儒家列聖做人的鑒誡宣示於形象，「金人」，是叫人「三緘其口」，謙虛謹慎；「石人」，主張人有所作為，匡正時弊；「玉人」，勸告人節制物欲，涵養性情。這組壁畫的主題思想與中國儒家提倡的倫理道德是一致的。摹本現存新疆博物館。

218　莊園生活圖

公元3—4世紀，長225cm，出自吐魯番哈喇和卓古墓。壁畫。描繪吐魯番地主莊園的生活場景。懸幔下，墓主人（莊園主）頭戴巾幘，身著大袖袍衫，雙手作揖，跪坐在前，其後妻妾家眷相隨。左側為庖廚和用具，廚娘正

忙於操作。右側有耕地，葡萄園，桑園，釀酒房，鞍馬，牛車，工匠等等。此壁畫用稚樸、簡練的筆法對莊園生活作了概括描繪，其藝術風格與甘肅嘉峪關魏晉壁畫相同，但繪畫水平又在其上。摹本現存新疆博物館。

219　六屏式花鳥壁畫

公元7—9世紀，長37.5cm，出自吐魯番阿斯塔古墓。此畫繪於阿斯塔那217號墓室後壁。採用現實生活中六曲屏風的形式，用紅色粗線條將壁畫隔成並列的六幅。內容為山水花鳥，畫面近景有百合、蘭花、鴛鴦、野雞、野鴨。色彩艷麗，造型逼真。遠景有群山流雲，飛燕翔翔。比例適度，筆法精煉。整個畫幅裝飾感極強。

220　墓主人生活圖紙畫

公元7—9世紀，出自吐魯番。紙畫。畫面描繪墓主人莊園生活的幾個場景：如宴飲、樂舞、農田、園林、牛車、庖廚等。此畫在佈局形式、繪畫技法等方面與哈喇和卓98號墓墓室壁畫（莊園生活圖）明顯不同。其線條較為流暢圓潤，簡潔準確，堪稱這一時期墓室畫的精品。現存印度新德里。

221　伏羲女媧絹畫

公元7世紀，長216cm，出自吐魯番阿斯塔那古墓。伏羲女媧手執規矩，上身相擁，下身化作蛇尾纏繞。整個畫面大面積平塗深藍色，並用紅、黃、白三色描繪日月及人物蜿蜒纏繞的身軀。伏羲、女媧粗眉、圓眼、勾鼻、朱唇，表情呆滯。與這一墓地同一題材作品中人物高眉秀目、豐頤櫻唇的形象特徵有所區別。現存英國倫敦。

222　伏羲女媧絹畫

公元7世紀，長221.5cm，出自吐魯番阿斯塔那古墓。人身蛇尾男女二人，上身相擁，下體相交。男為伏羲在右，頭戴幞頭，深目高鼻，上唇和下頦長滿濃密鬍鬚，左手執矩。女為女媧在左，束髮高髻，濃眉高揚，鼻直唇紅，右手執規。二人上穿大袖圓領袍衫，下著蓮花紋傘狀短裙。畫面上下分繪日月，周圍星辰環繞。此二人即華夏傳說中的人類始祖。此畫意在表現陰陽交合產生人類萬物，世代不絕。這一題材早在漢代中原墓室繪畫中已流行。但本圖在人物造型、運筆、敷彩等方面與漢風畫截然有別，具有鮮明的西域藝術特點。現存新疆博物館。

223　高昌景教壁畫

公元9世紀，出自吐魯番高昌故城。畫中描繪一群手持棕枝、身材矮小的信徒恭謹地站立在手持聖水杯身材高大的牧師身旁。此畫表現的是「聖枝節」（pamsunday）人們歡迎基督進入耶路撒冷城的情景。壁畫帶有明顯的拜占庭藝術風格，是研究景教在高昌流行的生動資料。現存德國柏林。

224　摩尼教典籍中插圖

公元9世紀，出自吐魯番高昌故城。紙質二件。左件正中墨書三行回鶻文字，一側樹下端坐兩排持筆書寫的教徒，均長髮披肩，白衣白冠。右件下部一側畫盛開花朵

的長籐。另一側用紅黑兩色書寫回鶻文字。上部殘存兩個跪坐的戴尖頭高帽的俗體人物，葦右側者彈奏琵琶。本圖選用金、銀、紅、綠等色，絢爛奪目。現存德國柏林。

225 摩尼教壁畫

公元9世紀，出自吐魯番高昌故城。壁畫左繪教祖摩尼，頭戴鍍金葉飾的主教冠，身穿白色長袍，領口和前襟有一條深色寬邊。身後從者為僧眾，均白衣白冠，長髮垂肩，袖手站立。教主與僧眾領下都用紅帶子繫結，顯得樸素無華。現存德國柏林。

226 舉哀圖

公元10—11世紀，吐魯番柏孜克里克石窟第33窟。壁畫。繪於洞窟後壁。下部的佛涅槃像已毀。圖中沙羅雙樹下，右側為悲哀的供養菩薩、天龍八部，左側是前往舉哀的十六國王子。中間光焰衝起，頂端繪含利塔。雙樹枝間繪二身散花童子飛天。圖中十六國王子的形象已完全中國化，其中有頭戴通天冠的漢族帝王，又有突厥、吐蕃、回鶻等各族王子。人物表情凝重，內心抑鬱，造型生動傳神。畫家以近乎寫意的筆致著意刻劃不同民族的形象特徵。這既是一幅宗教畫，同時又是一幅珍貴的歷史風俗畫。

227 貴婦禮佛像

公元9世紀末—10世紀中葉，出自吐魯番柏孜克里克石窟第20窟。壁畫。前一身為貴婦，體態豐腴，服飾衣著華麗，雙手托盤供奉三枚寶珠。其面型與中原漢族婦女相同，但服裝、飾物又有高昌回鶻人的特徵。其身後侍女正合掌禮拜。現存德國柏林。

228 天王像

公元9世紀末—10世紀中葉，出自吐魯番柏孜克里克石窟第20窟。壁畫。畫面正中為天王，立於須彌山上，身著鎧甲，頭後有項光。右手握寶珠，怒目圓睜，咄咄逼人。其左右文武侍從或跪或立，文臣持筆端硯，武將手握大斧，侍從托盤拿勺。畫面佈局嚴謹，線條精細華美，是一幅難得的精品。此畫是＜毗沙門天圖＞的一部分。現存德國柏林。

229 回鶻王供養像

公元10世紀，出自吐魯番柏孜克里克石窟第45窟。壁畫。畫中右下角的回鶻文題記指明，此人乃回鶻國王。頭戴金冠，身穿紅色圓領長袍，右手握拳，左手持花，雙眉微蹙，兩唇緊閉，二目炯炯，神情威嚴肅穆。身後有一門，上下左右極盡裝飾，富麗堂皇，烘托出主人地位的顯貴。此畫用筆細膩，一絲不苟，可稱上乘肖像畫。現存德國柏林。

230 回鶻王像麻布幡

公元9世紀，長142cm，出自吐魯番高昌故城。麻布幡。正反兩面各繪一幅站立執花的回鶻王像，頭戴尖頭高冠，身穿緊身長袍。并繪出人物飽經風霜，大度沈穩的性格特點。幡上方繪一結跏趺坐的小型坐佛像。回鶻王下身

兩側各繪一童子，以及幾行墨書的回鶻文題記。為摩尼教文物。現存德國柏林。

231 回鶻王侯家族群像

公元10—11世紀，出自吐魯番柏孜克里克石窟第169窟。本圖是窟內供養人列像中的一部份。共八人，臉型長圓，神色肅敬。均身穿長袍，但顏色花紋不同。右側四人戴三尖高帽，左側四人冠帽呈直立折扇形。髮式有兩種：一種額前將髮中分，頭後辮髮下垂；另一種前額留出劉海。每人手中持花一束。各人都有一條回鶻文名榜。這種人物眾多的王室貴族供養人列像，反映出高昌佛教的興盛。現存德國柏林。

232 龍騰圖

公元9世紀，出自吐魯番柏孜克里克石窟。圖中繪群山密樹旁一池碧水，煙波浩渺，游龍騰躍。畫面運筆雄健豪放，敷彩細膩絢麗。游龍尖嘴齜牙，長舌卷曲，龍髯飄動，利爪揮舞。氣勢凶悍矯健，充分顯示出藝術家高超的繪畫技藝。現存德國柏林。

233 飛天絹畫

公元8世紀，長35.3cm，出自吐魯番高昌故城。畫中散花飛天上身裸露，臂繞帔帛，下著紗裙，輕薄如煙籠水洗。周圍浮雲隨柔美飄逸的體態婉轉流動，輕盈妙妍。現存德國柏林。

234 僧統供養像

公元9—10世紀，出自吐魯番柏孜克里克石窟第20窟。圖中三僧內穿回鶻式圓領窄袖衣，外披交領廣袖中原式紫袈裟，雙手執花供養。上方有漢文回鶻文合壁的墨書。「僧統」系官名，說明三位高僧是管理僧眾事務的僧官。現存德國柏林。

235 回鶻公主供養像

公元9世紀末—10世紀，出自吐魯番柏孜克里克石窟第20窟。畫中兩身供養人袖手持花，立於飾有波浪紋樣的地毯上。人物皮膚白淨，體態豐腴，神情怡靜、溫婉。身穿茜色通裙大裾，頭戴如意雲金絲冠，髮卷外翻，四周插金鳳凰、花釵及步搖。金耳環下垂至肩，精巧別緻，富麗堂皇。現存德國柏林。

236 仕女圖

公元7世紀，出自吐魯番。絹畫。仕女臉型長圓，髮束雙髻，額間描紅，高眉細目，鼻樑端秀，小口朱唇。外穿翻領繡花衣。神態文靜高雅，端莊凝重。現存日本東京。

237 釋迦太子出遊圖

公元7—9世紀，吐魯番吐峪溝石窟出土。紙畫。相傳釋迦太子出遊時，分別見到孕婦、老人、病人、死人及修行者，感到人有生老病死四苦，於是起了出家修行之念。本圖描繪太子騎馬出城，前有二人肩抬死屍。圖中城樓、人物服飾、形象均為中原風格。現存日本東京。

238 護法神像（局部）

公元9—10世紀，吐魯番柏孜克里克石窟出土。絹畫。畫面左側存兩身著鎧裝、披紅袍，手握武器的護法神，粗眉倒豎、眉頭、鼻翼擠擰成團，眼睛怒睜裂成多邊形，神奇誇張。護法神左側頭光中繪兩人頭兩怪獸的神像。畫面右側殘存數十隻手，空手或握各種法器，可能是多手觀音像的一部份。現存德國柏林。

239　樹下人物圖

公元8世紀，吐魯番阿斯塔那古墓出土。紙質。草地間一顆樹下站立一對男女。男子頭戴尖頂帷帽，服飾類中原唐時的寬袍大袖。女子頭梳低鬟，身穿圓領長袍，足蹬黑靴。這種樹下人物圖的結構、佈局深受薩珊波斯圖案藝術的影響，在敦煌莫高窟壁畫中亦有所見。現存日本東京。

240　摩尼教經卷插圖（局部）

公元10世紀，吐魯番柏孜克里克石窟出土。紙質，畫中兩側存墨書粟特文字數行，上鈐紅色印記。中間繪一幅伎樂插圖，圖中兩樂伎吹笙簫，踏蓮花相對而立。正中書一行貼金箔的粟特文字。現存吐魯番博物館。

241　觀世音菩薩像

公元10世紀，吐魯番高昌故城出土。絹畫。菩薩頭戴花冠，冠後兩根紅飄帶垂至肩部，身穿繡花邊紅袍。身後有背項光。表情和善安詳。從人物的服飾看來，當為回鶻化的觀世音形像。現存德國柏林。

242　供養禮佛圖

公元9世紀末—10世紀中葉，出自吐魯番柏孜克里克石窟第20窟。畫面正中上下通欄繪說法傳教的大立佛，右側從上至下分繪兩身比丘、兩軀菩薩和兩身單跪托盤供養的俗體人物，盤中各放七個袋子。左側從上至下分繪金剛、菩薩、跪坐的俗體人物，馱供物的馬、驢、駱駝。整個畫面以紅色為基調，綠色、白色相間，色彩熱烈、絢麗、接近晚唐壁畫的敷彩。現存德國柏林。

243　供養人像（局部）

公元9世紀—10世紀，出自吐魯番柏孜克里克石窟第20窟。本圖系供養禮佛圖局部，描繪兩身遊牧貴族向佛奉金銀寶物的情景。兩人相貌略有差異，均雙手托盛滿寶物的金花盤，左膝單跪向佛，兩人身穿金花皮袍，腰繫皮帶，上別馬鞭，足蹬高筒皮靴。右側者頭戴黑皮金邊瓜皮小帽；左側者戴喇叭形皮帽，均梳長短不一的細辮髮。現存德國柏林。

244　眾人奏樂圖

公元10—11世紀，出自吐魯番柏孜克里克石窟第33窟。本圖所繪為外道婆羅門聽說佛涅槃後歡欣慶賀的場面。此畫運筆奔放流暢，勾線瀟灑有力，群像神態各異，造型逼真傳神，充份體現了古代畫工卓越的繪畫技巧。畫中樂器有琵琶、橫笛、鐃、鼓等，為研究高昌音樂史提供了寶貴的形象資料。現存日本東京。

245　延受命菩薩麻布畫

公元7—8世紀，長37.7cm，吐魯番交河出土。在正

方形的麻布上用淡茶色、黑色沿邊描出輪廓及對角線。在兩側三角形中各有一身菩薩坐像。披紅袈裟，坐蓮花座，座兩側繪出卷草。一身菩薩旁書「延受命菩薩」字樣，另一身僅寫一「延」字。「延受命菩薩」不見於正規佛典，屬於民間信仰。現存遼寧省旅順博物館。

246　長壽王菩薩絹畫

公元7—8世紀，長102.6cm，吐魯番出土。畫中菩薩頭戴珠冠，身披瓔珞，右手作印，面容慈祥，端莊。其服飾及冠中化佛與觀世音菩薩相同。菩薩右側有「南無延壽命長壽王菩薩」題記。現存遼寧省旅順博物館。

247　供養菩薩像

公元10世紀，出自吉木薩爾北庭回鶻寺廟。壁畫。畫面保存較好。畫中菩薩像成組呈排佈局，形象大同小異：長圓臉，彎眉，細眼，高鼻，朱唇小口；頭戴花冠，辮髮垂肩；上身袒裸，頸繫項飾瓔珞，臂腕佩釧，斜披絡腋或披半臂；雙手多合十，身後有圓形項光和背光，上有各色光輪。此壁畫風格、技法與柏孜克里克石窟同類壁畫極為接近。

248　王者出行圖

公元10世紀，出自吉木薩爾北庭回鶻寺廟。壁畫。圖中心為一交腳橫坐於白象背上的王者，鎧裝，頭後有圓形項光，左手按於左腿之上，右手伸二指舉於胸前；白象鞍轡俱全。王者和白象前後簇擁眾騎士。騎士鎧裝，腰間掛佩劍和弓箭，雙手合持長傘或旌旗；坐騎鞍轡齊備，行進於山巒草地間。壁畫中人物服飾，騎士裝束與敦煌石窟及安西榆林窟同時期壁畫比較接近。

編　織　類

249　禽獸紋錦（局部）

公元4世紀，吐魯番阿斯塔那古墓出土。藏青色錦地，棕、藍、綠色顯花，黃色線勾出圖案的輪廓。在由曲波線和直線構成的幾何紋中填以大小不一、上下相對的怪獸和相背的怪鳥紋。怪獸頭上長角，身後生翼，尾上卷或下垂，龍爪形足。怪鳥頭尾似禽，四足如獸作走狀。整個畫面橫向佈局，上下對稱，構圖繁縟，線條均勻流暢，色調和諧，是一幅難得的藝術珍品。現存新疆博物館。

250　織金錦

公元8—10世紀，殘長71.5cm，鄯善縣魯克沁出土。長方形。殘片，以黑、黃、青色絲線顯花。整個畫面以狩獵題材為主，花石點綴，充滿生機。現存吐魯番博物館。

251　毛繡殘片（局部）

公元前10世紀，哈密縣五堡古墓出土。毛布袍殘片。平紋，組織較粗疏。深絳色地，其上用黃、白、藍、綠色毛線繡出三角形圖案。色澤豔麗，構圖規整而不板滯，顯示出新疆地區早期毛繡技術的嫻熟。現存新疆博物館。

252 草編簍

公元前18世紀，高10cm，若羌縣羅布泊孔雀河古墓出土。芨芨草編織。直口，鼓腹，環底，頸部編有曲波紋和弦紋。簍口蓋褐色毛布。現存新疆考古所。

253 毛線編織帽、氈帽

公元前9世紀，且末縣扎洪魯克墓地出土。左件黑色線織成，口小頂略大，平頂上插一根草狀物。帽彈力很大，用四種不同的編結法結成，使帽形成紋路不同的四瓣形。這是我國發現最早的一件毛線編織帽。右件氈帽，白色以兩片羊毛氈縫合而成，口大頂小，圓頂上縫有棒狀角形飾，帽後開叉處有一繫帶。現存巴音郭楞蒙古自治州博物館。

254 尖頂氈帽

公元前9世紀，高29cm，且末縣扎洪魯克墓出土。為二片長三角形褐色氈片縫合而成。在帽內中部至頂部充填硬物，使帽挺直。底部兩側有遮耳。現存巴音郭楞蒙古自治州博物館。

255 毛織衣

公元前9世紀，長53cm，且末縣扎洪魯克墓地出土。以斜紋毛布裁剪為左右前襟，左右袖、背五片縫合而成。對襟，直筒形，橢圓形領，領下有一繫帶，袖窄短。做工較粗糙。現存巴音郭楞蒙古自治州博物館。

256 毛布男褲

公元2—3世紀，長115cm，尉犂縣營盤古墓出土。質地細膩柔軟，平紋組織，淺黃色，布滿豎條形褶紋。褲腿肥大，褲口有貼邊。褲腰系另縫合上去的。布料表面平整，開口處有一繫帶。現存巴音郭楞蒙古自治州博物館。

257 栽絨毯

公元2—3世紀，長260cm，寬95-100cm，尉犂墓地出土。長方形，中部為動物紋樣幾何形的立獅。用紅、白、藍、淺綠、黑等色毛絨栽絨編結成各種圖案，花紋由彩條和菱形格紋等構成邊飾，主體圖案是一雄獅，獅首右半殘缺，間夾「卍」字紋。此毯色澤穩重、柔和，莊重富麗。現存巴音郭楞蒙古自治州博物館。

258 「萬世如意」錦袍

公元2世紀，長133cm，民豐縣尼雅古墓出土。錦袍對襟，用紅、綠、藍、白多種彩色絲線顯花。窄長袖，束腰，斜擺式，錦上織有漢文「萬世如意」和變體卷雲紋。衣襟右下緣鑲貼的錦上有「延年益壽大宜子孫」吉祥語。色彩溫暖柔和，富麗高雅。這件錦袍對研究古代民族服飾具有重要意義。現存新疆博物館。

259 龍紋絲織帶（局部）

公元1—2世紀，尉犂縣營盤墓地出土。錦帶殘為兩段。以綠、黃、紅色絲線織出長方格龍紋。共三排，色彩各異。龍長頸、長嘴、昂首細腰、長尾高揚，四足作騰雲狀，形象生動活潑，雄健有力。在主題圖案中又夾織一組黃色幾何紋圖案。現存巴音郭楞蒙古自治州博物館。

260 印花棉布（殘片）

公元2世紀，民豐縣尼雅古墓出土。藍色地，白色顯花。左下方框內為袒胸露懷的半身菩薩，雙目斜視，神情恬靜溫婉，頸飾串珠，雙手捧盛滿葡萄的角形容器，身後有圓形項光。其右側為魚紋和鳥紋等圖案。現存新疆博物館。

261 「永昌錦」（局部）

公元2世紀，若羌縣樓蘭高台墓地出土。藍地上黃、褐、綠三色顯花。卷藤狀紋飾的彎曲處填有各種瑞獸和「永昌」漢字銘文。左起第一排為佇立的飛禽，第二排是長角生翼的怪獸，第三排為溫馴的小羊，第四排是回首作登山狀的猛虎。色彩深厚穩定而古樸，是研究中國早期織錦技術的珍品。現存新疆考古所。

262 「延年益壽大宜子孫」錦（局部）

公元2世紀，若羌縣樓蘭高台古墓出土。錦面棕褐色、黃、藍色線織花。紋樣系圖案化了的瑞獸和變體雲紋。均縱向排列，間織有「延年益壽大宜子孫」吉祥語。怪獸神態各異：左起第一排前蹄上抬作登山狀，第二排似在行走中抬頭回盼，尾上翹，與變體雲紋相連。第三排怪獸頸前伸，巨口大張，雙耳直立，背上有翼，尾上翹，尾端下垂，身軀上織斑點紋。現存新疆考古所。

263 「長壽明光」錦（局部）

公元2世紀，若羌縣樓蘭高台古墓出土。藍色地上黃、褐、綠三色顯花。以卷曲枝藤紋為主題圖案。卷藤紋彎曲處填有瑞獸和「長壽明光」漢字銘文。左側怪獸頭頂長角，背上生翼，巨口大張，四足作行走狀，中間虎紋形象的瑞獸抬頭回首作攀登狀，右側瑞獸抬頭回首作行走狀。造型簡練逼真，驕健生動·使畫面顯得更富有詩情畫意。現存新疆考古所。

264 魚禽紋錦（局部）

公元2世紀，若羌縣樓蘭高台古墓出土。錦面料染成褐色，魚用黃色線顯出，水禽則用藍色線織出，每兩條游魚之間夾有一對野鴨。紋飾清新典雅。現存新疆考古所。

265 三葉花緙毛（局部）

公元1—2世紀，若羌縣樓蘭高台古墓出土。彩色毛織物，古稱「罽」。採用「通經斷緯」織花法織成。紫紅色地上用黃、綠、藍等色顯花。圖中部是一較完整的桃花環，環中為一株三葉花。中間花葉上方有六顆似兩露的圓點紋，兩側花葉上亦有一顆圓點紋。花環外下方兩側各有一株盛開的花朵，右側是一豎排波浪紋。現存新疆考古所。

266 卍字邊幾何紋緙毛（局部）

公元1—2世紀，出自樓蘭地區。緙毛地為藍色，以白、紅、黃、綠色線顯花。幾何形圖案中填以花朵和變體鳥紋。邊用黃、綠色線顯出三角形紋。黃色線顯出卍字紋，色彩富麗高雅。現存瑞典斯德哥爾摩。

267 人首馬身毛織壁掛（部分）

公元1—2世紀，58×45.5cm，洛浦縣山普拉墓地出土。此壁掛出土時被剪裁為四塊，縫製成一條褲子，右褲腿為人首馬身，左褲腿為倒置的武士像。人首馬身的題材，見於希臘神話傳說，也稱「馬人」（centaur），但作為織物紋樣尚屬首見。壁掛以藍色為地，用十餘種顏色表現花紋圖案。採用通經斷緯的組織局部挖花方法織造。屬大型藝術壁掛，是高級毛織物中的精品。現存新疆博物館。

268　栽絨鞍毯

公元1—2世紀，76×74cm，洛浦縣山普拉墓地出土。此毯近正方形，出土時覆蓋於馬鞍上，故名「鞍毯」。以絳紅色為主色調，用秋香、淺黃、湖藍、墨綠、烟、黑色等毛線栽絨顯現花紋。中心圖案為橫列小菱形紋，內填以葉紋，或稱「有基樹紋」。四周有一組順式二方連續曲折紋與大樹葉紋組成紋樣，外框則以小色塊與斜紋組成連續幾何紋，四角綴穗。結扣為「土耳其式」。該毯圖案具有濃郁的地方特色，是迄今國內保存最完整的鞍毯。現存新疆博物館。

269　武士像毛織壁掛（部分）

公元1—2世紀，61×48.2cm，洛浦縣山普拉墓地出土。此壁掛原位在人首馬身之下。其織法同前圖。使用二十餘種顏色的細毛線織造。特別是武士面部各器官均使用退暈方法以表示明暗，具有立體感。顯然為希臘化影響之產物。現存新疆博物館。

270　人首馬身武士像掛毯復原像

經拼對復原，人首馬身及武士屬同一塊壁掛的上下部份，人首馬身在上，下為武士右手握矛圖。整體具希臘文化傳統，又揉進了犍陀羅藝術的表現手法。（新疆博物館黃小江復原）。

271　藍地白花紋棉布

公元1—2世紀，長11.5，殘幅寬41.2cm，洛浦縣山普拉墓地出土。藍地白花，平紋組織，一端遺有經頭。採用防染法，顯露出白色花紋圖案，由朵花、圈點、曲長線、鈎連等紋樣上下橫列組成圖案。是新疆現存最早的防染法棉布標本。現存新疆博物館。

272　狩獵紋印花絹片

公元8世紀，寬30cm，吐魯番阿斯塔那古墓出土。平紋印花絹織物。紋樣內容為騎士射獅，獵犬逐兔，獵鷹追飛鳥。圖案上下對稱，畫面動感極強。現存新疆博物館。

273　吉字紋錦（局部）

公元5世紀，寬30cm，吐魯番阿斯塔那古墓出土。錦為紅色地，藍、白色顯出圖案。紋樣有條紋，菱格紋和棘紋，紋樣中部夾織「吉」字紋。彩色清新典雅。現存新疆考古所。

274　夔紋錦（局部）

公元5世紀，吐魯番阿斯塔那古墓出土。織錦。藍色地、黃、白、紅、綠、粉紅色線顯花，提花準確，錦面結構細密，色彩豔麗，紋樣五彩繽紛。主題花紋是由夔龍形變體卷藤紋組成的圖案，橫向排列。在卷藤紋的彎曲處填飾雙角怪獸和菱形花朵。獸頸後有順風揚起的彩帶。風格

質樸，色彩莊重。這件作品採用波斯錦的斜紋組織緯線顯花的織法織成，帶有波斯薩珊王朝織錦的藝術風格。現存新疆博物館。

275　「富且昌宜侯王夫延命長」編織履

公元5世紀，長23，寬8.5cm，吐魯番阿斯塔那古墓出土。鞋底用粗麻線編織，呈土黃色。鞋幫用色澤鮮豔的彩色絲線編織，絲線顏色有紅、白、黑、藍、綠、杏黃、褐色等。從鞋尖向鞋口，圖案分別為紅地黃色忍冬紋，鋸齒紋，黃地寶藍色相對稱的忍冬紋，紅地綠色相對稱的雙葉紋和點紋，山紋兩側又用紅、藍、黃三色線織出「富且昌」、「宜侯王」、「夫延命長」漢文字樣。該品工藝之精，色澤之鮮豔，為全國之冠，是漢晉文獻中所戴「絲履」的重大發現。現存新疆博物館。

276　套環「貴」字紋綺（局部）

公元5世紀，吐魯番阿斯塔那古墓出土。平紋組織，淺絳色地上紫絳色顯花，圖案由各式團花套環組成，雙線中夾連續鈎藤紋或如意形相套連的圓環。環內夾以「貴」字，雙鳥紋。兩環相交處用小團花相接。套環連續成行，空隙處填充小團花裝飾。構圖複雜，富於浪漫氣息。線條圓潤，質地薄細透明，反映了這個時期我國傳統絲織技術有了高度發展。現存新疆博物館。

277　對鳥對羊樹紋錦（局部）

公元5世紀，吐魯番阿斯塔那古墓出土。織錦。錦地深綠，紋飾用紅、黃、棕、白色彩線織出中間是一排呈塔形的燈樹紋：樹下臥有一排對稱的長角羊：樹梢兩側是對稱的立鳥：圖上方的每組對鳥共銜忍冬紋，其間用一棵小花樹相間。圖案設計較規整，花紋簡約質樸，用色反差強烈。現存新疆考古所。

278　母女繡像

公元9-10世紀，17.5×4cm，吐魯番高昌故城出土。刺繡。表現一位回鶻公主和她的女兒。這個貴族特徵的婦人以手握著一枝花，髮飾很高，佩帶著裝飾品，長衫拖曳。小孩服飾神態與母親相似。此繡品繡工精良，華貴，是一件難得的藝術品。現存德國柏林。

279　刺繡鎧甲衣片

公元7—9世紀，長17-21.5cm，寬20cm，烏魯木齊阿拉溝石壘城出土。方形，棉布縫製而成。中部湖藍色地上用黃、綠色絲線繡花草紋，花草紋間鑲有數枚乳釘式銅飾。四邊用黃色棉布裹貼。現存烏魯木齊市博物館。

280　盤絲獅象紋錦

公元5世紀，長13cm，吐魯番阿斯塔那古墓出土。白地，花紋分為絳、綠、藍、黃四色。主體紋樣系兩列盤絲團窠，內填以正、倒相對的獅和象。團窠之間飾以復合忍冬四葉紋。現存新疆博物館。

281　紅地對馬紋錦（局部）

公元7—8世紀，吐魯番阿斯塔那古墓出土。此錦殘存紋樣為四方連續的團窠聯珠，之間以仰連相綴。內織有翼系綬雙馬相對連蓬卷葉紋。在四方連續的團窠間，填珠心

卷葉紋。現存新疆博物館。

282 飛鳳蛺蝶團花錦殘片（局部）

公元7—8世紀，吐魯番勝金口佛寺遺址出土。此錦花紋為六彩瑞花團窠和繞花飛舞的遍地金黃色飛鳳。鳳首頂花冠，頸下懸墜，長尾如藤曲卷，翩翩飛翔，姿態優雅。飛鳳間蛺蝶相隨，別有情趣。現存新疆博物館。

283 聯珠對雞紋錦（局部）

公元7—8世紀，吐魯番阿斯塔那古墓出土。黃色地，紅、白二色顯花，圖案橫向排列。橢圓形聯珠花環內是兩隻站立在方形物體上的對雞，頭頂華冠，項繫綬帶，雖用色不多，但美感極強。現存新疆博物館。

284 聯珠鷥鳥紋錦（局部）

公元7—9世紀，吐魯番阿斯塔那古墓出土。黃色地，紋樣用深藍、灰、白等色織出。橢圓形聯珠花環內織一立鳥，口銜串珠，項繫綬帶向後揚起。頸下和翅上飾有珠飾。雙翅上張，尾微下垂。色調高雅，佈局規整。現存新疆博物館。

285 聯珠鹿紋錦（局部）

公元7—9世紀，吐魯番阿斯塔那古墓出土。錦為土黃色地，黑、綠色顯花。紋樣簡練明朗。聯珠花環內飾一雄鹿，鹿體肥大，舉步輕捷，多枝巨形花角後彎，項繫綬帶後飄，身上飾有鋸齒紋，三角紋和圓圈紋、山形紋。這是一件具有薩珊風格的中國織錦。現存新疆考古所。

286 聯珠「胡王」錦（局部）

公元5世紀，吐魯番阿斯塔那古墓出土。採用倒置循環提花法織成上下對稱的圖案。米黃色地，絳紅，桔紅顯花。橢圓形聯珠花環內填飾正、倒相對的駱駝、牽駝人和漢字「胡王」。牽駝人手執長鞭，深目高鼻。花環之間飾以復合忍冬四葉紋。整個畫面形象生動，色彩深厚古樸，西域文化特徵濃郁，這是「絲綢之路」上文化交流的佳作，反映出與中國內地的密切聯繫，現存新疆博物館。

287 狩獵紋印花紗（局部）

公元7—8世紀，吐魯番阿斯塔那古墓出土。平紋組織。經、緯線排列疏鬆，構成方形小孔。在黑綠色地上顯淺綠色圖案。印花工藝為減劑印花法，使花紋自然出現深淺不同的效果。畫面以狩獵紋為主。襯以花卉樹木。天空有驚飛的鳥雀，地下有奔逃的鹿兔，獵者驅馬奔跑，有的張索欲投，有的彎弓射箭，有的持刀捕獵野獸。線條簡潔，敷彩單純明麗，形象生動活潑。現存新疆博物館。

288 獸紋錦（局部）

公元5世紀，吐魯番阿斯塔那古墓出土。用藍、黃、白、綠、褐色絲線織出獸紋。圖案縱向排列。動物有牛、獅、象。左起第一排牛首右側作行走狀，第二排臥地雄獅前足抬起作欲起狀，第三排行走的象背上飾有華蓋和人物。形象具體而簡練。這種形式的紋樣在中亞、西亞地區常見，表明吸取了中亞和西亞的紋飾和技法。現存新疆博物館。

289 騎士對獸紋錦（局部）

公元5世紀，殘長22.5cm，吐魯番阿斯塔那古墓出土。黃地，深青、淺藍、淺黃色顯花。以數個相切的圓環為圖案骨架，圓環內飾騎士射鹿、對象、對獅、對駝等紋樣。圓環之間填對馬和忍冬紋樣。圓環相切處又以仰蓮相綴，精細嚴謹。現存新疆博物館。

290 樹紋錦（局部）

公元5世紀，吐魯番阿斯塔那古墓出土。在黃、黑色彩帶上飾有上下兩排相錯的紅色樹紋圖案。在樹紋之間又飾有菱形格和格紋。紋飾較簡。完全圖案化。現存新疆博物館。

291 靈鷲紋錦（局部）

公元10—11世紀，尉犁縣阿拉干出土。米黃色錦面上以藍、白、黑色絲線織花，圖案設計精巧。圓球形聯珠花環內兩隻背立的鷲鳥，右翅振起，左翅下垂作舞狀兩尾相交下拽作花籃狀，中間織有花束。花環外相交和空隙處飾有方棋龜紋和四鳥相連的團花紋圖案。紋飾清新典雅。這件織物是一件完整錦袍的局部。現存北京故宮博物館。

292 地毯

公元19世紀，和闐徵集。毯面棕紅色中間以棕、白二色相錯顯出多種菱格圖案。菱格紋中有圓點紋和相套黃色格紋，中間再飾四瓣形花朵。邊飾折線紋、葉狀紋、花朵紋等。整個畫面色彩柔和，構圖規整，織毯技術嫻熟。現存新疆博物館。

293 菱形格絹（局部）

公元18世紀，長310cm，和闐織造。亦稱艾特萊斯綢。為多色平紋印花絹織物。圖案對稱。在紫色地上飾紅、白、深綠、淺綠、深藍、淺藍和桔黃色花紋。中部為連續菱形格紋，每個菱形格又套飾兩端的凸飾的菱格紋。兩側飾有對稱的顏色各異的折線彩帶，彩帶內散填圈紋。色彩絢麗。現存新疆博物館。

木 器 類

294 木雕人物椅腿

公元3—4世紀，高34.5cm，民豐縣尼雅遺址出土。使用浮雕與線刻相結合的技法雕成，通繪朱紅彩，略帶黑色造型生動，立體感強。左為女性，右為男性均頭戴冠帽，面部線條明快，眼鼻口耳清晰，男唇上有髭。身側有雙翼。兩者下身為馬蹄形上下身交接處雕刻成半開半閉的蓮花形。頭後有榫口插入榫頭，可起連接作用。頭冠頂部的鉤手，不僅是帽子的一部份，還可起固定椅墊的作用。整個造型明顯具有印度和希臘羅馬的藝術風格。現存英國倫敦。

295 半身木雕女像

公元前9世紀，高57.5cm，若羌縣孔雀河古墓溝出土。整木雕刻。頭戴圓帽。腦後垂著編織的髮辮臉部較光滑，未雕五官。體扁平，乳房下垂。無手。出土時身前背後尚有毛織物殘片。該像雕刻簡略，樸拙，可能是祭祀用的女神像。現存新疆考古所。

296　鳥柄木碗

公元前9—公元前8世紀，長17cm，和靜縣察吾呼溝古墓出土。以木削製而成。敞口，環底，沿較厚，腹外連一鳥首形柄，曲頸，頭下垂。頭上透鑽一圓孔。現存巴音郭楞蒙古自治州博物館。

297　男女木雕像

公元前10—9世紀，女高14、男高12cm，哈密焉布拉克古墓出土。用原木刻成，造型古樸。除面部的嘴眼用陰刻方式表現出來，略具神態外其餘部份雕刻僵直刻板。男不粗壯，女不纖細。但性器均被明顯誇張。現存哈密博物館。

298　羊形柄木梳

公元前9世紀，長12.4cm，哈密五保墓地出土。用木刻削而成，製作粗糙，刀痕明顯。梳柄刻成羊形，昂首，大角後卷，軀短肥。下部穿孔，中套皮繩。梳齒7枚，齒粗且疏。現存新疆考古所。

299　木耜

公元前10世紀，長38.5cm，哈密五保古墓出土。木質，乾裂有朽痕，長方形，上端有柄，面微弧曲。上端有修補痕，刃部有使用痕跡。現存新疆考古所。

300　木鉢木勺

公元1世紀，鉢徑34、勺長28cm，洛浦縣山普拉古墓出土。鉢用木鏇製。敞口，平沿，淺腹，環底，有鏇痕。勺用圓大剖成。勺部口徑11—12cm，深6cm，環底，長柄。柄末端下垂呈鈎狀。現存新疆博物館。

301　蛇形弓、箭

公元前5世紀，弓長121、箭長79cm，鄯善縣蘇貝希古墓出土。弓用硬木條、樹膠。牛筋、獸角等製成，剖面呈三角形。箭以木幹製成，鏃與幹結為一體，分單翼雙翼。弦為牛筋。現存新疆考古所。

302　漆花木梳

公元1—2世紀，高9cm，洛浦縣山普拉古墓出土。以木刻削而成。半圓形柄，黑地彩繪紅、黃、綠色增月形和圓點紋。柄齒間飾三排圓點紋，梳齒61枚，齒細且密。製作精巧，表面光滑。現存新疆博物館。

303　木雕飾板

公元2—3世紀，長30cm，民豐縣尼雅遺址採集。為一木雕小門扇。圖案分上下兩部分，上為一深目高鼻人牽一駁物大象，下為一四足怪獸。周刻幾何紋邊飾。現存和闐博物館。

304　佉盧文木牘

公元1—3世紀，長27.5cm，民豐縣尼雅遺址出土。胡楊木加工製成，長方形，函盒中部下切凹槽，內書佉盧文字。函蓋置於函盒凹槽內，背部隆起，鑿三道捆扎用的槽和一長方形封泥凹槽。涵蓋兩端橫書佉盧文字。現存和闐

博物館。

305　木几

公元1—2世紀，長36.5cm，洛浦縣山普拉古墓出土。以木刻削製成，幾面較平，邊緣起棱。四足雕刻精緻，上飾刻劃紋。現存新疆博物館。

306　木碗、木杯

公元3世紀，高6.4—13cm，尉犂縣營盤遺址出土。四件。均鏇製。單耳木碗斂口，曲腹。漆碗，略殘，內外壁髹黑漆。大環圓形敞口，束腰，底腰部兩條平行凸弦紋。木環，敞口，平底旋製。現存巴音郭楞蒙古自治州博物館。

307　斷頭菩薩立像

公元8世紀，殘高24cm，巴楚縣庫姆阿克大佛寺出土。木雕。頸戴項圈，上身赤裸，斜披綬帶。雙手殘，下身著拖地長裙，腰繫圍裙，裙帶下垂。赤足立於底座上，座飾仰覆蓮瓣紋。現存德國柏林。

308　木雕菩薩立像

公元12世紀，高9cm，吐魯番高昌遺址出土。木雕。頭戴寶冠，高髻，面部豐滿、祥和，戴項鏈，上身著低領衫，束寬腰帶，肩坡綬帶。下著拖地長裙。手均殘。赤足立於覆蓮瓣紋的橢圓形座上。整體造型具有密教風格。現存德國柏林。

309　坐佛像

公元9世紀，高15cm，吐魯番高昌故城出土。高浮雕式，木質雕像。佛盤膝坐於蓮花寶座上，袒右臂，外披扁衫，雙手相疊，其頭和身後有頭光和背光。光輪邊緣有一圈裝飾圖案，為透雕的渦狀卷草紋。佛面部豐腴，形象生動，神態慈和莊嚴神聖。雕像造型精美，藝術價值甚高。現存德國柏林。

310　擊腰鼓天人木雕

公元6—7世紀，高10.9cm，拜城縣克孜爾石窟出土，這是一奏樂天人，頭帶寶冠，有頭光結跏而坐，左腋夾腰鼓，右手殘缺，但仍能窺其擊打的喜悅神態。木雕奏樂天人在龜茲出土文物中尚屬罕見，現存德國柏林。

311　佛立像

公元7世紀，高18cm，拜城縣克孜爾石窟出土。木雕。身略右側，高肉髻。白毫相。身著右袒肩條紋袈裟。右臂垂於身側，手握袈裟，左臂微屈，赤足立於方座上。現存德國柏林。

312　交腳菩薩像

公元7—8世紀，高16cm，拜城縣克孜爾石窟出土。木雕。有背光，束髮，髮帶垂肩，首微低，面容和善。戴項圈。上身袒裸。高胸束腰，右小臂已失，左手置於腿上，下身著貼身小褲，作交腳坐式。現存德國柏林。

313　木雕佛首

公元5—6世紀，高11cm，巴楚縣吐木休克遺址出土。面部呈橢圓形，眉目端莊，鼻樑挺直，嘴角略凹。頭髮呈波浪形，有頂髻。木雕表面包金箔。此件作品刀法細膩，

雕刻精湛。佛表情安詳、凝重，富於智慧。其造型受犍陀羅藝術影響，又體現出中原佛教造像特徵。現存德國柏林。

314　觀音立像

公元7世紀，高38cm，鄯善縣吐峪溝出土。木雕。頭戴寶冠，上飾十個面部表情各異的人頭。菩薩面相豐腴，雙目低垂作俯視狀。上衣右袒，下著寬裙，戴項圈、瓔珞和綬帶，佩臂釧。左手殘損。右手置於體側，赤足（殘）。雕刻精緻，神態莊嚴肅穆。現存德國柏林。

315　力士木雕像

公元8世紀，高25.6cm，焉耆縣七個星佛寺遺址出土。木雕。手殘。昂首挺胸，雙目圓睜怒視前方。力士頭戴小帽，身著豎條紋衣，下擺垂於兩腿之間。腰繫布捋腰帶，胸前紅帶兩周，帶頭下垂。身後披風飄舉，披風結繫於頷下。腿繫護腿，足蹬尖頭靴。雕飾精美，質感很強。現存英國倫敦。

316　彩繪木雕佛龕

公元7—8世紀，高28.2cm，焉耆縣七個星佛寺遺址出土。立柱形佛龕，內分上中下三層。上層雕刻一立佛，右側一持華蓋立侍。佛上身赤裸，下繫短裙，手施無畏印，有頭光。中層左側亦為一手施無畏印立佛，立於蓮座上。右側上下排列兩合掌菩薩，呈跪姿。菩薩前面一人匍匐於地，頭觸佛足。下層分左右兩區。左區為一持杖立佛，右區為兩供養人像。佛和菩薩形象具有濃厚的印度風格，兩供養人衣冠整齊，又帶有中原漢風。現存英國倫敦。

317　木雕桌腿

公元1—4世紀，長67.8cm，高60cm，民豐縣尼遺址出土。保存較好。共有四腿，四側板，用榫鉚套合成形。其上雕刻紋飾，分區佈置，周圍用連珠紋隔開，最多見的是四瓣花紋，刻於側板和腿上部，並配置長方形、正方形或三角形框。長側板中心紋飾類似石榴。腿上部還飾有八瓣蓮花紋和經幡圖案；頂面上有鉚頭，其上承接的桌面無存。現存英國倫敦。

318　木雕佛像

公元3—5世紀，高25cm，巴楚縣托庫孜薩來遺址出土。高浮雕式木雕。有背光，佛頭戴寶冠，面相呈圓形，上身著圓肩緊身衣，佩戴手釧、手鐲，下身著貼身小褲，雙手合掌，作結跏趺坐式。雕刻粗獷笨拙。現存巴楚文化館。

319　塔式彩繪木舍利盒

公元8—9世紀，高13.4cm，鄯善縣吐峪溝石窟出土。鏇製。上下兩半球體以子母口扣合。白地上飾紅、綠、黃、黑色三層仰覆蓮瓣紋。頂有六層塔式蓋鈕，大盤圈足。造型別緻新穎，具有濃厚的宗教色彩。現存德國柏林。

320　彩繪木舍利盒

公元8世紀，高25cm，拜城縣克爾石窟出土。鏇製。

由幾部分套接成型，子母口扣合。盤狀蓋，頂隆呈圓錐狀。深直腹，平底。紅褐地，黑彩，通體飾帶短垂線的弓形紋和「⌣」紋。現存德國柏林。

321　木雕坐佛

公元5世紀，高16cm，巴楚縣吐木休克遺址出土。高肉髻，面相清瘦，雙目低垂。上身著圓肩僧衣，結跏趺坐，雙手相疊作禪定印。雕刻簡練，無華麗裝飾。現存德國柏林。

322　彩繪馬夫木俑

公元7—9世紀，高56cm，吐魯番阿斯塔那古墓出土。彩繪木雕。通體分十塊刻成，粘合成型後施彩。人物特徵應「胡人」：頭戴高尖頂折沿氈帽，身著翻領長袍長靴。眉毛密而修長，大眼，鼻樑長挺，唇上下有鬚，雙手作握攬物體狀。人物造型氣宇軒昂，頗富神采。現存新疆博物館。

323　彩繪木鴨

公元7世紀，左長15、右長14cm，吐魯番阿斯塔那古墓出土。兩件。雕刻極為簡練，繪紅黑彩。左件頭大，長弧形喙，頸粗，頸下呈船形，圓頭尖尾，微上翹，作游泳狀。右件喙殘，圓眼立頸，頸下亦呈船形，作游泳狀。現存英國倫敦。

324　木牛車

公元6—7世紀，通高53cm，吐魯番阿斯塔那古墓出土。車體呈箱形，前後有出入口，頂部露天，車輪正圓，各有輻條十二，牛用一整木雕成，著黑色，是研究當時交通工具的資料。現存新疆考古所。

325　彩繪木罐

公元7—9世紀，通高7cm，吐魯番阿斯塔那古墓出土。以木鏇製成。子母口，扁圓鼓腹，平底，蓋上有傘形鈕，外表塗黑，蓋繪卷草紋。罐繪寶相團花和雲氣紋。色彩附著不牢，專為死者製作的冥器。現存新疆博物館。

326　彩繪仕女木俑

公元7—9世紀，高54cm，吐魯番阿斯塔那古墓出土。用一段整木雕成，後施繪彩，色彩多已剝落。仕女髮束「驚鵠髻」，體態豐腴，衣袖寬肥，為盛唐貴婦典型形象。現存新疆博物館。

327　彩繪女木俑

公元7—9世紀，高29.5cm，吐魯番阿斯塔那古墓出土。木刻彩繪。頭及軀體均以木雕刻而成，唯手及長裙用襯紙做成。臉部經過打磨施彩。頭梳高髻，兩手交疊腹前，面部刻劃細膩，色彩鮮艷明麗，表情溫順安靜。在製作上採用了多種材料，技法高超、嫻熟。現存新疆博物館。

328　彩繪天王踏鬼木俑

公元7—9世紀，高86cm，吐魯番阿斯塔那古墓出土。由三十餘塊分別雕成後套接成形。繪紅、黃、綠、藍、紫和黑色。天王高髻束帶，身著鎧甲，右手上舉，左手彎曲前伸，著紅花褲，繫扶腿，足蹬靴。右足下踏一醜

陋小鬼。造型威嚴，氣勢雄偉，形象地反映出天王勇猛的
姿態。現存新疆博物館。

石 雕 類

329 阿勒泰市阿維灘石人

公元6—8世紀，高160cm，圓柱形礫石雕成。臉橢圓
形，高顴骨，深目高鼻，八字鬍。頜部鬍鬚濃密。身體部
份僅刻劃出兩手，右手托杯狀物於胸前，左手置於腹部。
現存阿勒泰博物館。

330 清河縣什巴爾庫勒鹿石

公元前8世紀。高300cm，這是一通兩面雕刻鹿紋的
方柱狀鹿石。橫截面正方，邊長23cm。一面上端刻帶柄
圓圈，下雕五鹿。首鹿較小，反向面下，四鹿依次朝上重
疊排列。另一面雕刻六鹿。已圖案化，皆鳥喙狀長嘴，角
長繁枝連弧後延，後肢曲，前肢或直或曲作奔跑狀，鹿紋
鹿石是亞洲北方草原的代表性文物之一，多分佈於阿爾泰
山地東部及蒙古高原西部。該鹿石發現於查干敦楞鄉境
內。現存阿勒泰博物館。

331 富蘊縣恰爾格爾鹿石

公元前8世紀，高290cm。這是一通四面雕刻的刀形
鹿紋鹿石。截面長方，寬40、厚20cm。兩寬面雕刻鹿
紋；另一面僅見連點和鹿紋。鹿紋已圖案化，依次朝上重
疊排列，長角繁枝連弧後延，喙狀長嘴，曲肢，或上視或
回首作奔跑狀以表現其一定的寓意。鹿紋雕刻精細流暢，
是鹿石中的佳作。該鹿石發現於恰勒格爾，現存阿勒泰文
管所。

332 獸頭柄石杯

公元前6—公元前5世紀，徑13—15cm，阿勒泰縣克爾
木齊古墓出土。係用石英質岩石鑿刻而成。厚重，粗糙，
直腹平底，柄呈獸頭形。現存新疆考古所。

333 石雕女像

公元前18世紀，高27.5cm。若羌縣孔雀河古墓溝出
土。白石雕刻而成，外表打磨光滑。方頭，眉、眼、嘴、
鼻均用黑色豎橫線表示，頸部陰刻三道弧線表示服飾領
口，胸部刻乳房。束腰繫帶，下肢簡略，造型奇特精美。
現存新疆考古所。

334 石祖

新石器時代，長13cm，木壘縣四道溝遺址採集。以
長圓形礫石雕刻而成，造型古樸。前端呈弧形。上豎刻兩
道凹槽。反映古人對男性生殖器的崇拜。現存木壘博物
館。

335 石臼

公元前15世紀，徑12.7cm，長5.5cm，和碩縣新塔那
遺址出土。經鑿後磨製而成。斂口，弧腹，環底，較厚
拙。微向下彎。現存新疆考古所。

336 踞猴石燈

公元1世紀，高30cm，巴里坤縣大河鄉出土。青石雕
成。形態為一猴踞跪於方座上頭頂鉢形燈盞，前肢上舉扶
持。雕刻簡樸，粗放，形象地表現出猴在困壓之下流露出
痛苦神情。現存哈密博物館。

337 昭蘇縣1號石人

公元7—9世紀，高145cm，條形礫石雕刻而成。僅刻
頭、面部，長方形臉，尖頷，高顴骨，圓目，長鼻，唇微
啟，唇上有翹八字鬍。神態莊嚴冷峻。現存昭蘇喇嘛廟。

338 昭蘇縣2號石人

公元7—9世紀，高110cm，礫石雕刻而成。臉部刻
眉、目、鼻、口及小八字鬍。軀體僅以陰線刻出雙手，左
手握刀，右手托杯置於胸前。現存昭蘇喇嘛廟。

339 昭蘇縣3號石人

公元7—9世紀，高108cm，礫石雕成。圓臉，高顴
骨，刻有臉、嘴、鼻。頸部陰刻許多短鬚。軀體部份加
刻劃。技法笨拙。現存昭蘇喇嘛廟。

340 昭蘇縣小洪那海石人

公元7—9世紀，高230cm，礫石鑿刻。頭戴圓帽，髮
辮後垂至腰。長方形臉，高鼻深目，唇上有八字鬍，腰間
繫帶，上墜飾物，右手執杯形彎曲於胸前，左手置於腹
部。身下刻有粟特文。現存昭蘇種馬場。

341 溫泉縣阿爾卡特石人

公元6—8世紀，高285cm，石人圓臉、睜目、闊鼻、
嘴緊閉，有兩撇八字鬍鬚。身穿翻襟圓領大衣，腰繫寬
帶，右手舉杯，左手執刀。腰間另有佩刀一把。形象威嚴
莊重。現存新疆博物館。

342 阿勒泰市汗德特石人

公元7—9世紀，高130cm，係選取長方形條石用淺浮
雕法製成。長方形臉，兩道彎眉與長鼻相連，細目，唇上
有翹八字鬍。頸肩分明，身體部份僅刻劃兩手。右手托杯
狀物舉於胸前，左手置於腹部。凸突面均施朱彩。現存新
疆考古所。

343 博樂縣蘇里科克石人

公元7—9世紀，高160cm，石人用長條石雕刻。橢圓
形臉，面部較平，眉、目、鼻八字鬍突出，呈浮雕狀。頸
下刻一道凹槽。右手托一杯置於胸前。現存原地。

344 額敏縣種羊場石人

公元7—9世紀，高110cm，用紅灰色砂岩雕刻而成。
方臉，尖頷，高鼻深目，兩道劍眉與鼻相連，顴骨較高，
唇上有八字鬍，須頸以下未經雕刻。現存塔城博物館。

345 烏蘇縣奧瓦特石人

公元7—9世紀，高90cm，石人係用一條狀礫石雕刻
而成，僅刻出頭、面部。臉形橢圓，雙目微張，隆準闊
鼻、厚唇，口略啟，八字鬍鬚，頷下陰刻桃狀頸飾。雕刻
簡潔，形象生動。現存原地。

346 阿勒泰市布提伊爾敏女石人

公元7—9世紀，高60cm，圓臉，顴骨較高，圓眼，

闊鼻，口微閉。胸前刻乳房，右手置於胸前。現存切不爾切克鄉提伊爾敏原地。

347 托里縣石人
公元7—9世紀，高190cm，用整塊條石雕刻，面部略呈倒三角形，高鼻深目，八字鬍鬚，頸部以下未經雕刻。形象威嚴。現存原地。

348 吉木乃縣森塔斯湖石人
公元7—9世紀，高250cm，頭呈圓形，上戴方帽，面部磨鑿呈桃狀，隆鼻，眼、口漫漶不清。肩部以下未經雕刻。現存沙窩子山森塔斯湖原地。

349 阿合奇縣阿文庫石人
公元7—9世紀，高62cm，橢圓形臉，尖頜，彎眉，大眼，長隆鼻，八字鬍上翹，頜上刻有菱狀髯。現存原地。

350 昭蘇縣空古爾布拉克石人
公元7—9世紀，高110cm，係用長方形青石陰線刻成。僅刻出頭面部。面龐橢圓形，兩道彎眉與鼻相連。頭上刻幾道豎線組成三個三角狀，表現髮冠。雙耳墜環。現存原地。

351 伊吾縣科托果勒石人
公元7—9世紀，高90cm，採用天然礫石線刻成。僅刻出眉、鼻、眼和臉龐輪廓。現存原地。

352 高昌石幢
公元4—5世紀，殘高66cm，吐魯番高昌故城出土。石幢形體小巧，鐫刻精緻，是寺院供奉之物。砂岩質，頂部殘失，存塔頸，覆鉢，經柱，基柱四部份。塔頸上刻出「大」形裝飾。下為覆鉢式塔腹，周開八座帶火焰狀龕楣的穹頂龕，上飾大瓣覆蓮。龕內刻有高浮雕佛像七身，彌勒一身，皆作禪定印，雕像造型簡潔粗疏，古拙有力。中部經柱為圓柱形，周陰刻經文35行，內容為《增一阿含經》前半部份。書法規整，挺拔剛勁，是典型的北朝體。經柱下的基柱呈八面形，每面陰刻天人一尊，有頭光，上身裸，下著裙，手中各持供物。天人上方各刻一八卦符號，將佛與黃老道術放在一起頂禮膜拜，反映出佛教文化與漢文化對高昌藝術的共同影響。現存德國柏林。

353 石面具
公元10—13世紀，高23.5cm，新源縣鞏乃斯河南岸出土。砂岩質，鑿刻成形，打磨光滑，面具呈橢圓形，雙目凹陷，瞳孔凸起，中穿一孔。寬隆鼻，闊嘴微啟，造型抽象，立體感強。面具邊緣有一周凹槽，當供附著之用。現存新疆考古所。

354 九層小石塔
公元18世紀，高15cm，和靜巴倫台徵集。雕刻成形後打磨光滑。通體呈乳黃色，塔身呈六棱柱形，共九層。塔檐上翹，上刻瓦棱。自第二層以上每層每面壁上均刻一龕形小窗。作工精巧。現存巴音郭楞蒙古自治州博物館。

泥　塑　類

355 泥塑天人像
公元6—7世紀，高40cm，焉耆縣七個星佛寺遺址出土。高髻，圓臉，彎眉秀目，直鼻櫻唇，上身袒裸，瓔珞垂胸，細腰露臍，短裙飄逸。天人體態婀娜，神態怡靜高雅，與古希臘維納斯殘像似有異曲同工之妙。該作品受犍陀羅藝術影響，堪稱西域藝術之精品。現存英國倫敦。

356 泥塑小飛天
公元6世紀，高14cm，和闐縣卡得魯庫出土。半浮雕狀。小飛天有頭光，束髻，全裸體，上腹繫束帶，雙手攜花帶作展翅狀，造型優美，動感強。現存英國倫敦。

357 人首牛頭陶杯
公元3—4世紀，長19.5cm，和闐縣約特干遺址出土。細泥黃陶質。上塑人首，下塑牛頭，器頂繫一圓形注口，中空。人戴螺形高帽，廣額隆眉，高鼻，長翹鬍美鬚髯，眼目傳神，形神華肖。器下部塑一彎角牛頭，牛嘴作口。這種造型奇特的杯，古人用來注神酒，希臘人稱為「來通」（rhyton），相似的器物在鄰近地區也有發現。現存新疆博物館。

358 伎樂陶殘片
公元4—5世紀，高12cm，和闐縣約特干遺址出土。兩個扇形小龕內各有持不同樂器藝人（饒和橫笛）。扇形龕被低矮的印度式圓柱支撐著，上部有蓮珠的帶狀飾，兩龕之間有一花形裝飾。構圖受犍陀羅風格影響。現存英國倫敦。

359 陶鳥
公元2—3世紀，高10.8cm和闐縣約特干遺址出土。高冠，長喙，有凸出的雙耳。冠和尾的紋樣似為變形蓮瓣紋。胸毛為按捺紋，表現手法高超。現存英國倫敦。

360 人首陶杯
公元3—4世紀，殘長17cm，和闐縣約特干遺址出土。細泥橙黃陶質，上端係圓形注口，中空。頭戴螺形高帽，窄額，隆眉，鼓目高鼻，鬍稍翹呈八字形，長鬚髯。下部出口殘失，但仍可見兩角，原亦塑有動物形象。此件與圖357號屬同一類器物。現存新疆博物館。

361 人頭像
公元3—4世紀，高13cm，和闐縣約特干遺址出土。陶製，呈黃色。殘毀比較嚴重。眉毛粗密，眼睛大張，鼻子高挺而粗壯。嘴唇上下皆有濃密的鬍鬚。塑造精美，風格粗獷有力。現存和闐博物館。

362 陶製帝王像
公元2—3世紀，高12cm，和闐縣出土。陶製，呈金黃色。塑一端坐在寶座之上的帝王形象。面部不甚清晰，右手放置在扶手上。下身衣衫及踝，赤腳。背後是高大的靠背。現存韓國漢城。

363　佛面範

公元4—9世紀，殘高25，寬23cm，皮山縣杜瓦出土。石膏範。佛相面部端重平和，眉目修長，眼微睜，鼻樑細長高挺，直通額際。口形小巧閉合，下頜豐腴。整體造型豐滿圓潤。現存和闐博物館。

364　蓮花坐佛

公元3—4世紀，高26cm，洛浦縣熱瓦克寺院遺址出土。泥塑坐佛，呈黃棕色。佛陀盤坐，兩手相疊置於腹前，兩腳相交。上有頭光，身後是一朵蓮花，以佛為中心花瓣向四周呈放射狀開放。佛面相豐腴，神態慈和，刻劃較細膩。現存和闐博物館。

365　泥塑立佛像

公元5世紀，高20cm，和闐縣喀拉墩遺址出土。立佛，施無畏印。肩後噴出火焰，象徵超人的力量，頭上有頭光，背光被火焰圍繞，雙肩扛火，腳踏波浪，衣褶雕塑細緻入微。整個雕塑具犍陀羅藝術風格。現存英國倫敦。

366　陶塑婦人半身像

公元1—3世紀，高12.4cm，和闐縣約特干遺址出土。中空，嘴半張，由口可通至塑像內部。前額髮短而齊，兩側的長髮披至肩上。項鏈下垂至胸前。上身著緊身套衣。風格上融入了西亞雕塑傳統，充滿了古樸原始的風韻。現存英國倫敦。

367　雄性陶猴

公元7—8世紀，高6.8cm，和闐縣約特干遺址出土。係用粘土捏製燒造而成，猴造型為跪坐，右手掌撫於胸前，左手持住性器。周身剔刺出許多小孔，雙目炯炯有神，形象風趣。現存遼寧省旅順博物館。

368　坐佛像

公元7—8世紀，高102cm，焉耆縣七個星佛寺遺址出土。泥塑。佛盤腿坐在四方形高台座上。高髮髻，面龐豐潤，神態端莊，眉目修長，眼光下視。身著百褶長衫，祖右臂，右手半舉，左手放置腿部。此像面部塑造極富神韻，手法高超。現存德國柏林。

369　菩薩頭像

公元4—5世紀，巴楚縣托庫孜薩來寺院。泥塑。菩薩臉型長圓豐潤，廣額寬頤，彎眉秀目，隆鼻厚唇，卷髮下垂至頸。面部表情溫婉怡靜，慈祥親切，具有一種人神融和所構成的特殊神態。現存法國巴黎。

370　惡鬼頭像

公元8—9世紀，高30.3cm，吐魯番勝金口佛寺出土。泥塑。惡鬼題材在中亞佛廟中很流行。這個頭像戴著寬大而低垂的帽子，眉下眼球向外暴凸，鼻子適中，嘴巴富於表情。著意於表現一種恐怖和幽默的藝術氛圍，再配以冷調的色彩，產生了一種假面似的效果。現存德國柏林。

371　菩薩頭像

公元6世紀，高27cm，拜城縣克孜爾石窟出土。泥塑彩繪。臉型寬圓，短鼻，眼微斜視，眉毛繪成弧形線狀，卷髮後披。頭冠由一紅綠色圓及其頂上兩個傾斜盤狀裝飾物組成。現存德國柏林。

372　天人半身像

公元7—8世紀，高52cm，焉耆縣七個星佛寺遺址出土。彩繪泥塑。臉部豐滿。髮頭上束；兩臂殘毀，胸、頸、肩部裝飾有多層瓔珞、珠串、釧環等物。塑造精緻華美。現存德國柏林。

373　天部全身像

公元7世紀，高72.7cm，巴楚縣吐木休克遺址出土。彩繪泥塑。為站立的全身天部造像。面部豐滿圓潤，頭髮卷曲，眼光平視有神，身穿綠色袒右肩長衫，胸前有一花圈裝飾物，右手抬起，手指張開，掌心向前，左手殘毀。右腿直立，左腿屈弓，衣裙線條曲折而富有神韻，整個造型端莊秀美。現存德國柏林。

374　泥塑立猴

公元5—6世紀，高23cm，巴楚縣托庫孜薩來遺址出土，整個造型為擬人化的猴頭人身，手扶一根大棍，棍下端為一圓球形，被雙腿交叉夾住。形象怪誕，似為佛教體裁中的某種怪獸動物。現存巴楚縣文化館。

375　菩薩頭像

公元6—7世紀，庫車縣庫木吐拉出土。泥塑。束髮高髻，臉略長，彎眉，細眼、端鼻，朱唇，蝌蚪狀鬍鬚。此類菩薩造型在克孜爾壁畫中常見。現存日本東京。

376　人首象身泥塑

公元7—8世紀，高63.5cm，拜城縣克孜爾石窟出土。為一人首象身的半人半象彩繪泥塑。上部為人頭，自脖頸以下的身軀部份塑造為大象形象：肩臂處為象耳，兩乳處塑成象眼，腰腹部塑成一只象腳，象鼻則從象腿左側盤繞一周後在右側探出鼻尖。人和象體之後為一長方體形背座。此像造型奇詭獨特，色彩線條富於變化。現存德國柏林。

377　大佛頭像

公元3—5世紀，高約50cm，若羌縣米蘭佛寺遺址出土。泥塑，為佛頭部造像。面相端正，弧線形長眉，眼帘微啟，鼻子隆直，上與眉線相接。嘴唇閉合，下頜比較渾厚，線條豐滿圓潤，著意表現佛慈悲祥和的神韻。現存新疆考古所。

378　彩塑菩薩頭像

公元6—7世紀，高30cm，焉耆縣七個星佛寺遺址出土。頭戴金冠，微睜雙眼，眉呈弧曲線狀，面目慈祥，前髮中分，重疊後攏。臉型豐滿圓潤，受中原雕塑風格影響。現存英國倫敦。

379　男子頭像

公元6—7世紀，高14cm，焉耆縣七個星佛寺遺址出土。此為婆羅門男性頭像。挽髻，濃鬍，表情寧靜，皺眉作沉思狀。現存英國倫敦。

380　菩薩頭像

公元7—8世紀，高20.5cm，焉耆縣七個星佛寺遺址出土。頭髮捲曲呈波浪狀，成束下垂。面部圓潤豐滿，雙眼微閉，做沉思狀。現存英國倫敦。

381 武士像

公元6—7世紀，高42cm，焉耆縣七個星遺址出土。上戴頭盔，身穿鎧甲，手持長矛、圓盾，嘴唇緊閉，目瞪直視前方。形象勇武威嚴。現存英國倫敦。

382 舞女俑

公元7—9世紀，高56cm，吐魯番阿斯塔那墓地出土。頭部泥塑彩繪，身軀以木棍支撐，胳膊用紙捻做成，外罩彩錦衣袍。肩披彩色紗巾。臉部形象刻劃細膩優美。現存新疆博物館。

383 男裝仕女頭像

公元7—9世紀，高16.5cm，吐魯番阿斯塔那古墓出土。彩繪泥塑。上為男式髮飾的幞頭打扮，初看似男子。但細眉秀目，在眼底鼻側繪綠、紅彩色小朵花鈿。現存新疆考古所。

384 思維女俑

公元7—9世紀，高13cm，吐魯番阿斯塔那古墓出土。彩繪泥塑，為一女子沉思形象。上梳高髮髻，頭向右偏。右手支撐臉頰，左手置於膝上，手中似握有一物。身著衣衫和長裙，席地而坐，右腿支起。整體造型表現處於沉思狀態。現存新疆博物館。

385 彩繪宦者俑

公元7—9世紀，高34.5cm，吐魯番阿斯塔那古墓出土。木身泥頭，屬「半身俑」式。雙臂用紙捻做成，下身採用木棍作腿、足。身著黃色綺袍。束髮髻。面部雕成後以經打磨處理，然後施彩。刻劃細膩生動。形神兼備，將宦者的可惡嘴臉表現得淋漓盡致。現存新疆博物館。

386 青鬼頭像

公元8—9世紀，高21.7cm，吐魯番勝金口佛寺出土。泥塑。其恐怖效果通過眉、目、牙等的特殊處理方法表現出來。暴凸的眼珠，濃密緊擰的眉毛，眼光斜視，大嘴張開，露出一顆尖牙，尤其是在前額正中又著意塑造了第三隻眼睛，使整個形象更顯得猙獰可怖。現存德國柏林。

387 武士頭像

公元8—9世紀，高22cm，吐魯番出土。彩繪泥塑。上戴頭盔，臉龐寬大豐滿，眼球暴凸，闊鼻，嘴角緊閉下撇，表現武士發怒的狀態。此像用色單純，採用了一定的誇張手法，著意於刻劃人物的神態。造型逼真生動。線條粗獷有力。現存韓國漢城。

388 彩繪文吏俑

公元7—9世紀，高24.2cm，吐魯番阿斯塔那古墓出土。彩繪泥塑。為文職官吏形像。右手握筆，左肋挾文卷。頭梳髮髻，身著長袍。施色單調。現存新疆博物館。

389 人物俑

公元7—9世紀，高24、29、28cm，吐魯番阿斯塔那古墓出土。三件，彩繪泥塑。左側人物為一士兵形象，戴盔著甲，左手作拄劍狀。其餘二人面部、髮飾等基本相同，唯中間一人著白色長袍，左手持盾，右手作握攮器物狀；右側人物著棕色長袍，雙手相握靠在腹部。現存新疆考古所。

390 單峰駝

公元7—9世紀，高72cm，吐魯番阿斯塔那古墓出土。泥塑，單峰駱駝昂首站立，外表塗紫褐色，多已脫落。在塑造方法上，採用傳統的木骨—草秸支架泥塑成型法。其中頭部的塑造較為精細。腿部塑出了凸凹的肌肉線條。現存新疆博物館。

391 泥牛俑

公元7—9世紀，高31cm，吐魯番阿斯塔那古墓出土。彩繪泥塑，牛頭昂起前伸，似被牽引前行。脖頸粗壯，肩背部暴凸，呈一峰狀，後腿叉開，保持站立時的姿態。現存新疆考古所。

392 彩繪胡人俑

公元7—9世紀，高110cm，吐魯番阿斯塔那古墓出土。彩繪泥塑。頭髮束髻、冠以巾幘，著對襟翻領長袍、皮靴。鼻樑高挺，亂髯濃鬚。其塑造採用木、草秸支架、草泥成型的傳統方法。現存新疆博物館。

393 彩繪打馬球俑

公元7—9世紀，高26.5cm，吐魯番阿斯塔那古墓出土。彩繪泥塑。騎者右臂揚起，手中握一弧形木杆做擊球的動作。胯下白馬四蹄騰起，作奔馳狀。馬球運動起源於波斯，唐代時傳入中國，成為當時貴族生活中的流行時尚。這件泥塑將騎者和馬的姿態準確、生動地表現了出來，富於動感。現存新疆博物館。

394 馬形陶燈

公元9—13世紀，高13.4cm，吐魯番英沙爾古城出土。陶質，呈灰紅色，馬昂首而立，短鬃上揚，背部有鞍，富於裝飾圖案。在馬鞍正中塑燈一盞，侈口，呈碗狀。馬尾粗壯，拖達地面。馬體造型粗壯肥碩，是實用的工藝品。現存吐魯番博物館。

395 人首豹身鎮墓獸

公元6—9世紀，高86cm，吐魯番阿斯塔那古墓出土。彩繪泥塑。此鎮墓獸頭作人形，上戴兜鍪如武士，面目威嚴，軀幹似豹，足如馬蹄，作蹲踞狀。尾部細長如蛇緊貼身後。這件作品是人和幾種動物形象的組合，既威嚴又恐怖，產生一種強烈的威懾效果。現存新疆博物館。

396 鎮墓獸

公元7—9世紀，高75cm，吐魯番阿斯塔那古墓出土。彩繪泥塑，為墓中避邪之物，造型取多種動物的特徵組合而成：獅首、牛蹄、豹身、狐尾，是一種臆造的怪獸形象。眼珠碩大，暴凸，鬃毛聳立，在體側又各塑出一隻眼睛。此像構思新奇怪誕，塑造手法細膩精微。現存新疆博物館。

397 騎馬武士俑

公元7—9世紀，高39.5cm，吐魯番阿斯塔那古墓出土。彩繪泥塑，為隨葬的儀仗兵馬俑之一。武士頭戴尖頂軟盔，穿深褐色長袍，外罩軟甲。端坐馬上，左手握疆，右手作提鞭狀。馬成黑色，體形高大健美。人與馬均保持靜態。現存新疆考古所。

398　女士半身像

公元8—9世紀，高43cm，巴楚縣吐木休克遺址出土。泥塑女子半身像。髮飾很高，前額上梳高而寬的瀏海，兩側的頭髮整齊下垂成為披肩髮式。面部豐滿圓潤，富於質感和美感。弧線狀的長眉，眼睛修長，鼻子窄而高挺，與眉線相連。嘴閉合，唇厚而潤，表現了女子特有的矜持神韻。自脖頸以下塑造比較粗率，僅在胸部粗線條地刻出肉褶線和乳房。現存韓國漢城。

399　雜技馬舞俑

公元7—9世紀，高12.8cm，吐魯番阿斯塔那古墓出土。彩繪泥塑。塑造的雜技動作形象。馬體中空，四肢為人腿，表明二人在下表演馬舞。馬背上騎一綠衣人，兩手伸張亦在表演動作。現存新疆博物館。

400　彩繪馬俑

公元7—9世紀，高56cm，吐魯番阿斯塔那古墓出土。彩繪泥塑。馬昂首張口，作嘶鳴狀。頭較小，脖頸粗壯。背上有裝飾精美的鞍具，胸部佩一圈紅纓，臀部圓突。整體造型高大肥壯健美，很有力度感。現存新疆博物館。

401　騎馬仕女俑

公元7—9世紀，高39cm，吐魯番阿斯塔那古墓出土。彩繪泥塑，為一騎馬出行的仁女。頭戴高頂寬沿涼帽，眉目修長，面部豐腴，身著衫褲，一手執疆，一手提鞭。這種服飾裝束是當時的時尚。馬的形體高大肥壯。造型逼真。現存新疆考古所。

402　黑人百戲俑

公元7—9世紀，高12.5cm，吐魯番阿斯塔那古墓出土。彩繪泥塑，塑造一個正在表演動作的男子。上身赤裸，下身著桔紅色短褲，赤腳，雙手正擰棒舞弄。皮膚施黑彩，短卷髮，嘴唇粗厚，臉部線條刻劃較粗，比例勻稱，形象活潑生動。是一非洲黑人形象。現存新疆博物館。

403　舞獅俑

公元7—9世紀，高13cm，吐魯番阿斯塔那古墓出土。彩繪泥塑，表現雙人舞獅的形象。此俑塑造方法比較獨特，即用摻有毛絨的細泥塑成外殼，以防乾裂：在軀體外表用梳狀物劃出彎曲的細條紋，形似獅毛。脊背中部塑一條裝飾帶並向兩側各垂下四條。通體施白彩，只在頭部施局部紅、黑彩。風格粗獷質樸。現存新疆博物館。

404　彩繪舞蹈泥俑

公元7—9世紀，高10.2cm，吐魯番阿斯塔那古墓出土。彩繪泥塑，表現一位正在表演搏擊動作的糾糾武士。眼珠暴凸，張口作呼嘯狀，鬍鬚濃密誇張，張臂，揮拳，蹲襠，作搏鬥姿勢。此像造型，刻劃生動細膩。現存新疆博物館。

405　彩繪勞作俑群

公元7—9世紀，高9.7—16cm，吐魯番阿斯塔那古墓出土，彩繪泥塑，一組四件，均為從事不同家務勞作的婦女形象。自左至右依次表現從春糧、簸糧、磨面、烙餅的過程：第一人雙手握杵春糧；第二人跽坐，手端簸箕：第三人作推磨狀，第四人席地而坐，腿上置麵板，雙手作擀麵狀。此群俑像不刻意求精，而求神似，表現了另一種藝術風格。同時也反映了唐代生活勞動情景。現存新疆博物館。

406　雞首人身俑

公元7—9世紀，高80cm，吐魯番阿斯塔那古墓出土。彩繪泥塑，為大型十二生肖俑中酉的標誌。造型上為雞首，自脖頸以下為人身，著綠色無領大襟窄袖衫，喇叭式長裙，雙手相握，籠在袖中。此像構思新穎奇特，塑造精美。現存新疆博物館。

407　豬首人身俑

公元7—9世紀，高75cm，吐魯番阿斯塔那古墓出土。彩繪泥塑，為大型十二生肖俑中亥的標誌。上為豬首，自脖頸以下為人身著橙蔥色無領大襟寬袖衫，喇叭式長裙。雙手相握，籠在袖中，塑造手法細膩逼真，尤其是豬臉部特徵及衣袖褶紋，質感很強。現存新疆博物館。

玉　琢　類

408　雙龍玉牌

公元10—12世紀，長20cm，伊寧縣出土。白玉透雕。整體呈長方形，雙龍身體彎曲並相互纏繞，龍頭回首相對，龍身刻劃卷渦紋。現存伊犁博物館。

409　臥虎玉硯

公元18世紀，長20.5cm，吐魯番征集。白玉雕刻，長方形，一側為圓角長方形硯池。另一側橫臥一隻猛虎，虎的雙足前伸，後足跪屈，昂首雄視前方。虎肌肉發達，齒爪鋒利，顯得威猛有神。現存新疆博物館。

410　項珠飾品

公元1—4世紀，若羌縣樓蘭遺址採集。項珠以紅、藍、綠、黃、青、黑色瑪瑙和玉石磨製而成，有圓柱形、圓形、橢圓形數種，中均穿孔，便於串連佩帶。現存新疆考古所。

411　玉璧

銅石並用時代，直徑7cm，且末縣北大沙漠採集。圓餅形，厚2.5cm，磨製而成，比較規整。中心圓形鑽孔，直徑1.8cm，色黃變藍，有一塊褐色斑塊。現存新疆考古所。

412　串珠

公元前18世紀，若羌縣孔雀河古墓出土。軟玉，淡黃色，透明度較差。呈圓柱形和菱形，中有孔。現存新疆考古所。

413　人形花押

公元4—5世紀，高2cm，吐魯番高昌故城出土。琥珀色瑪瑙淺浮雕，仰面呈橢圓形周有邊框，正中刻一站立人像，頭側向左，長髮，高鼻深目，戴圓形耳環，下頦鬍鬚前翹，身著雙襟雙邊短袍，腰繫帶，左手平伸向前部，右手握一杖形物置於腰側。現存吐魯番博物館。

414　人形花押

公元4—5世紀，高2.2cm，巴楚縣出土。琥珀色瑪瑙雕刻而成。仰面呈橢圓形，上刻人物側面肖像，深目高鼻，頭戴寬沿帽，腰繫圍裙式裝飾，肩上擔著魚等物品，足蹬長靴，邁步行走狀。具有美索不達米亞印章的風格。現存新疆博物館。

415　雙龍耳玉杯

公元18—19世紀，高5.5cm，烏魯木齊徵集。玉雕。薄胎，敞口，深腹，小圈足，雙龍形耳，龍前爪抓住杯口，頭俯於杯沿，身體彎曲成弓形，後足連於杯腹壁上，尾部卷曲呈草葉紋。雕刻工藝精湛。現存新疆博物館。

416　虎噬羊鎮子

公元18世紀，長24cm，吐魯番徵集。玉雕。底盤上浮雕一隻猛虎，身體跪伏，右前爪捕獲一羊，口噬其羊，羊仰天哀鳴，作掙扎狀。立體感強。現存新疆博物館。

417　白玉透雕椅扶手

公元18—19世紀，高34cm，喀什市徵集。以整塊漢白玉透雕而成。扶手雕出與後靠背銜接的榫頭，聯幫間雕以菱格紋。鵝脖部雕一盆花，花蕊伸出前垂，起到良好的裝飾作用。現存新疆博物館。

418　白玉盤

公元18世紀，直徑22cm，和闐徵集。玉雕。盤內用凸線隔成兩個部份。內刻兩行銘文：一為阿拉伯文，一為波斯文，大意是：「除了阿里再無其他勇猛的英雄，除了其寶劍再無其他銳利的刀劍。願萬能的真主保佑我們，消災除難，解脫一切苦源」。現存新疆博物館。

419　桃形雙聯玉洗

公元18—19世紀，高6cm，喀什市徵集。羊脂玉雕成。洗池間二桃相聯，兩桃上部之間聯結仰首老虎一隻，柄部透雕纏繞的花枝。雕刻精美，設計巧妙，具有極高的工藝價值。現存新疆博物館。

420　三嘴白玉吊燈

公元12—15世紀，長23cm，喀什市徵集。漢白玉雕刻而成。略呈三角形，中為十二瓣花飾，頂有圓孔穿通。邊伸出三個燈嘴。構思奇巧實用。現存新疆博物館。

建 築 類

421　樓蘭佛塔

公元3—4世紀，殘高10.4cm，位於若羌縣樓蘭古城遺址中。塔為夯土、土坯壘砌而成。底層為夯土，邊長19.5米，其下鋪一層10cm的紅柳。中部為夾雜有土坯的夯土。上層全用土坯壘砌。在每層土坯間夾10—15cm厚的紅柳枝。在佛塔右側還有一個較小的土台遺跡。

422　霍城吐虎魯鐵木耳麻扎

建於1365年，位於霍城縣東北38公里。禿黑魯帖木爾(1329—1362)為成吉思汗第七世孫，察合台系後王，新疆地區最早接受伊斯蘭教的蒙古可汗。陵墓高約15.5米，面寬10.8米，進深15.8米，磚木結構，穹窿頂。正面牆壁用藍、白、紫三色釉磚鑲砌裝飾。門拱上有古蘭經經文，兩旁為阿拉伯文書寫的讚頌銘文。建築風格為阿拉伯建築形式，是新疆著名的伊斯蘭教古建築。

423　交河故城

公元2—公元14世紀，吐魯番市西10里。城址座落在一狹長的孤島式台地上，四周是河床，崖壁峭立，相對高度30餘米。在崖壁東、南鑿崖為門。城中央有一條縱貫南北的大道，長350、寬6米，兩旁是高而厚實的土牆，但有巷口與幹道相連，形成縱橫交錯的居住院落。故城建築可分三區：西側北部為寺院區，東側北部為居住區，東側南部多大型建築，北端為塔林和墓葬區。是我國保存最好的、年代較早的古城之一。

424　交河故城大佛殿佛龕、佛像（殘）

公元9—10世紀，吐魯番。交河故城佛殿中央有一夯土築成的塔柱，塔柱須彌座以上四面開龕，龕內泥塑呈坐姿的佛像，均殘。龕壁、像表的彩繪被風沙剝落殆盡。這種供養佛像的塔柱是印度佛教建築精舍的一種演變形式，與中原唐代寺院殿中設施有所不同。

425　交河故城塔林

公元5—6世紀。位於故城遺址西北部，以一個金剛寶座式大塔為中心，在四角分列25個小塔，共為101塔組成規整的塔群。塔林全用大土坯砌成。

426　高昌故城

公元4—14世紀，吐魯番市東北火焰山鄉。城略呈方形，現存城址周長約5公里，分為外城、內城、宮城三部份。宮城位於最北，內城在宮城南側。現還有2座高塔。城內建築遺跡遍佈，曾為吐魯番地區統治中心。

427　高昌故城城牆

公元5—13世紀。圖為高昌故城西部的一段城牆，由夯土構築，牆外有馬面，高10米，用於戰時防御，馬面下半部尚可辨出柱孔遺痕。古城牆雖已是殘垣斷壁，但從其規模仍可想見當年的壯觀與宏偉。

428　高昌故城佛塔

約公元7—9世紀，殘高7米，吐魯番高昌故城東南隅。底部為兩層方形台基及一層圓形基座，上為圓形塔身。塔身上部已坍塌，目前殘存三級。均為土坯砌築。位於塔後的穹窿頂式建築，內壁尚殘存有零星佛教壁畫。

429　拜城克孜爾石窟

公元4—8世紀。位於縣城東木札提河北岸的懸崖間，已編號洞窟236個，是古龜茲境內規模最大的石窟寺，也是我國開鑿年代最早的石窟。按洞窟的形製和用途，可分為專供禮拜供養佛像的中心柱窟和大像窟，供誦經坐禪的方形窟，以及供生活起居的僧房等。其中以中心柱窟數量最多。以大像窟建築最為宏偉。立佛遺跡高達十餘米，其氣勢之恢宏不難想見。

430　中心柱窟窟形

公元4—5世紀，克孜爾石窟第100窟。圖中所示為該窟中心柱石壁正面，正中開一大龕，兩邊各開一小龕，龕中塑像不存，其下兩側均開一通向後室的甬道。這種中心柱窟在克孜爾數量最多。平面一般呈長方形，中部偏後鑿出直通到頂的方形塔柱，將洞窟分成前後兩室。前室高大開闊，後室低矮狹窄。

431　若羌米蘭佛塔

公元3—4世紀，現高約3.5m，若羌縣東米蘭佛寺遺址中。圓柱形佛塔周圍，有一道方形圍牆環繞。在塔身底部及圍牆內側均繪有佛教等內容的壁畫。其中著名的有翼天使壁畫即出自該塔及另一座佛塔之中，1989年在該塔又新發現多幅「有翼天使」壁畫。

432　民豐尼雅佛塔

公元3—4世紀，殘高約5米，民豐縣城北約120公里尼雅遺址。土坯建築，結構可分為三層。底、中兩層為基座，基本呈正方形。上層呈圓柱形，為一種已增高了的覆鉢狀塔身。佛塔南部已坍毀，西部破損較重。

433　喀什莫爾佛塔

公元5—6世紀，喀什市東北30公里哈諾依遺址中。現存塔基一座，殘塔一座。均用長方形和楔形土坯砌築而成。塔基為方覆斗形，殘存有壁龕。佛塔為正方形基座，圓腰、覆鉢狀塔身，殘高12.8米，底座最大邊長12.3米。是西域佛教建築中重要遺跡。

434　洛浦熱瓦克佛寺

公元5—6世紀，洛浦縣北約50公里的大沙漠中。寺院呈正方形，土坯砌築。佛塔居中，殘高約10米，周圍有邊長約60米的正方形圍牆，牆高2.8米。塔基下部殘毀，上部呈正方形，頂部呈圓柱形。在塔基下部及圍牆部份殘存有彩繪塑像，受破壞嚴重。

435　庫車昭怙喱佛塔

公元6—7世紀，高約7.5米，庫車縣城北20公里蘇巴什遺址。此塔下部為高方形基座，基座上是圓柱形加覆鉢式頂的塔身。土坯建築。在此佛塔中，曾出土邊一個精美的舍利盒。

436　鄯善烽火台

公元7—9世紀，高13.65米，鄯善縣連木沁鄉巴哥莊西北5.5公里。土坯建築。呈四方台形，上小下大，有中心柱，為空心建築，在其南壁及東壁各有一券頂洞室。外體建築之間有夾道相隔。整體堅實，風格粗獷。

437　庫車克孜爾朶哈佛塔

公元2—3世紀，高約15米，庫車縣城西北10公里處。從現存來看，為一四台狀夯土建築，土層中夾有蘆葦和樹枝，以起到加固作用。這座佛塔受侵蝕嚴重。但其建築高大堅固，附近就是克孜爾朶哈石窟。

438　艾提尕爾清真寺

初建於公元1426年，喀什市中心艾提尕爾廣場西側。前後經過多次擴建修整，現存為1872年擴建後的規模。總面積16000多平方米，是新疆最大的清真寺。由禮拜殿、教經堂、門樓及一些附屬建築組成。大門樓高約12米，兩邊各有一18米高的尖塔，塔頂有召喚樓和新月。門樓之後為一大拱拜，其頂部亦有尖塔和新月。建築高大雄偉，莊嚴肅穆，是新疆伊斯蘭教建築藝術的代表作之一。

439　艾提尕爾禮拜寺敞廊

艾提尕爾禮拜寺為建築群體，內有花園、淨身池，還分成內外寺及敞廊和封閉的講堂。敞廊即禮拜殿，正面寬160米，進深16米，由140根大木柱支撐房頂部，寬敞壯觀，可容數千人同時禮拜。

440　阿巴霍加陵墓

又稱為香妃墓。初建於公元1640年前後，位於喀什市郊。為明末清初喀什伊斯蘭教伊禪派首領玉素甫霍加及其後裔的家族陵園。磚木結構，通高26米，底寬約35米，進深29米，四角各有一個圓形塔柱，柱頂各有一小巧玲瓏的召呼樓和新月。陵墓頂部是用表磚砌成的半圓形大穹窿，直徑17米，頂端也有小樓和新月。通體用綠、藍、黃等釉磚貼面。富麗堂皇，莊嚴肅穆，為新疆伊斯蘭陵墓建築之冠。

441　庫車大寺

公元1935年重建，庫車城內。為庫車著名大禮拜寺，相傳初建於16世紀，1931年毀於大火，同年開始重建，1935年完工。占地21畝，設有禮拜殿、宣禮塔、門樓、望月樓、宗教法庭、宿舍等。宣禮塔高18米，大殿由88根木柱支撐，雕樑畫棟，裝修華美。

442　蘇公塔清真寺

公元1777年修建，通高37米，吐魯番城東2公里。又名額敏塔，為清代乾隆年間吐魯番郡王額敏和卓及其子蘇來滿修建。分為塔及所屬的清真寺兩大部份。塔由基台、基座、塔身、望月樓組成。所屬清真寺亦為新疆地區較典型的伊斯蘭教建築。在塔門外側立有建塔石碑一方，用漢文、察合台文陰刻，記敍了建塔經過。此塔是新疆境內伊斯蘭教建築中現存規模最大的磚塔，其建築結構和造型美觀別緻，具有濃厚的伊斯蘭藝術風格。

443　蘇公塔（額敏塔）身

全塔用灰黃色條磚疊砌，外表分層砌出三角形、四瓣花形、水波形、菱格形等十四種平行的幾何圖案，及富裝飾效果。內部設有螺旋形階梯72級通達頂部。

444　塔塔爾寺

公元1901年建。長35、寬10、高7米，塔城市區。又稱紅寺。門向西，建築分兩部份：下部是建築主體，呈長方形，四角有圓柱：上部為穹窿圓頂，呈毯廬狀。風格別緻。

445 艾買爾太陵墓

公元1934年建。高約10米，布爾津縣杜拉特鄉。艾買爾太據說是當地的一位哈薩克族將軍。死後葬於此地。陵墓為磚結構，門向西開，分前、後兩室。前室為圓柱形體穹窿頂，仿帳篷形狀；後室近似四方形磚塔，頂上豎有一彎新月。風格較為獨特。

446 哈密回王墳

公元1840年建。哈密回城西1公里。由大拱拜（第七、八世回王陵），小拱拜（一至六、九世回王陵）及大禮拜寺三座建築組成。圖為第七世回王陵。大拱拜門向西開，上覆穹窿頂，四角有塔柱，外牆及頂部以琉璃磚瓦裝飾。

447 惠遠新城鐘鼓樓

公元1882年建。霍城惠遠新城中心。此樓為東方傳統的樓閣式建築，磚木結構。底部為四方形高台，上建三層飛簷樓閣。氣勢雄偉。惠遠城在公元1884年前曾是伊犁將軍駐地，是清代新疆的軍事政治中心。

448 昭蘇聖佑廟大殿

公元1898年建。昭蘇縣城西北1公里。聖佑廟為喇嘛教建築。由照壁、山門、大殿、後殿及左右配殿幾部分組成，其中大殿是其主體建築，磚木結構，上下兩層，平面呈正方形，殿堂用木柱架排列支撐，大出簷，在裝飾上雕樑畫棟，屬於傳統的東方建築。在西北邊陲草原獨樹一幟。

449 烏魯木齊紅山寶塔

公元1788年建，高約12米，位於市中心紅山頂部，又稱鎮妖塔。為八角十一級樓閣式風水塔，由青磚砌成，原取「寶塔鎮河妖」之意，現為烏魯木齊美景之一。登山臨塔，邊城景物盡收眼底。

450 烏魯木齊文廟

公元1922年建。位於烏魯木齊市區內，是烏魯木齊現存比較完整的一座清代風格的建築群。原為上帝廟，主祭上帝，配享孔子，1945年改大殿為孔子大殿。整個建築包括前後兩部份，前部有山門、邊門、廂房、前殿及鐘鼓樓；後部為東西廂房及後殿。佔地面積2800平方米。

PHOTO INDEX

STONE IMPLEMENTS

001, Microlithic Arrowheads

The Neolithic Age L. 2. 9—5. 5cm Lopnur

These five arrowheads, made of jade and flint by using the technique of "pressing—carving", vary in shape. They include (from left to right) : 1. triangle arrowhead with a hollow bottom, 2. round—headed arrowhead, 3. arrowhead with a handle, 4. laurel—leaf—shaped arrowhead, 5. spearhead with a hollow bottom.

002, Stone Spearhead

The Neolithic Age L. 7. 9cm Lopnur

The flint spearhead is in the shape of laurel leaf. It was made by using the technique of "pressing—carving"; on one end was processed the handle. Now it is preserved in Xinjiang Institute of Archaeology.

003, Bola

The Neolithic Age D. 7cm Toksun

This yellow—brown stoneware, found at the Xiaocaohu Site, was made by using the technique of carving and polishing. There are some colliding traces on the surface. It is preserved in Xinjiang Museum , now.

004, White Jade Axe

The Neolithic Age L. 11. 6cm Lopnur

The jade axe was carved and polished entirely; its edge was polished sharply. The texture of the jade is very pure. It is a valuable handicraft aritcle, and is preserved in Xinjiang Institute of Archaeology, now.

005, Microlithic Necleuses

Later Mesolithic Age to early Neolithic Age L. 3. 5,6cm Shanshan

The two microlithic necleuses, in the column shape, were found at the Microlithic Site, Dikaner, and are preserved in Turfan Museum now.

006, The Stone Hoe in the Triangle Shape

The Bronze Age W. 22, H. 17cm Tacheng

This milky yellow stone hoe, excavated from the Wei Xiao Site, Tacheng, was polished in the shape of the triangle. In the center of it, there is a hole; the "bottom—side" of the "triangle" was polished to the blade. The technology of polishing was ripe. It is preserved in Xinjiang Institute of Archaeology, now.

007, Stone Hoe

The Bronze Age L. 17. 5cm Fukang

The oblate stone hoe, found at Sangong Township, was made by using the drilling and polishing technique. One of the ends was polished to the blade, and another was drilled a hole. It is now preserved in Xinjiang Institute of Archaeology

008, Stone Sickle

The Neolithic Age L. 15. 3cm Shufu

This sandstone sickle, now preserved in X. M, was unearthed in 1972 at Ak Tala Site. It is curve in shape. The inner side was polished to the blade; and one of the ends was polished to the point.

009, Blue Jade Axe

The Bronze—Stone Age L. 8. 8cm W. 4. 3cm Hoxud

The axe, made of blue jade, was polished on both sides of blade. It is a very exquisite tool and handicraft article. Now, the jade axe, excavated from the Xintata Site, is preserved in Xinjiang Institute of Archaeology

010, Stone Hoe in the Shape of Crane—Mouth

The Bronze—Stone Age L. 13. 1cm Hami

The stone hoe, collected at Banfang Valley, looks like the mouth of a crane. In the center, there is a drilling hole, and there is a hollow groove around the edge of the hoe. This kind of stone hoe is less to find up to now.

This one is preserved in Hami Museum now.

POTTERY

011, Painted Pottery *Dou* (stemmed dish)

5c B. C. H. 18. 2cm Shanshan

The upper part of the vessel takes a bow-like shape, with a sharp—edged rim, contracted mouth, swollen belly and a single handle. The bowl's outer surface was richly ornamented with black designs, i.e. evenly placed wave patterns under the rim, and oblique parallel lines on one side of every wave patterns. The lower part of the vessel is a long circular leg. This is the precious one of the painted pottery articles that have been found in Xinjiang. It is preserved in Turfan Museum now.

012, Pottery Jar with a Wide Flared Mouth

5c B. C. H. 26cm Kizil

This is an unusually shaped vessel which is rarely seen in Xinjiang. It has a square—edged rim, wide flared mouth, contracted neck, flat bottom and a long and thin handle. The outer surface of the neck was ornamented with one row of discrete embossed nipple protrusion. It is preserved in Xinjiang Institute of Archaeology, now.

013, Painted Pottery Cup with a Single Handle and a Spout

10—5c B. C. H. 12. 5cm Chawuhugou

The cup has a sharp—edged rim, open mouth, thick neck, swollen belly, flat bottom and a single handle on its shoulder. The outer surface was ornamented by plain red color on the lower belly and colored pattern above. The pattern consists of two parts, i.e. eight horizonal rows of solid reversed triangles near the handle, and deformed rectangular spirals under the spout. It is preserved in Xinjiang Museum now.

014, Grey Pottery Cups

10c B. C. H. 12cm (right one) and 2. 3cm (left one) Tacheng

Both made of peculiarly ill — levigated clay, the two cups have almost the same shape with a square — edged and slightly inwards turning rim and a flat bottom. The left bigger one's outer surface was ornamented with stamped zigzag lines below the rim. The right smaller one's outer surface was wholly ornamented with stamped finger—print. They are preserved in Tacheng Museum now.

015, Pottery Cup with Triangle Designs

15c B. C. H. 9cm Hoxud

Made of black clay, the cup has an outwards turning mouth, a vertical belly and a flat bottom. Around the upper part of the belly there incised a few triangle designs. The cup was unearthed from the Xintala Site.

016, Pottery Pot With Four Mouths (damaged)

10—5c B. C. H. 34cm Tacheng

Being hand — made of ill — levigated red clay, the jar has a swollen belly, four mouths, a badly damaged, possibly flat, bottom, Its total height is 34cm and the biggest diameter at the upper part of the body is 44cm. Among the four mouths, the biggest one is located in the middle, with a outwards turning rim, a mouth diameter of 17cm and two bulged ridges under the rim. The rest of three mouths symmetrically surround the contral biggest one, and each has a inwards turning rim and a mouth—diameter of 7. 5cm. Showing a unique form, such kind of jars have never been found in Xinjiang before. It is preserved in Tacheng Museum now.

017, Stamped Pottery Jar

12—7c B. C. H. 17cm Altay

Showing an olive—like shape, the jar has a swollen belly, conical bottom and sharp — edged rim. The outer surface was ornamented with stamped decoration, i. e., finger—print on the rim and groups of parallel arc lines on the belly. Its shape and printed design share some characteristics with that of the typical articles of the Karasuk Culture in Kazakhstan. It is preserved in Xinjiang Institute of Archaeology, now.

018, Handleless Painted Pottery Pot

10—5c B. C. H. 35. 6cm Hejing

The vessel has a square—edged and slightly everted rim, round shoulder, swollen belly and flat bottom. Its outer surface was richly ornamented with peculiar dark red designs. It is preserved in Xinjiang Institute of Archaeology, now.

019, Pottery Jug with a Single Handle and a Spout

10—5c B. C. H. 11. 5cm Hejing

The vessel has a round — edged and outwards turning rim, flat bottom, and a large, upwards protruding like a bird's beak, spout.

The mouth diameter is bigger than that of the body. The outer surface was ornamented with a circle of embossed decoration around the neck. It is preserved in Bayingolin Museum now.

020, **Painted Pottery Jar with Lying Camel Decorative Design(damaged)**

　　10—5c B. C.　H. 21. 3cm Hejing

　　Being hand—made of ill—levigated red clay, the jar has a square—edged rim, sloping shoulder and flat bottom. Its outer surface was ornamented with lying camel design around the neck. It is preserved in Xinjiang Institute of Archaeology, now.

021, **Painted Pottery Cup with a Single Handle**

　　10—5c B. C.　H. 14. 2cm Hejing

　　The cup has a round—edged rim, slightly opened mouth, swollen belly, flat bottom and a short horizonally outwards protruding spout. The outer surface was richly ornamented with parallel zigzag lines and one row of regularly placed deformed bird figures that were contained in a band obliquely extending downwards from the belly. It is preserved in Xinjiang Institute of Archaeology, now.

022, **Painted Pottery Jar with Double Handles**

　　5c B. C.　H. 16cm Hami

　　Being hand—made of well—levigated red clay, the jar has a round—edged and slightly outwards turning rim, bevelled shoulder, swollen belly, flat bottom and double handles. Its outer surface was richly ornamented with red designs, i. e several evenly placed parallel vertical bands extending downwards from the rim (and narrowing)to the bottom, and many crop seedling like design filled in between these bands on the belly. Such kind of pottery vessels, with the same shape and decoration have also been found in Gansu and Qinhai provinces. It is preserved in Hami Museum now.

023, **Painted Pottery Bowl**

　　5c B. C.　H. 6. 4cm Hami

　　Made of well—levigated red clay, the bowl has a square—edged rim, flat bottom with a central hole, and a broad vertical ring handle. Its outer surface was ornamented with two circles of continuing zigzag lines under the rim and many discrete zigzag lines below. It is preserved in Hami Museum now.

024, **Painted Pottery Jar with a Single Handle**

　　3c B. C.　H. 18cm Barkol

Being hand—made of poorly levigated red clay, the vessel has a square—edged rim, slightly opened mouth, long neck, sloping shoulder, swollen belly, flat bottom and a broad vertical ring handle on its belly. The outer surface was ornamented with red parallel zigzag lines contained in three bands separately on the rim, upper belly and lower belly. The handle surface was also ornamented with the same kind of parallel zigzag lines. It is preserved in Xinjiang Museum , now.

025, **Painted Pottery Pot with a Long Neck and Double Handles**

　　5c B. C.　H. 19cm Hami

　　With a round—edged and slightly outwards turning rim, long neck, swollen belly, flat bottom and double handles on its belly, the vessel was ornamented with irregular triangle design on the rim's inner and outer surfaces. It is preserved in Hami Museum now.

026, **Painted Pottery Pot with Double Horizonal Ring Handles**

　　5c B. C.　H. 16. 7cm Hami

　　The vessel has a round—edged and slightly inwards turning rim, swollen belly, flat bottom and two horizonal ring handles. The outer surface was ornamented with wave—like black zigzag lines on the red ground. It is preserved in Hami Museum now.

027, **Pottery Jar With a Large Spout**

　　10c B. C.　H. 39cm Baicheng

　　The jar has a round—edged and slightly outwards turning rim, contracted neck, sloping shoulder, swollen belly, round bottom and a large upwards protruding spout. The outer surface was ornamented with plain red above its neck and solid triangle design below. It is preserved in Xinjiang Institute of Archaeology, now.

028, **Pottery Jar with a Single Handle and a Spout**

　　10c B. C.　H. 28cm Baicheng

　　The jar has a round—edged rim, thick neck, slightly swollen belly, small flat bottom and a short upwards protruding spout. Its rim and upper belly outer surface were ornamented with zigzag lines and dots. It is preserved in Xinjiang Institute of Archaeology, now.

029, **Painted Pottery Jar**

　　5c B. C.　H. 22. 5cm Baicheng

　　The vessel has square—edged and everted

rim, swollen belly, round bottom, broad vertical ring handle and a mouth 34cm in diameter. The outer surface was richly ornamented with two rows of solid triangles on the upper part of the body and parallel zigzag lines below. It is preserved in Xinjiang Institute of Archaeology, now.

030, Painted Pottery Cup with a Single Handle and Flat Belly

5c B. C. H. 10. 2cm Shanshan

With a square—edged rim, flat belly and flat bottom, the cup was richly ornamented with black designs, i. e. one row of solid reversal triangles on the rim's inner and outer surface, another row of bigger solid reversal triangles on the belly's outer surface. It is preserved in Xinjiang Institute of Archaeology, now.

031, Painted Pottery Cup with a Single Handle

5c B. C. H. 11. 3cm Shanshan

The cup has a square—edged and slightly outwards rim, swollen belly, round bottom, and a single handle extending downwards from the rim to the bottom. Rim inner surface was ornamented with one row of small triangles. The whole outer surface was ornamented with parallel vertical red bands narrowing to the bottom. It is preserved in Turfan Museum now.

032, Pottery Pitcher in the Shape of a Gourd

5c B. C. H. 4. 2cm Shanshan

The vessel has a round—edged rim, long and thin neck, small mouth, swollen belly and a round bottom. Its outer surface was ornamented with irregularly incised cord pattern. This is one of the rarely seen pottery articles found in Xinjiang. It is preserved in Turfan Museum now.

033, Long—necked Pottery Flask

1c A. D. H. 20cm Shanshan

The vessel has a square—edged rim, open mouth, long and narrow neck, round shoulder, swollen belly and a small flat bottom. The belly outer surface was ornamented with embossed vertical ridges and semicircles. It is preserved in Xinjiang Museum, now.

034, Painted Pottery Bowl with a Single Handle

5c B. C. H. 10cm Shanshan

The bowl has a square—edged and slightly everted rim, big mouth, swollen belly, small flat bottom and a horizonal ring handle. Its outer surface was ornamented with one row of long and slender red reversed triangles under

the rim. It is preserved in Turfan Museum now.

035, Painted Pottery Jar with a Spout and Human Figure Decoration

10—5c B. C. H. 23cm Luntai

The jar has a round—edged and vertically upwards turning rim, swollen belly, flat bottom and a short upwards protruding spout. Its outer surface was richly ornamented with beautiful designs, i. e. triangles filled in blank with parallel lines on the upper and lower part of the body, and several different designs including one half—length human figure, drawn in profile in rhomboid blank on the middle body. It is preserved in Bayingolon Museum now.

036, Painted Pottery Cup

5c B. C. H. 18. 5cm Luntai

The vessel has a sharp—edged rim, circular mouth, thick and long neck, swollen belly and flat bottom. The outer surface was ornamented with one row of ladderlike solid squares contained in a band obliquely extending downwards from the rim to the bottom, and plain red outside the band. It is preserved in Bayingolin Museum now.

037, Painted Pottery Dou (Stemmed Dish)

5c B. C. H. 19. 6cm Urumqi

Being hand—made of poorly levigated red clay, the vessel has a bowl—shaped upper part and a long circular leg as the lower part. The bowl has a square—edged rim, single handle and a slightly opened mouth. Its whole surface was covered by red slip. The rim's outer surface was ornamented with irregular vertical black lines. It is preserved in Xinjiang Institute of Archaeology, now.

038, Painted Pottey Jar with a Single Handle

5c B. C. H. 12cm Urumqi

The jar has a square—edged rim, slightly opened mouth, swollen belly, single handle and a small flat bottom. The outer surface was richly ornamented with elegant black designs, i. e. one row of small and slender reversed triangles under the rim and parallel zigzag lines on the belly. It is preserved in Xinjiang Institute of Archaeology, now.

039, Painted Pottery Jar with a Single Handle

5c B. C. H. 13. 6cm Urumqi

Being hand—made of poorly levigated red clay, the jar has a square—edged rim, open mouth, long neck, swollen belly, sloping shoulder and a round bottom. The outer surface was richly ornamented with net pattern on the neck and parallel lines contained in one row of connecting reversed triangles on the belly. It is preserved in Xinjiang Museum , now.

040，Painted Pottery Jar with a Single Handle

5c B. C. H. 16. 6cm Urumqi

The jar has a square — edged rim, long neck, swollen belly and a flat bottom. Its outer surface was ornamented with red branch pattern. It is preserved in Xinjiang Museum , now.

041，Painted Pottery Jar with a Single Handle

4—5c B. C. H. 11. 5cm Urumqi

Being hand—made, of poorly levigted red clay, the jar has a sharp— edged rim, slightly opened mouth, sloping shoulder, flat bottom and a single broad vertical ring handle. The outer surface was richly ornamented with two rows of connecting solid triangles on the neck and three big spirals on the belly. It is preserved in Xinjiang Museum , now.

042，Painted Pottery Pot

3—2c B. C. H. 29cm Zhaosu

The vessel has a round — edged rim, slightly opened mouth, slightly contracted neck, swollen belly and a round bottom. The outer surface was richly ornamented with decorative designs, i. e. reversed triangles under the rim, blank, solid or red point filled—in net patterns on the neck, and parallel zigzag lines on the belly. It is preserved in Xinjiang Museum now.

043，Cocoon—shaped Pottery Flask

1c A. D. H. 20cm Zhaosu

Being an imitative work of the nomadic people's leather bottle, the vessel takes a cocoonlike shape with two bulged ridges on the opposite side of its shoulder, There are some drilled holes on the ridges. Such kind of vessels have also been found in the ancient tombs of Qin Dynasty in Guanzhong areas, Shaanxi Province. It is preserved in Xinjiang Museum , now.

044，Pottery Candle Stand with Two Holders

1c A. D. H. 8. 3cm Zhaosu

Like a stemmed dish, the upper part of the stand takes a bowl like shape, while the lower part of the stand has a short stem and a ring foot. It is preserved in Xinjiang Institute of Archaeology now.

045，Painted Pottery Pot

2—1c B. C. H. 24cm Zhaosu

The vessel has a square — edged rim, slightly opened mouth, contracted neck, round shoulder, swollen belly and a flat bottom. The outer surface was richly ornamented with dark red designs, i. e. two different designs, one being net design, the other being semicircle design, contained in fourteen squares on the upper belly, and plain red outside the squares. It is preserved in Xinjiang Museum now.

046，Painted Pottery Cup with a Single Handle

3c B. C. H. 12. 5cm Xinyuan

Being hand—made, the vessel has a square —edged rim, slightly contracted mouth, slightly swollen belly, flat bottom and a single handle. The outer surface was ornamented with irregular net patterns. It is preserved in Xinjiang Institute of Archaeology, now.

047，Painted Pottery Pot

5c B. C. H. 35cm Qapqal

The vessel has a square—edged rim, open mouth, slightly contracted neck, square shoulder, swollen belly and a flat bottom. The outer surface was richly ornamented with elegant red designs, i. e. chessboard (or checked) pattern on the shoulder and neck, solid rhombus form and other local style designs on the belly. Such kind of decorative patterns are rarely seen on the articles of the same period in Xinjiang. It is preserved in Xinjiang Institute of Archaeology, now.

048，Handleless Painted Pottery Pot

5c B. C. H. 12. 5cm Qapqal

The vessel has a square—edged rim, short neck, swollen belly and a flat bottom. The outer surface was ornamented with red net designs on the upper part of the body and plain red below. It is preserved in Xinjiang Institute of Archaeology, now.

049，Painted Pottery Bowl

5c B. C. H. 12. 4cm Qapqal

The vessel has a round—edged and vertically upwards turning rim, slightly swollen belly and round bottom. The outer surface was richly ornamented with red designs, i. e. regular undulate mountain pattern on the lower part of the body and branch pattern above. It is preserved in Xinjiang Institute of Archaeology, now.

050，Pottery Pot with Black Slip

2c A. D. H. 22. 8cm Minfeng (Niya)

The vessel has a square—edged and everted rim, open mouth, contracted neck, sloping shoulder, swollen belly and a flat bottom. The outer surface was ornamented with two rows of triangles on the shoulder, the lower row being solid triangles, the upper row being reversed triangles with dots filled in. It is preserved in Xinjiang Museum, now.

051, Pottery Cup with Black Slip

5—6c A. D. H. 12. 3cm Yanqi

Being hand—made and hard—fired, the cup has a square—edged rim, flat belly, flat bottom and bigger mouth diameter than bottom diameter. It is preserved in Bayingolin Museum now.

052, Pottery Pot with Incised Decoration

7—9c A. D. H. 23cm Qira

Made of well leivgated red clay, the vessel has a sharp—edged and everted rim, swollen body and flat bottom. The outer surface was richly ornamented with incised decoration, i. e. zigzag lines on the rim, neck and shoulder, one row of paired leaves, with their butts above and tips below, on the belly. It is preserved in Hotan Museum now.

053, Single—handled Pottery Pot

7—9c A. D. H. 27. 5cm Turfan

Made of red clay, the vessel has a wide flared mouth, a long neck, a single handle, a short spout and a flat bottom. A figure, in the shape of a bodhisattva's face, was attached on the neck. It is preserved in Lushun Museum, Liaoning Province.

054, Oblate Pottery Amphora

11c A. D. H. 26cm Hotan

With a white color, the vessel takes an oblate spherical shape with two loop handles and tube form neck. The inner and outer surface were ornamented with incised concentric lines. It is preserved in Hotan Museum now.

055, Three—handled Pottery Vase

6c A. D. H. 45cm Hotan.

Fashioned on the wheel from reddish brown clay, the vessel is a wide—grithed, three—handled vase, the upper half of which, below the rim, is richly decorated with ornaments borrowed from classical antiquity. On each of the handle is a small female head in the Indian style. One row of rosettes are impressed in three trapezoids. The bulbous part of the body bears the most important decortation, namely seven circular medallions in relief and honeysuckle design outside. Each medallion is bordered by two concentric circles, separated by a beaded ring. Three different design appear in the medallions: the first is a female figure, standing and facing side, with a pitcher and goblet; the second is a seated man facing side, with nimbus and goblet; the third is a lion's head. All ornaments were mould—made or stamped with dies and applied to the vase before it was fired. The vase is preserved in Berlin now.

056, Pottery Shard with Brahman Figure Decoration

3—5c A. D. L. 28cm Shufu

The shard is from the belly of a pottery article. The outer surface was richly ornamented with medallions, twisting branche design, dragon design, petal design etc. in relief. Each medallion is borderd by two concentric circles and separated by a beaded ring. Inside the beaded ring is a head portrait of Brahman with a treasured crown on his head. It is preserved in The Cultural Centre of Shufu County now.

057, Pottery Incensory

7c A. D. H. 25. 7cm Kizil

Unearthed at No. 6 cave of Kizil Thousand—Buddha Grottoes, the vessel was wheel—made of pooly levigated red clay, the outer part of which has an open mouth, square—edged rim and flat bottom, while the inner part of which has an open mouth, contracted neck and five oral form holes on the upper belly as the pass of incense smoke. Its outer surface was covered by greenish glaze. This kind of incensories were dipicted on many murals in Kizil Thousand—Buddha Grottoes. It is preserved in Xinjiang Institute of Archaeology, now.

058, Pottery Vase with Two Handles and Embossed Decoration

3—5c A. D. H. 14cm Hotan

The vessel has a square—edged and outwards turning rim, long neck, bevelled shoulder, swollen belly and a ring foot. On each of the upper and lower part of each handle is a circular medallion in relief. The rim inner surface and shoulder outer surface were ornamented with rows of dots in relief. Both the outer surfaces of the neck and belly were ornamented with one row of embossed circular medallions.

There are two concentric lines on the upper belly. It is preserved in Seoul, South Korea now.

059, Pottery Jug

1c A. D. H. 10. 6cm Hotan

Rim damaged, the vessel has a swollen belly, sloping shoulder and a flat bottom, The whole outer surface was uniquely ornamented with regularly incised stripes. On the handle is a monkey sculpture, holding something in its hands. It is preserved in London, now.

060, Pottery Jar with a Single Handle

7—9c A. D. H. 14. 3cm Hoxud

The vessel has a square—edged rim, open mouth, contracted neck, swollen belly, flat bottom and a small ring foot. The outer surface was ornamented with two incised lines on the shoulder. It is preserved in Bayingolin Museum now.

061, Painted Pottery Pitcher with a Single Handle

7c A. D. H. 24. 5cm Turfan

The vessel has an open mouth, contracted neck, swollen belly and flat bottom. The outer surface was richly ornamented with one row of green dots under the rim, one row of linked red rings, filled in by green dots, on the neck, one row of cloud design on the shoulder, lotus petals on the middle belly, and arcs and dots below. It is preserved in Xinjiang Museum, now.

062, Pottery Urinal

7—8c A. D. H. 9cm Hami

The urinal is tortoise—shaped with a loop handle on each side of the toroise's forwards extending head, and a circular button—shaped handle surrounded by one row of medallion designs on the back. It is preserved in Hami Museum now.

063, Pottery Boshan Incensory

3—4c A. D. H. 14cm Ruoqiang

Made of black clay, the incensory can be divided into two parts: a plate form pedestal, and a conical form burner with a removable conical cover. As the pass of smoke, there are many evenly drilled holes on the cover. It is preserved in Seoul, South Korea now.

064, Pottery Jar

7—8c A. D. H. 30cm Barkol

The jar has a square—edged rim, open mouth, contracted neck, sloping shoulder, swollen belly, small flat bottom and two handles. It is preserved in Hami Museum, now.

065, Pottery Pitcher with a Bird—head—shaped Mouth

7—8c A. D. H. 27cm Turfan

With a yellowish color, the vessel has a swollen belly, big flat bottom, bird—head—shaped mouth, and a bulged ridge on its shoulder opposit to the handle. The outer surface was ornamented with incised parallel lines on both sides of the bulged ridge and an incised lotus flower below the ridge. The vessel's elegant shape shows an influence of Persian tradition, in making bird—head decorated gold and sliver vessels. It is preserved in Seoul, South Korea now.

066, Pottery Sarira Vase with Embossed Decoration

1—2c A. D. H. 20cm Hotan

The vessel has a contracted mouth, swollen belly, bevelled shoulder and a circular leg. The outer surface was richly ornamented with embossed or incised decoration, i. e. one row of incised circles under the rim, vertical lines bordered by dots on each side on the shoulder, one row of circular medallions in relief, bordered by two incised lines on the belly, and crescent moon design above the medallions. There are also some symmetrically placed Persian style embossed human head decoration on the belly's outer surface. It is preserved in London, now.

067, Pottery Sarira Casket with a Contracted Mouth

7—8c A. D. H. 30cm Kuqa

Shaped like a peach, the vessel has a circular contracted mouth with fitted cover, large flat bottom and the biggest diameter at the upper part of the body. It is preserved in Xinjiang Museum now.

068, Pottery Coffin

5—7c A. D. D. 30cm, L. 66cm Shanshan

With a tubular shape, the coffin has a rectangular opening and tile—like cover. The cover was cut off from the coffin body before fired. There are three long longitudinal and two short transverse embossed ridges on the coffin's outer surface near the opening, and one long longitudinal embossed ridge on the bottom's outer surface. The ridges take a rope—like shape and have stemped prints on it. In the coffin is a reburial matural human being's skeleton.

069, Painted Pottery Sarira Casket

4—5c A. D. H. 24cm, Kalpin

The casket has a cylindrical shape with a flat bottom, a circular opening, 10cm in diamenter, at the top and fitted conical cover. The shoulder's surface was ornamented with reversed lotus flower designs on redish brown ground, whereas the body's surface was ornamented with white rhomboid patterns, and red dots at the point of intersection, on black ground. It is preserved in Xinjiang Museum , now.

070, Celadon Plate

13—14c A. D. D. 34cm Huocheng

It is a shallow plate with a flat bottom and a dragon design in the middle. The ancient city of Alimali had ever been the capital city of Jagatai Khanate and was in the midway between the Oriental and the Occidental civilization centres. Thus the unearthed article can tell us something about the relation between the East and the West of that time. It is preserved in Xinjiang Museum , now.

071, Celadon Bowl of Longquan Ware

13—14c A. D. D. 34cm Huocheng

With a yellowish color, the vessel has a round—edged rim, open mouth and ring foot. It is preserved in Xinjiang Museum , now.

072, Yellowish—Brown Glazed Pottery Vase

13—14c A. D. H. 30cm Hotan

The vessel has a square—edged rim, contracted neck, swollen belly and a ring foot. The outer surface was richly ornamented with three groups of mountain designs on the neck, two incised lines on the upper and lower part of the belly and flying bird patterns between. It is preserved in Xinjiang Museum , now.

073, Blue and White Porcelain Vase

18—19c A. D. H. 46cm Xinjiang

The vase has a round—edged and vertically upwards turning rim, round shoulder, flat bottom, two loop handles on the shoulder, and the biggest dimeter at the upper belly. The outer surface was richly ornamented with the mountain and river patterns on the neck and belly. It is preserved in Xinjiang Museum, now.

BRONZES

074, Bronze Figure of a Warrior

5—4c B. C. H. 40cm Xinyuan

This hollow bronze figure, casted by composing patterns, was unearthed from the southern bank of Kunes River. The warrior wears a wide—brim hat with a high winding hook on the top; squats down on the left leg but kneels down on the right. Both of the hands are in the posture of holding something. It is preserved in Xinjiang Museum , now.

075, Bronze Tray with High Base

5—1c B. C. H. 32cm Urumqi

The square, casted bronze tray was unearthed from the Ancient Tombs of Ala Gully, Nanshan. In the center, there are two animals which look like the lion. The high base is square and hollow. Now it is preserved in Xinjiang Museum

076, Bronze Necklace

5—4c B. C. D. 38cm Xinyuan

This bronze necklace was cast in the shape of double tigers with their heads facing each other and bodies joining together. It was found at the southern bank of the Kunes River, and now it is preserved in Xinjiang Museum

077, Bronze Necklace Decorated with Double Winged Animals

5—4c B. C. D. 42. 5cm Xinyuan

On the hollow ring, found at the southern bank of the Kunes River, there are two animals facing each other. The heads of the animals are in the shape of the tiger's head; but there are double wings on their backs. Now it is preserved in Xinjiang Museum

078, Copper Cauldron with Three Legs

5—4c B. C. H. 44cm Xinyuan

This kind of cauldron was used to cook rice in ancient China. It was cast; the belly is bulgy, and the bottom is round, and there are two doubles of ears on the belly. It was unearthed at the southern bank of Kunes River, and now is preserved in Xinjiang Museum

079, Bronze Cauldron with Two Upright Handles and a Circular Leg

5—1c B. C. H. 57cm Urumqi

The casted bronze cauldron was found at the Nanshan Tree Farm, Urumqi. It has straight mouth, deep belly, and round bottom. On the mouth, there are two upright handles in the rectangle shape, decorated with three mushrooms on each of them. On the surface of the cauldron was decorated with some kinds of geometric figures. Now it is preserved in Xinjiang Museum .

080, **Copper Cauldron**

5—1c B. C.　H. 50cm Barkol

The casted copper cauldron, excavated from the Lanzhou Wanzi Site, Barkol, has two ring—shaped handles, a deep belly, round bottom, and a high, bell—like circular leg. Now it is preserved in Xinjiang Museum

081, **Bronze Cauldron**

5—1c B. C.　H. 76cm Xinyuan

The cast bronze cauldron has a deep belly and two ears and a high, hollow base in the bell—shape. It is preserved in Ili Museum now.

082, **Bronze Tray**

5—1c B. C.　L. &W. 76cm H. 23cm Qapqal

This square tray, unearthed at Wusun Mountain, has two side ears on the surface and four legs which were cast in the shape of human face and camel's foot. It is preserved in Xinjiang Museum , now.

083, **Copper Plaque**

5—1c B. C.　L. 13cm Mori

The casted, penetrating copper plaque is in the shape of rectangle. There is a horse in the left side that bitting the fore leg of the horse. It was found at the Eastern Town of Mori. Now it is preserved in Mori Museum.

084, **Bronze Buckle**

8—5c B. C.　W. 6. 4cm Hejing

The casted bronze buckle, excavated from the Ancient Tombs of Chawuhu Gully, is in the shape of a bow with two heads of birds at each end. It is preserved in Bayingolin Museum now.

085, **Bronze Plaque**

2—1c B. C.　L. 11. 5cm H. 5. 5cm Turfan

This penetrating bronze plaque was cast in the shape of a tiger, who holds a sheep in its mouth. On the back of the plaque, there are three knobs in the ring — shape. This bronze plaque with the Ordos — style was excavated from the Aiding—Lake Ancient Tombs, Turfan. Now it is preserved in Turfan Museum.

086, **Bronze Plaque**

2c B. C.　W. 6cm Urumqi

This cast, penetrating bronze plaque in the trapezium—shape, was found at Wulabai, Urumqi. The central pattern is two sheep which are facing each other. Now the plaque is preserved in Urumqi Museum.

087, **Copper Plaques Decorated with Tigers' Patterns & Golden Leave**

6—5c B. C.　L. 4. 76cm Shanshan

These rectangle — shaped copper plaque, excavated from the Subashi Ancient Tombs, were covered with golden leaves. In the center of the plaques, there is a pattern of a tiger, who holds up its tail. On the back of the plaques, there is a knob. These decorations of copper plaque now are preserved in Turfan Museum.

088, **Copper Plaque**

5—1c B. C.　D. 7. 3cm Mori

The round, cast, penetrating copper plaque, decorated with the patterns of a wild boar in the center and five wild boars arond it, was found at the Eastern Town, too. Now, it is preserved in Xinjiang Institute of Archaeology

089, **Bronze Axe**

10—8c B. C.　L. 24cm Tuoli

This axe was collected at Tuoli. At the end, there is an ellipse— shaped hole decorated with the patterns of trees leaves. It is preserved in Tacheng Museum now.

090, **Bronze Axe**

5c B. C.　L. 17cm Baicheng

The casted bronze axe, excavated from the Ancient Tombs of Kizil Reservoir, has a ellipse—shaped hole near one of the ends; the edge is long, narrow and flat. It is preserved in Xinjiang Institute of Archaeology, now.

091, **Bronze Axe**

10—8c B. C.　L. 21cm Barkol

The casted bronze axe unearthed at Kuisugeda is in the hexahedron shape with a round hole at one end, and a narrow edge. It is preserved in Hami Museum now.

092, **Bronze Adzes**

The Bronze Age L. 4. 5, 5. 5cm (from left to right) Tacheng

All of the Bronze adzes are long and norrow and the edges are in the arc—shape. They are preserved in Tacheng Museum now.

093, **Bronze Knives**

8—5c B. C.　L. 13. 5—17. 5cm Hejing

These three knives, excavated from the Ancient Tombs of Chawuhu Gully, Hejing, were forged. All edges of knives are sharp and in the arc shape. Between the handle the and edge, there isn't the hand — guard. It is preserved in Bayingolin Museum now.

094, Copper Hamess

8—5c B. C. L. 17. 5cm Hejing

It is one of the hamesses that is held in horse's mouth. Being excavated from the Ancient Tombs of Chawuhu, Hejing, it is preserved in Xinjiang Institute of Archaeology, now.

095, Bronze Axe with a Perpendicular Handle

8—5c B. C. L. 10cm Hejing

The bronze axe is in the shape of rectangle, with a perpendicular handle. It was also excavated from the Ancient Tombs of Chawuhu Gully, Hejing. Now it is preserved in Xinjiang Institute of Archaeology

096, Bronze Sickles

The Bronze Age L. 24, 23. 5, 22cm (From top to bottom) Tacheng

Being collected at Tacheng, these sickles were made by forging, in the shape of axe. At the end of the handle of each sickle, there is a small hole. They are preserved in Tacheng Museum now.

097, Copper Dagger—Axes

5—1c B. C. L. 16. 1—15. 1cm (From left to right) Shanshan

Both of the dagger—axes were cast with the composing patterns. They have the long and straight parts of the edge, the sharp point, the protruding "ridge", and the perpendicular hollow handle. They were excavated from the Yanghai Ancient Tombs, and now are preserved in Turfan Museum.

098, Bronze Knife

5—1c B. C. L. 23cm Xinyuan

Being found at Chabu, the cast knife has a straight handle decorated with some patterns of the crisscross lines and semicircles and a sheep head at the end. Its edge is wide and short. Now this bronze knife with the artistic style of the hordes in the grasslands of Northern Asia, is preserved in Xinjiang Museum .

099, Bronze Knife

8—5c B. C. L. 12. 2cm Hejing

The cast and forged knife has a straight back, a wide edge and a flat handle decorated with a standing animal which looks like the bear. It was excavated from the Ancient Tombs of Chawuhu Gully, and now is preserved in Xinjiang Institute of Archaeology.

100, Bronze Knife

8—5c B. C. L, 36cm Hami

The handle of this knife was made in the shape of a deer's head. It was found at Hami. Now it is preserved in Hami Museum.

101, Bronze Knife

1c B. C. L. 41cm Toksun

At the end of the handle, there is a ring and a hand—guard between the handle and the edge. It is preserved in Xinjiang Museum now.

102, Bronze Crossbow

1—4c A. D. L. 12, H. 17. 7cm Ruoqiang

The bronze crossbow was riveted with some different parts. It should be made in Zhongyuan (the Central Plain) and found at Alagan, Ruoqiang. Now, it is preserved in Xinjiang Museum .

103, Short Sword

13—14c A. D. L. 30cm Qapqal

On the surface of the handle of the sword, unearthed at the Hainuke Ancient Town, were decorated with some patterns of the wild boars. The copper sword is now preserved in Ili Museum.

104, Small Bronze Spearhead

1—3c A. D. L. 11cm Ruoqiang

The casted copper spearhead in the shape of the willow leaf, collected around the Loulan Ancient City, has a protruding "ridge" in the middle of the body; the handle is very short. Now it is preserved in Xinjiang Institute of Archaeology.

105, Bronze Spearhead

8—5c B. C. L. 17cm Hejing

The casted bronze spearhead excavated from the Ancient Tombs of Chawuhu Valley has a edge in the shape of the willow leaf. The hollow handle is very long. It is preserved in Bayingolin Museum now.

106, Copper Arrow—Heads

5—1c B. C. L. 4. 8—5. 9cm Shanshan

Each of the two casted copper arrow—heads, excavated from the Yanghai Ancient Tombs, has a protruding "ridge" with two "wings" on both sides, and a round, hollow hole. Now the two arrow—heads are preserved in Turfan Museum.

107, Copper Mirror Decorated with a Curly Animal Pattern

8—5c B. C. D. 9cm Hejing

The round mirror was also excavated from the Ancient Tombs of Chawuhu Gully. In the center of its back, there is a knob, decorated with the pattern of a curly animal around it. This mirror is the earliest one among the mirrors which have been found in Xinjiang. Now it is preserved in Xinjiang Institute of Archaeology.

108, Copper Mirror with a Handle

　　8—5c B. C.　L. 17cm Hejing

The round mirror with a handle has no decorative pattern. It was excavated from the Ancient Tombs of Chawuhu Gully, and is preserved in Bayingolin Museum.

109, Copper Mirror with a Sheep — Shaped Handle

　　1c A. D.　H. 16cm Barkol

The difference of this round mirror is that it has a handle in the shape of a big — horn sheep. It is preserved in Xinjiang Museum .

110, Copper Mirror

　　5—1c B. C.　D. 12. 5cm Baicheng

This round mirror excavated from the Ancient Tombs of Kizil Reservoir is plain without decorative pattern. The back is in the shape of a shallow tray, which has a knob in the center. It is preserved in Xinjiang Institute of Archaeology.

111, Copper Mirror

　　1c A. D.　D. 10cm Hejing

This round mirror with the Zhongyuan style has a round knob in the center of its back. Around the knob are two square patterns; inside them are the inscriptions in Chinese characters of the twelve Earthly Branches, used in combination with the Heavenly Stems to designate years, months, days and hours. Then, around the square patterns, there are the Sishen, the four supernatural beings symbolizing the four guardians of the sky and the earth, and also the four seasons, and twenty — eight inscriptions in the official script, Li, an ancient style of calligraphy current in the Han Dynasty. (206B. C. — 220A. D.). This mirror is preserved in Hejing Museum.

112, Copper Mirror with the Story of *Xuyou* and Saofu

　　7—9c A. D.　D. 15cm Turfan

The mirror is in the shape of eight—petals flower. On the back, there is round knob in the center. On the left of the knob, there is a man who is sitting down the tree on the bank of the river and reeling the silk; on the right, there is

a man who is leading an ox. It is the story about Xuyou, Fanshu, and Saofu living in the ages of Yao, a king in the remote antiquity in China. The mirror is preserved at Seoul, Korea, now.

113, Copper Mirror with the Story of *Liuyi*

　　10—12c A. D. D. 10cm Fukang

This round mirror was unearthed at Sangong Township, Fukang. In the center of its back, there is a knob, decorated with the patterns of men, tree, river, and horse, etc, around it. There are a big tree upwards facing each right. On the right, there is a man who is facing to the women; under the knob, there is a man leading a horse. It drew its material from the prevalent story of Liuyi among the people in ancient China. This mirror is now preserved in Xinjiang Institute of Archaeology.

114, Copper Mirror Decorated with the Patterns of Plants and Beasts

　　7—9c A. D. D. 9. 7cm Urumqi

The round mirror, unearthed at the Wulabai Ancient Town, has a round knob on its back, decorated with two circles and some patterns of the plants and beasts around it. It is preserved in Urumqi Museum now.

115, Copper Mirror

　　7—9c A. D. D. 11cm Korla

The mirror found at Korla City is in the shape of the flower with eight — petals. In the center of the back there is a round knob decorated with the patterns of four celestial beings riding the cranes around it. It is preserved in Bayingolin Museum.

116, Copper Mirror Decorated with Birds and Beasts Patterns

　　7—9c A. D. D. 23cm Jimsa

The mirror is in the shape of the flower with eight — petals. In the center of its back, there is a round knob decorated with the patterns of two lion — like beasts and two birds, and some bees, plants, flowers, etc. around it. This mirror of inner China style was unearthed at the Beiting Ancient City. Now it is preserved in Xinjiang Museum .

117, Seated Buddha

　　7—8c A. D. H. 42cm Qira

This exquisite and valuable copper statue of Buddha was found at Damagou, Qira. Now it is preserved in Hotan Museum.

118, Head of Buddha

3—4c A. D. H. 17cm Hotan

This gilt copper head of Buddha, found at Hotan, is preserved at Tokyo. The Buddha has a wide forehead decorated with the Hua Dian, a kind of the decorative patterns on face in ancient China, a straight nose, and closes his mouth; these give us a dignified and deep impression.

119, Copper Figure of Mani

7—9c A. D. H. 8cm Turfan

This hollow copper figure of Mani, who was the founder of the Manicheism, is a personal collection. The face of Mani is thin with a long beard on his chin. He wears a crown and dresses a kasaya, and sits on the lotus — throne.

120, Vajrapani

15—18c A. D. H. 16cm Usu

The gilt copper statue of a vajrapani, with the distinct characteristics of the Esoteric Sect. culture, is one of the collections of the Tacheng Museum. The vajrapani rides a horse with the upper part of his body uncovered. He raises his right hand; an implement is held in his left hand. The image is fearsome with the Death's heads worn on his crown and hung on his hip.

121, Seated Bodhisattva

12c A. D. H. 17cm Hami

The gilt copper statue, with the Esoteric Sect. style, shows a bodhisattva who seats on a lotus throne. He wears a crown, and uncovers the upper part of his body. His left hand is in the mudra of preaching, and the right hand is in the mudra of touching earth. This statue, collected at the Xishan Township, is preserved in Hami Museum now.

122, Standing Buddha

6—7c A. D. H. 9. 5cm Turfan

The head of the bronze figure of Buddha is encircled by a large nimbus. He wears a kasaya, holding an alms bowl in the left hand. The figure was found at the Gaochang (Khocho) Ancient City. Now, it is preserved at Berlin.

123, Standing Bodhisattva

7—8c A. D. H. 8. 8cm Turfan

The gilt bronze bodhisattva wears a crown on his head. His face is chubby, and the eyes stare downwards. The upper part of his body with a necklace is bare, and the lower body wears a narrow, small skirt. The raising hand in the right holds something that looks like a horsetail whisk; the left hand carries a bottle. He stands with bare feet on the lotus—throne. The figure is now preserved at Berlin.

124, Gilt Bronze Bodhisattva

7—9c A. D. H. 9cm Kuqa

The bronze figure of bodhisattva, found at the Subashi Site, wears a crown on his head. He raises his left hand, and stands on the lotus —throne with bare feet. There are two hollow, round storeys of base downwards the lotus — throne. Now it is preserved in Xinjiang Institute of Archaeology.

125, Copper Incense Burner

16—17c A. D. H. 15. 4cm Hami

The copper incense burner has a rectangle —shaped mouth, and two high, upright handles on its belly. It also has four legs; there are some inscriptions in Arabian characters on its belly. Now, it is preserved in Hami Museum.

126, Copper Lion

7—9c A. D. L. 9. 7cm Jimsa

Being unearthed at the Beiting Ancient City (Bishbalik), the copper lion was casted in the shape of a lion. The lion is in the posture of running to attack something with the opening mouth, the bending legs, and the big, strong tail raising to touch the back of the head. Now it is preserved in Xinjiang Museum .

127, The Xuan De Incense Burner with Arabian Characters

15c A. D. H. 9cm Turfan

This copper incense burner was collected at Turfan. On the surface of the belly, there are three groups of Arabian characters which mean that "Mohammed is the Emissary of Allah", etc. In the middle of the bottom, there are six Chinese characters that mean " made in the years of Xuan De, the great Ming Dynasty". It is now a personal collection.

128, Copper Bowl

13—14c A. D. D. 21. 5cm H. 13cm Hotan

The copper bowl with two ring — shaped ears, collected at Hotan, was made by forging and carving. On the surface, there are the decorative patterns of flowers and plants, and the Jagatai (Caqadai) characters. It is preserved in Hotan Museum now.

129, Copper Paperweight

7—9c A. D. H. 7cm Jimsa

Being unearthed from the Beiting Ancient

City, the gilt copper lion was cast in the posture of squatting down, with a large mouth and opening eyes and a ball pressed by both forelegs. It is preserved in Xinjiang Museum now.

130, Copper Pot and Basin

17—18c A. D. H. of pot 40cm, Bore of basin 32cm Kashi

The two copper wares, collected at Kashi, were made by using four kinds of technologies: mould pressing, forging, engraving, and riveting. Many kinds of decorative patterns and Uighurian characters were engraved on the surfaces of the pot and basin. They are the type of the technology and industrial art of the Uighur nationality, and now preserved in Xinjiang Museum.

131, Karakhanid Coin

10—13 A. D. D. 2.3—3.2cm Artux

Made of copper, the coin has a nearly circular form and double—line—edged rim. It was inscribed with, in Arabic alphabet, an Islamic phrase meaning "Allah is the only one suppernatural being" on the obverse, name and title of its isseur on the reverse. The batch of coins was made by striking and pressing technique which is belonged to Greek heritage, defferent from that of Chinese heritage represented by the typical coins of circular form with a square central hole. This coin is preserved in Xinjiang Institute of Archaeology, now.

132, Sino—Kharosthi Coin

3—4c A. D. D. 1.8cm Hotan

Circular and holeless like a round flapjack, it was made of copper by striking technique. On the reverse are Chinese characters "六铢钱" (means the coin weighing 6 *Zhu*, or 12.5 grams). On the obverse is a horse figure surrounded by Kharosthi characters. That is why the coin is also called the "Hotan Horse Coin". It is preserved in Xinjiang Institute of Finance Research now.

133, Kushan Coin

2—3c A. D. D. 2.7cm Loulan

On the obverse (left) is a standing king's figure surrounded by Greek inscriptions of the king's name. On the reverse (right) is a deity on camel back holding in his hand a three—point spear. It is preserved in China Historical Museum now.

134, Gaochang "*jili*" Coin

5—7c A. D. D. 2.6cm Turfan

Made of copper, the circular coin has a square hole in the middle and thickened inner and outer rim. On the obverse is one circle of clockwise inscribed Chinese characters "高昌吉利" (means lucky Gaochang); on the reverse is plain. It is preserved in Turfan Museum now.

135, Kuchean *Wu—chu* Coin

4—7c A. D. Kuqa

Belonged to circular form with square central hole coinage system, the coin was made of copper by casting method. It is also known as the so—called Sino—Kuchean coin and has thickened inner and outer rim. On the obverse are Chinese seal characters (a style of Chinese calligraphy, often used on seals) "五铢" (means the coin weighing 5 *Zhu*, or about 10.4 grams). On the reverse are Kuchean characters ")0". This kind of coins have more than ten varieties differing in size and weight. It has been regarded as the coin (widely used in the ancient kingdom of Kuchean) modelled in type on Chinese Wu—chu. It is preserved in Xinjiang Institute of Archaeology, now.

136, Turgis Coin

8c A. D. D. 2.3cm Mori

Made of bronze by casting technique, the coin has a round shape, thickened inner and outer rim and a square hole in the center. On the obverse are one circle of Sogdian scripts meaning " Heavenly Turgis Khanate Coin". On the reverse is a crescent—moon—shaped seal symbol. It is preserved in Mori Museum now.

137, Golden Horse and Eagle—Deer

8—5c B. C. L. 53cm Akqi

The two ornaments, excavated from the Kulansarike Ancient Tombs, were forged and moulded of the goldleaves. The left is in the shape of a horse which has a holding head, the erecting ears, the short mane, and in the running posture. The right is a deer with an eagle standing on its back. They are the culture relics of the nomadic nations in ancient Northern Asia. Now they are preserved in People's Bank of China, Akqi Branch.

138, Golden Fingerring Inlaid with Rubies

1c A. D. D. 2.2cm Zhaosu

This elegant, valuable fingerring was excavated from the Xiatai Ancient Tombs of Wusun. It is preserved in Xinjiang Museum.

139, Golden Buckle with Dragons' Patterns

1c B. C. L. 9. 8cm, W. 6cm Yanji

On the front of the golden buckle, there are the dragons' patterns inlaid with rubies and emeralds. The elegant and valuable buckle was unearthed at Yongning. Now it is preserved in Xinjiang Museum.

140, Golden Earring

5—1c B. C. D. of the ring 1. 3cm Tekes.

This earring with a eardrop welded with eight hollow golden balls was excavated from the Ancient Tombs of the First Grazing Land, Tekes. It is preserved in Xinjiang Institute of Archaeology now.

141, Golden Flower

5—4c B. C. L. 5. 9cm Shanshan

The golden flower, excavated from the Yanghai Ancient Tombs, has a round stamen with six long and six short petals. It is preserved in Turfan Museum now.

142, Golden Earring

5—1c B. C. L. 2. 5cm Urumqi

The earring with a hollow pagoda—shaped eardrop was excavated from the Ancient Tombs of Wulabai Reservoir, Urumqi. It is preserved in Xinjiang Institute of Archaeology, now.

143, Golden Plaques and Belt

5c B. C. D. of plaques 6cm L. of belt 26cm Urumqi

On the surface of the two round plaques were moulded in the tigers' patterns. These golden handicrafts were found at the Ancient Tombs of Ala Valley, Nanshan. Now they are preserved in Xinjiang Museum.

144, Golden Chain

5c B. C. L. 25. 4cm Urumqi

The golden chain, hanged with some jades wrapped up by the golden leaves, was excavated from the Ancient Tombs of Ala Valley, Nanshan. Now it is preserved in Xinjiang Museum.

145. Golden Plaque in the Lion Shape

5—1c B. C. L. 20cm Urumqi

This plaque excavated from the ancient tombs of Ala Valley, was made of the goldleaf. The lion is in the posture of running quickly to bite something. This exceptional article of virtu is preserved in Xinjiang Museum now.

146, Silver Tray Engraving Ostriches Patterns

4—7c A. D. Bore 21cm Yanji

This tray was unearthed at Laocheng Village of Qigexing. It has a big mouth, a shallow belly, and a round bottom. Inside the tray there are engraved patterns of seven ostriches inlaid with the gold. It is now preserved in Bayingolin Museum.

147, Double Golden Heads of Ox

5—1c B. C. L. 3. 5cm Turfan

This hollow golden heads of ox was made of the golden leaf by mould pressing and excavated from the Aiding—Lake Ancient Tombs. It is now preserved in Xinjiang Institute of Archaeology.

148, Silver Bowl

4—7c A. D. H. 7. 4cm Yanji

Being forged of silver and unearthed at Laocheng Village of Qigexing Township, the bowl has some inscriptions of the Sogdian characters on the round and hollow base. It is preserved in Bayingolin Museum now.

149, Golden Earrings

5—1c B. C. D. 2. 6cm Hami

Being excavated from the Ancient Tombs of Linya, Hami City, the two ring — shaped earrings are preserved in Xinjiang Institute of Archaeology, now.

150, Jagatai Golden Coin

13—14c A. D. D. 3. 2cm Bole (Bortala)

Made by striking and pressing technique, the circular coin was inscribed on both sides. The inscription on the obverse means "Mohammed is an envoy from Allah. We are all very grateful to Allah". The inscription on the reverse means "The highest—ranked imams are supernatural beings second only to Allah. Allah is the guard of our religion and head of his belivers". This coin is preserved in Bortala Museum now.

151, Eastern Roman (Byzantine) Empire Golden Coin

7—8c A. D. D. 2. 2cm Turfan

On the obverse is a crown — capped head portrait of the Eastern Roman King with some decorations around his neck. On the reverse is a standing female figure with wings on her back and a stick — shaped cross holding in her right hand. The coin is preserved in Xinjiang Museum now.

152, Persian Silver Coins

3 — 4c A. D. D. 2. 6cm (left) and 3cm (right) Turfan

Circular and holeless, the batch of coins were made by striking and pressing technique.

The left one is the silver coin of Persian Ardashir II and the right one is the silver coin of Persian Shapar II. There is a half—length king's portrait on the obverse of two coins, and an inscription around the portrait on the obverse of Shapar II silver coin. They are preserved in Xinjiang Museum, now.

153, Hotan Silver Coin

18c A. D. D. 1. 6cm Hotan

Made by striking technique, the coin has a circular and a value of one *qian* (1mace, or 5 grams) silver. Its form is also known as Habibulla 1mace small "tanga" coin. There are inscriptions on both the obverse and reverse. On the obverse are Arabian inscriptions meaning "We have only one Allah. Mohammed is an envoy from Allah. 128th year in Hui calender". On the reverse are Jagatai inscriptions meaning "Made in Hotan". It is preserved in People's Bank of China, Xinjiang Branch now.

154, Jagatai Silver Coins

13—14c A. D. D. 1. 8—2. 0cm Changji

Made by striking and pressing technique, the circular coin has inscriptions on both sides. Inscribed on the obserse are the making locality and mintage symbol in the central part, around them with inscriptions meaning "Allah is the only supernatural being…". On the reverse are two lines of inscriptions meaning "The heighest and most fairly", around them with the Hui calender time in smaller characters. It is preserved in Xinjiang Institute of Archaeology now.

ROCK CARVINGS

155, Reproduction Worship

10c B. C. Hutubi

In the middle of the picture, there is a female figure with two heads and a body. At both sides of her there are two men. The left one has a head of man on his chest. This rock carving was found at Kangjiashimenzi, Hutubi.

156, Dancers

10c B. C. Hutubi

This rock carving, one of the main parts of the rock carvings, found at Kangjiashimenzi at the northern foot of the Tianshan Mountains, shows five women who are dancing. The women' faces are thin with sunken eyes and high noses, and small mouthes. They wear the

high hats decorated with two feather; the right hands raise up, but the left hands hang down.

157, Double Horses

10c B. C. Hutubi

This rock carving of two male horses, facing each other, with the heads and legs joining together, expresses the thought of reproduction worship, too. It is one part of the rock carvings of reproduction worship, Kangjiashimenzi.

158, Persons and Tigers

10c B. C. Hutubi

On the upper part of this rock carving, there are three standing persons; the left one is a man, who directs his long penis to the women. Under the persons are two tigers. This rock carving is one part of the rock carvings of reproduction worship, Kanjiashimenzi.

159, Reproduction Worship and Grazing

5c B. C. Tacheng

In this rock carving, found at Baerdakuer, Tacheng, there are persons (male and female), horses, goats, wolves and a yak. The main part, on the right, is the men and women, who were carved in the gesture of sexual intercourse, standing, etc. On the left are the men, who ride the yak and horses, and a man stands in front of them. In the middle of rock carving, there are several goats, wolves and a row of dancing children. This rock carving expressed the thought of the reproduction worship of the ancients.

160, Two Horses and a Goat

8—9c B. C. Altai

This rock carving was found at the Duoate Valley. All of the two horses and a goat were depicted in the posture of running.

161, Celestial Being

Primitive Society Period Fuyun

Inside a cave in Tangbaleng, Fuyun County, there incised many colorful religious patterns and symbols. This one, related to Shamanism probably, is one of them.

162, Reindeers

8c B. C. Fuyun

This rock carving was found at the Bulate Grazingland, southwest to the Fuyun Town.

163, Herding

8c B. C. Altai

In this rock carving, showing the scenes of herding, there are one man and some animals, such as ox, goat, dog, and elephant. The man stands in the front of animals, with his hands raising, in the posture of driving. This rock carving, reflecting the life of herding, was found at the Duolate Valley.

164, Acrobatics

5c A. D. Altai

This rock carving, found at Queergou, Lamazhao Township, depicts the scenes of the acrobatic performance. A tall man, who is lifting a child in each hand, stands on the goat's horns; an old man sits on the man's head, with arms akimbo. This simple and unadorned rock carving expressed a primeval style of the rock art.

165, Goats

About 1c B. C. —1c A. D. Altai

These goats were carved simply and directly, and the style of this rock carving, found at the Duoate Valley, is also primeval.

166, Running Deers

5c B. C. Altai

This rock carving shows a group of deers which were running quickly. It was found at the Queergou, Lamazhao Township.

167, Cavalrymen

9c A. D. Hami

This rock carving shows the cavalrymen who are fighting with long weapons.

168, Cavalrymen and Horses

7—8c A. D. Barkol

In this picture, there are three horses and two cavalrymen who hold the weapons. The rock carving was found at the top of a hill, near the Baqiangzhi Village, 38km northeast to the Barkol Town.

PAINTINGS

169, A Gandharva

7c A. D. Kizil, New cave 1

In this wall painting, the gandharva wears a one — pearl crown with the hairs hanging down shoulders; on his neck, chest, shoulders, and arms, etc, are necklaces, ribbons, bracelets, long and narrow embroidered cape, etc. His left hand is in the posture of strewing flowers. This strong, tall gandharva is different to those ones of India—style with the full breasts and plump bellies.

170, The Lying Woman

5c A. D. Kizil, cave 84

In this wall painting. the nude woman lies on her back with her face turning to the right. Her hands put on her right leg which curls a bit. The lying posture of her was painted very gracefully and lively. Now, this wall painting is preserved at Berlin.

171, Painting from Budddhist Stories

6c A. D. L. 12cm Qira

There are four Buddhistic figures in this painting. From left to right, the first one and second one are Bodhisattvas. The third one had one head and four arms, who should be a vajrapani. The fourth one is similiar to the first one in wearing and dressing, who should be a devata. This painting on wooden plank, found at Dandan—oilik, is preserved at London, now.

172, Camels

7—8c A. D. L. 14cm Minfeng

This sketch, painted on paper, shows a camel which is feeding its baby. It was found at Andier, and now is preserved at London.

173 174, Painting on Wooden Plank

7c A. D. L. 33cm Qira

On the front and back of this plank, there are two kinds of paintings. On the front was painted a Bodhisattva with one head and four arms, in the Persian style. But, on the back of the plank, a devata in the Indian style was painted; it has three heads and four arms. This painting on wood, found at Dandan — oilik, now is preserved at London.

175, The Goddess Hariti

8c A. D. Yutian

Hariti is a female devil in the mythology of ancient India; afterwards, she was vanquished by Buddha. This wall painting shows Hariti and her children. Now it is preserved at New Delhi.

176, Head of Buddha

7—8c A. D. Qira

The wall painting was unearthed from Damagou. The Buddha faces left; his eyes and eyebrows are very thin and long, and the nose, mouth are very dainty too. His face, neck, and shoulders are mellow and full. All of these express not only a very ripe artistry but also a unique style of the Buddhist paintings. Now the painting is preserved at New Delhi.

177, Worshipping Bodhisattva

7—8c A. D. Qira

This fragment shows a bodhisattva facing left who is worshipping the Buddha. He wears a flower crown and some ornaments such as the necklace, bracelet, etc. He puts his hands together, and raises his head. This wall painting with a distinctive style of paintings in ancient Hotan, now is preserved at New Delhi.

178, Winged Angel

4—5c A. D. Ruoqiang

The portrait of a winged angel, painted on the wall of a stupa of the Buddhist Temple Site, Milan, with the Gandhara — style of paintings, shows an winged angel. Now, the wall painting is preserved at London.

179, Portraits of Buddha and Six Bhiksus

4—5c A. D. Ruoqiang

The wall painting, found at Milan Buddhist Temple Site, shows the portraits of Buddha and six bhiksus (Buddhist monks) behind him. The Buddha has big eyes and moustaches, simply dressed without any embellishment. This painting shows a unique style of Buddhistic painting. Now it is preserved at New Delhi.

180, Vairocana

7—8c A. D. Qira

In this figure, the Buddha has a nimbus behind him, and some patterns on his bare body, such as the sun, moon, pestles, pearls, horse, etc. His face is round; the eyes, eyebrows, noes and mouth are all small and concentrated. This wall painting, found at Damagou, is preserved at New Delhi, now.

181, Stories about the Causes

4—5c A. D. Kizil, cave 171

This wall painting was painted at the surface of the cave's ceiling, and arranged in the rhombus shape. It is about the stories of the causes, with the figures of the Buddha and all living creatures. The artistic characteristics of this wall painting is the arrangement of painting in the rhombus shape, which was invented by the painters of ancient Kuqa.

182, Standing Buddha

6c A. D. H. 46cm Baicheng

The Buddha stands on a lotus throne with bare feet. He wears a kasaya, with his left shoulder uncovered, and holds an alm—bowl in his right hand. There are halos behind his head and body. This painting on wood was found at Kizil Cave Temple. Now it is preserved at Berlin.

183, Devatas

4c A. D. Kizil

This wall painting shows two devatas, who are snuggling under the bodhi tree, looking like a couple of lovers. The left one, with the upper part of the body uncovered, wears a crown and some ornaments such as ribbons, caletes, cape, etc; the right is playing the *Konghou*, an ancient plucked string instrument in China. Now, this painting is preserved at Berlin.

184, The Cowherd Nanda

4—5c A. D. Kizil, cave 47

The fragment, now preserved at Berlin, shows that the cowherd Nanda, who, resting on his gnarled stick, watches over his animals as he listens devortly to the words of the Buddha. So deep is his concentration that he is oblivious of the poor frog he is crushing beneath his stick. The frog, so the legend goes, would have escaped if it had not meant disturbing Nanda's attention; the frog will be rewarded by being reborn as a god, while Nanda will enter the Buddhist order.

185, The Bodhisattvas Playing Instruments

4c A. D. Kizil, cave 38

In this wall painting, the two bodhisattvas are playing instruments, the Pipa and flute. They were depicted beautifully and finely.

186, Scenes of Buddha Vanquishing the Daughters of Mara

4—5c A. D. Kizil, cave 76

In this wall painting, describing the scenes of the daughters of Mara tempting Buddha, the Buddha sits in the center. At the left, there are three standing, beautiful girls, who are daughters of Mara; the front one, with bare body, draws her left hand to Buddha in the posture of "finger — sword". At the right are three ugly old women with white hairs, who had been vanquished by Buddha with his superhuman strength. Now this wall painting is preserved at Berlin.

187, Gandharvas

6—7c A. D. Kizil, cave 8

This fragment shows two flying gandharvas. The upper one holds up a tray with the flowers; the other one plays the Pipa, a plucked string instrument with a fretted fingerboard in China. Around them are the rhombus —shaped mountains, trees, and lake, etc.

188, Bodhisattva

4c A. D. Kizil, cave 38

The bodhisattva sits on a square pedestal with legs crossd. The upper part of his body is bare, with wearing some ornaments such as necklaces, ribbons, and bracelets, etc. He wears a three — pearls crown, and puts his hands together in front of his chest.

189, Devatas

4—5c A. D. Kizil, cave 76

All of the two devatas have the head—halo behind their head. The left one holds a lotus flower in one hand; the right one, with the upper part of his body uncovered, puts the palms together. Now, this wall painting is preserved at Berlin.

190, Dancer and Musician

10c A. D. Kumtura, cave 73

This fragment of wall painting shows a dancer and a musician who are dancing and playing. The musician on the left is playing the *Sheng*, a reed pipe wind instrument in China. Now, this wall painting is preserved at Berlin.

191, Group of Bodhisattvas (part)

4—5c A. D. Kumtura, cave 21

This cave was found in 1977. The wall paintings on the ceiling are colorful and well preserved. A lotus was painted on the center of the ceiling. Thirteen trapezoid pictures, painted with a bodhisattva respectively, radiate from the lotus. This picture is one of them. Its vivid description of the bodhisattva, thin and fine strokes and reasonable tone make it a wonderful work of wall painting.

192, Gandharvas (Facsimile)

8c A. D. Kumtura, cave 16

The two gandharvas were painted in flying posture. They wear the long skirts. Under their bodies are waving clouds; the opening lotus flowers surround them. All of these give us a very strong feeling of moving.

193, Gandharvas

7c A. D. Kizil—Kargha, cave 30

This wall painting is one part of the scenes of Gandharvas. The Gandharvas were painted in the gesture of flying from the sides to the center. They are dancing, or strewing flowers, or playing the *Pipa*, etc.

194, Jataka Story of the Royal Monkey

4c A. D. Kizil, cave 38

This wall painting shows the story of the royal monkey from the stories of Jataka. When the royal monkey led the small monkeys to eat the fruits in an orchard, they were found and pursued by the king and his attendants. In order to help the small monkeys to cross over a river, the royal monkey dropped into the river and died.

195, Ajatasatru

6—7c A. D. Kizil, cave 205

Ajatasatru was the king of ancient India. He dreamt that the Buddha died, and he was very painful. His minister showed him a painting on Buddha's Life and hinted that the Buddha had been in Nirvana. This wall painting shows the story. In the right is the Ajatasatru, who was put in a jar to have a bath; in the left are Ajatasatru and his wife, his attendants, who are listening to the minister. This kind of content of wall painting has only been found at Kizil, but this one had been destroyed in the war.

196, Scene from the Vishvantara Jataka

4c A. D. Kizil, cave 38

This wall painting shows the scene of that the prince Vishvantara is selling his sons to a Brahman. The Vishvantara was painted in the bodhisattva's image. Now this wall painting is preserved at Berlin.

197, Seated Vajrapani

4c A. D. Kizil, cave 77

This wall painting shows a Vajrapani with an Indian look on his face, i. e. the curved eyebrows, big eyes, long nose, and the moustaches. He seats. on a square pedestal, and wears a pearl — crown, with the hairs hanging down shoulders. In his left hand is held a vajra—pestle. Many kinds of ornaments, such as necklace, cape, bracelet, etc. , are worn on his body. This wall painting is preserved at Berlin, now.

198, The Bodhisattva Preaching

4—5c A. D. Kizil, cave 17

This wall painting, the best one of the preaching scenes which have been protected up to now in Kizil, was painted on the wall under the semicircular top. In the center, the cross—legged bodhisattva sits on a high square pedestal, in the posture of preaching, surrounded by five cross — legged, hearing bodhisattvas at his each side.

199, Three Half—Figures

4—5c A. D. Kizil, cave 224

In this wall painting, the left figure is the King Ajatashatru, who has a head—halo and a canopy and wears a crown with three pearls. At the King's left is his wife, who has a head—halo, too. The right one is the King's minister Varshakara. Behind them were painted the palace. This wall painting is preserved at Berlin, now.

200, The King and His Wife

6c A. D. Kizil, cave 205

In the middle of this wall painting, the king stands with a sword and a incense burner held in his hands. At his left is his wife; at his right, there are two bhiksus, who are explaining and publicising the Buddha's dharma to them. All of the king and his wife have head—haloes behind their heads. Now, this wall painting is preserved at Berlin.

201, Two Donors

6—7c A. D. Kizil, cave 189

The two standing donors wear long robes with the turndown collar and edged lace. A knife is worn on the belt of each donor. Each of them is given a lotus flower in the hands. Now, this wall painting is preserved at Berlin.

202, Paintings of Dancing and Playing on a Reliquary

7c A. D. H. 31. 2cm Kuqa

The reliquary, made of wood, is in the shape of cylinder, with a lid in the shape of the circular cone. On the surfaces were painted the scenes of dancing and playing instruments. It was found at the Coqur Temple Site (the Subashi Ancient Town). Now it is preserved at Tokyo.

203, The Dancers and Players

This is one part of the facsimile of the paintings on the surfaces of the reliquary. It shows the scenes of dancing and playing instuments. It was copied by Li Yao Tian.

204, Scenes of Buddha Cremated

6c A. D. Kizil, cave 205

This wall painting, preserved at Berlin, depicts the scenes of the Buddha cremated by his disciples, after he entered into the Nirvana. The Buddha lies on his right side in a coffin, wrapped up with a kasaya; his expression is very serene. The Ananda, his disciple, stands and holds the cover of the coffin in his hands. Around Buddha are the Buddhist monks and

devatas, who are worshipping or crying or strewing flowers for Buddha.

205, Scenes of Contending for Buddha's Relics

6c A. D. Kizil, cave 205

This fragment of wall painting shows the story of that the eight kingdoms sent their armed forces to kusinagara, where the body of Buddha had been cremated, and contend for the Buddha's relics. It is preserved at Berlin, now.

206, Farming

7c A. D. Kizil, cave 175

This fragment of wall painting shows two farmers who are digging the ground by using the farm tools which are called "Kantuman" and used up to now in southern Xinjiang. On the right side is a standing Buddha.

207, Group of Donors

8—9c A. D. Yanji

The wall painting, excavated from the site of Buddhist Temple, Qigexing, is composed of two men and two women. The lined face and bent back of the first man on the left clearly reflect old age; on his head he wears an unusual, high, black hat. Next to him on his left stands a taller woman in short—sleeved yellow jacket. The next figure is again that of an man, who wears a hat like a crown. The female figure on the right is identical with the other woman. This wall painting is now preserved at Berlin.

208, Bhiksuni

8—9c A. D. Yanji

This wall painting was found at the Buddhist Temple Site, Qigexing. The Bhiksuni, with the upper part of her body uncovered, puts her palms together. Now, it is preserved at London.

209, The Bhiksus in Teaching

8—9c A. D. Yanji

The fragment, found at Qigexing, shows four young bhiksus who are taught by an old bhiksu. Above them, there is a flying gandharva who is strewing flowers. This wall painting is preserved at London, now.

210, A Young Woman Playing Weiqi

7—9c A. D. Turfan

This painting on silk, shows a young women who is playing Weiqi, a game played with black and white pieces on a board of 361 crosses. She wears a cape and a green shirt; all of her face and body are full and beautiful. A piece of Weiqi is in her right hand and she is hesitating about what move to make. This painting, found at Astana, now is preserved in Xinjiang Museum .

211, A Young Woman

　　7c A. D. Turfan

　　Young woman is the traditional theme in Chinese paintings. In this painting on silk, the young woman had her hairs tied together behind her head; her cheeks were painted in red color. She stands with folded arms. There are a row of Chinese characters on the left of the woman. This painting is preserved at Stockholm, now.

212, A Boy

　　7－9c A. D. Turfan

　　The boy wears a pair of trousers, and takes a small dog in his left arm. His right hand raises upwards. This lively and interesting silk painting of a boy, found at Astana, is preserved in Xinjiang Museum now.

213, A Young Maidservant Holding a Tea－tray

　　7－9c A. D. H. 81cm Turfan

　　In this painting on silk, the maidservant stands with a tea－tray in her hands. It was found at the Astana Ancient Tombs, No. 187, and now is preserved in Xinjiang Museum .

214, A Female Dancer

　　7－9c A. D. H. 47cm Turfan

　　In this painting on silk, the woman has a high hair worn in a bun, and wears a red, long skirt. On her forehead is painted a ornamental pattern, which is called *Hua Dian* in China. It is preserved in Xinjiang Museum , now.

215, A Young Maidservant

　　7－9c A. D. H. 61cm Turfan

　　The painting on silk, found at the tomb No. 187, Astana Ancient Tombs, shows a young maidservant. She has the lower hairs tied together with red strings, and wears a purple robe. Now, it is preserved in Xinjiang Museum .

216, A Groom Leading a Horse

　　7－9c A. D. Turfan

　　The groom wears a white and black boots. His left hand holds a whip and his right hand leads the horse. This painting on silk, found at Astana, is preserved in Xinjiang Museum now.

217, Paintings about Warning

　　7－9c A. D. L. 4m Turfan

　　These are the paintings about the ethics and morals; they adopted the layout in the form of the six－sides screen. The left one is a vessel containing water, which warns people to make modest and honest remarks. The right one is painted a box and a sheaf of silk, which means that how to conduct oneself in society. The four figures in the middle are the images of the ethics and morals. The wall paintings were found at the back wall of the tomb No. 216, Astana Ancient Tombs.

218, Scenes of Living in the Manor

　　3－4c A. D. L. 2. 25m Turfan

　　This painting, painted at the back wall of the tomb No. 98, Kharakhoja Ancient Tombs, shows the scene of a landlord living in his manor. In the front is the landlord, making a bow with hands folded in front. His wife and children follow him. In the right part of the painting, there are fields, vineary, mulberry field, winery, horse, ox and cart, craftsmen, etc.. The style of this painting is similar to the wall paintings of the *Jiayuguan* Ancient Tombs in the Wei and Jin Dynasties.

219, Flower－and－Bird Painting

　　7－9c A. D. L. 37. 5cm Turfan

　　This traditional Chinese flower－and－bird painting, painted on the back wall of a tomb of the Astana Ancient Tombs, No. 217, adopted the layout in the form of the six－side screen. Each side of "screen" is painted with one or two birds and flowers.

220, Painting on Paper

　　7－9c A. D. Turfan

　　This painting on paper portrays several scenes of a landlord living in his manor, such as the banquet, dancing, fields and gardens, etc.. It is now preserved at New Delhi.

221, Silk Painting Portraying *Fuxi* and *Nuwa*

　　7c A. D. L. 216cm Turfan

　　Fuxi and *Nuwa* are the ancestors of mankind in Chinese ancient fables. In this painting, they were depicted with human heads and snakes' bodies, embracing and entwining each other, with a sun above them in the horizon and a moon under them. In their hands are held a pair of compasses and a rule which symbolize the principle of the universe. This painting on silk, found at Astana, is preserved at London, now.

222, Silk Painting Portraying *Fuxi* and *Nuwa*

　　7c A. D. H. 221. 5cm Turfan

This painting on silk portraying *Fuxi* and *Nuwa* is similar to that one. *Fuxi*, on the right of the picture, is male, holding a rule in the hand. *Nuwa*, on the left, is female, holding a pair of compasses. In the philosophy of ancient China, people consider that all of the thing in the world are born of the combining of the *Yin*, the female or negative principle in the nature, and *Yang*, the male or postive principle in the nature. This painting, expressing this question, found at Astana, now is preserved in Xinjiang Museum .

223, **The Nestorian Wall Painting**

9c A. D. Turfan

This fragment of wall painting found at Gaochang Ancient City, shows the scenes of that the Christians wellcame the Christ to Jerusalem in the Pamsunday. The tall missionary, holding a holy cup in the hands, stands on the left; in the front of him, there are three Nestorians, who are standing respectfully. This wall painting with the Byzantinism of art is preserved at Berlin, now.

224, **Fragments from a Manichaean Book**

9c A. D. Turfan

The left one was painted with two rows of Manichees, who are sitting abreast under the trees with white hat and clothes; in the middle of them, there are three rows of Uighurian characters. In the right one, there are two persons, patterns of plants and five rows of Uighurian characters. The two fragments on paper, found at Gaochang, now are preserved at Berlin.

225, **The Manichaean Wall Painting**

9c A. D. Turfan

On the left of the fragment, Mani, the founder of Manichaeism, wears a crown decorated with goldleaves, and a white robe. All of his disciples, following him, wear white hats and clothes, with the long hair hanging down their shoulders. This wall painting was found at the Gaochang Ancient City. Now it is preserved at Berlin.

226, **Scenes of Grieving for Buddha**

10—11c A. D. Bezeklik, cave 33

This wall painting shows the scenes of that the disciples of Buddha are grieving over the Buddha's death. On the right are the bodhisattva and devatas; the left are the princes of the sixteen kingdoms. The figure of Buddha has

been destroyed.

227, **Lady Worshipping Buddha**

10c A. D. Bezeklik, cave 20

On the right of the wall painting, there is a standing lady wearing a luxurious suit of clothes. Her face, looking like a woman of Han nationality, is full and round; her body is also full. A tray with three pearls in it is held by her hands. Behind her is a maidservant who puts her palms together. Now, this painting is preserved at Berlin.

228, **The Vaishrvana and His Attendants**

9—10c A. D. Bezeklik, cave 20

The fragment of wall painting shows the Vaishravana and his civil and military attendants. This kind of image of Vaishravana has also been found in the Buddhistic paintings in India and Tunhuang.

229, **Uighurian Prince**

10c A. D. Bezeklik, cave 45

The prince stands before a door or window opening, between red curtains which have been tied back on either side. He wears a long, belted robe; his head is crowned with a high tiara fastened under the chin with a red band. Prince Alp Arslan ("brave lion"), whose name and title can be read on the cartouche located below the elbow, holds the stem of a flower in his left hand. Now, this wall painting is preserved at Berlin.

230, **Uighurian Prince**

9c A. D. L. 142cm Turfan

This large banner, painting on ramie, possibly a votive offering, with the portrayal of a Uighurian prince on both sides, consists of three parts: the long, narrow, rectangular banner itself, the triangular segment at the bottom with a wooden stick to weigh it down. On the prince's head is a three— pronged cap; he has a beard covering his chin and framing his checks. His fine robe, patterned with a large floral design, is modeled on the typical dress of China. It is a long—sleeved, round—necked garment reaching to the feet. In his hands the prince holds a stem with several blossoms. On each side of him, there are a child and some Uighurian inscriptions. The banner, found at Gaochang (Khocho), is preserved at Berlin, now.

231, **Group of Uighurian Royal Kinsmen**

10—11c A. D. Bezekik, cave 16

The fragment, including eight persons, is one part of the donors of the Uighurian royal kinsmen. All of the donors dress long robe, hold a flower in the hands; there is a list of names posted up in Ughurian characters around each head of them. Now, this wall painting is preserved at Berlin.

232, **Dragon in a Lake**

9c A. D. Bezeklik

Stylized mountains, their valleys wooded with various kinds of trees, encircle a lake from which is emerging a two horned dragon with slender wings. In view are the monster's forequrters, its claws, and its head and neck with white mane. Anger is visible in the eyes, and its jaws are widely open. Now this wall painting is preserved at Berlin.

233, **A Gandharva Steming Flowers**

8c A. D. L. 35. 3cm Turfan

This fragment of a silk painting depicts a gandharva floating aloft; his robe and scarf stream behind him in the wind. He carries in his right hand a bowl, out of which he has just plucked a handfull of flowers with his left hand. This fragment, found at Gaochang (Khocho), is preserved at Berlin, now.

234, **Three Buddhist Monks**

9—10c A. D. Bezeklik, cave 20

The three Buddhist monks, wearing the purple kasayas, stand and hold the flowers in their hands. Above their heads, there are three lists inscribing their names and status in Chinese and Uighurian characters. This wall painting is preserved at Berlin, now.

235, **Uighurian Princesses**

9—10c A. D. Bezeklik, cave 20

Two Uighurian princesses with East Asian features walk solemnly toward the left over a wave — patterned carpet with borders on each side. They are wearing wide, sand — colored robes without a pronounced waistline. The V—shaped neckline is edged by a collar embroidered with red spiral lines. Each woman has been given a flower in their hands. Now, this wall painting is preserved at Berlin.

236, **Head of a Young Woman**

7c A. D. Turfan

This fragment of painting on silk is preserved at Tokyo, now.

237, **The Excursions of Prince Skayamuni**

7—9c A. D. Turfan

According to the biography of the Buddha, when Sakyamuni was a prince, one day he went on a tour by riding a horse. At the gate of a town, he saw two persons who were lifting a dead body and passing in front of him. So he was engendered the desire of abandoning. This painting on silk, found at the Tuyugou (Toyok), shows this story. Now it is preserved at Tokyo.

238, **Lokapalas**

9—10c A. D. Turfan

This fragment of the painting on silk, was found at Bezeklik. On the left, there are two Lokapalas who wear the armours and hold the arms in their hands. At the left of them there are a Lokapala with two man's heads and two figure of the Avalokiteshvara with a thousand arms. Now, this painting is preserved at Berlin.

239, **Figure Painting**

8c A. D. Turfan

This painting on paper shows a man and a woman, who stand under a tree. The man wears a high and pointed hat and a spacious robe; his left hand drews the woman's hands behind him. This painting on paper, found at Astana, is preserved at Tokyo, now.

240, **Manichaean Painting on Silk**

10c A. D. Turfan

In the middle of this fragment, there are two figures who are standing on the lotus pedestals facing each other and playing the instruments. On the sides of them, there are several rows of Sogdian characters. This painting is preserved in Turfan Museum now.

241, **Avalokiteshvara**

10c A. D. Turfan

In this fragment of painting on silk, the bodhisattva wears a crown with flowers, and a red robe. Behind his head, there is a halo. This wall painting of Avalokiteshvara, who has the evident Uighurian features, was found at Gaochang (Khocho). It is now preserved at Berlin.

242, **Scenes of Buddha with Worshippers**

9—10c A. D. Bezeklik, cave 20

In the center of this wall painting is the standing Buddha, who is preaching. On his left there are two bhiksus, two bodhisattvas, and two donors who are worshipping the Buddha by kneeling their legs, and holding the trays with their hands. On the right of Buddha are the va-jrapani, the bodhisattva, the donor, etc. This wall painting with the style of the Gaochang Uighurian Kingdom Age, is preserved at Berlin, now.

243, Donors
9—10c A. D. Bezeklik, cave 20

The fragment shows two noblemen, who are worshipping Buddha. They kneel down on their left legs, and hold the trays full of trea-sures with their hands. The two men wearing the hat, robe, long boots and horsewhip on their belt, have dense beards and moustaches on their face. Now this wall painting is pre-served at Berlin.

244, Scenes of Playing Instruments
10—11c A. D. Bezeklik, cave 33

This fragment shows the scenes of that the Brahmanic heretics were playing instruments to celebrate the Buddha's death. The wall paint-ing is preserved at Tokyo, now.

245, Bodhisattvas
6—7c A. D. L. 37. 7cm Turfan

On a piece of square liner, two bodhisattvas were drawn at each side of the di-agonal in pale yellowish brown and black. These two bodhisattvas, sitting on lotus pedestals, wear red robes. There are also vine patterns and several Chinese characters in the picture. According to the characters, the bodhisattvas are the figures of folk belief. This picture is preserved in Lushun, Liaoning Province.

246, Silk Painting of a Bodhisattva (King of Langevity)
7—8c A. D. L. 102. 6cm Turfan

The bodhisattva, kind and decorous in ap-pearance, wears a crown decorated with pearls, jewelled necklaces and strings of ornaments. His dress and the figure of Buddha on the crown are the same with those of Avalokites-vara. There is an inscription at the right side of the bodhisattva. Now it is preserved in Lushun, Liaoning Province.

247, Bodhisattvas
10c A. D. Jimsa

This wall painting was found at the Ruins of the Gaochang Uighur Royal Temple. The bodhisattvas, with the same image of the curved eyebrows, thin eyes, high nose, small mouth, etc, were arranged in rows. The style

of this painting is similiar to the wall painting of the bodhisattva of Bezeklik.

248, The Procession Scene of a King
10c A. D. Jimsa

The painting was painted on the wall of the Gaochang Uighur Royal Temple, located at the west of the Beiting Ancient City (Bishbalik). In the center is the king who is sitting on the back of an elephant. Around the king are the warrior attendants, riding the horses, wearing the armours and swords, bows, etc.

WOVEN WARES

249, Part of the Brocade with Bird and Beast Designs
4c A. D. Turfan

On the dark blue ground, normal and re-versed jacquared wefting with brown, blue, green and yellow threads formed elegant, upper—lower symmetrical, geometric designs, i. e. grotesque beasts and birds filled in the blanks of geometric designs. The beasts have horns on head, wings on back, and dragon — claw — shaped feet. The grotesque bird has a bird's head and four beast's feet. this precious bro-cade is preserved in Xinjiang Museum now.

250, Satin dorure de Nankin (damaged)
8—10c A. D. L. 71. 5cm Shanshan

On the silver grey ground are black, yel-low and blue polychromatic patterns, with a hunting scene as the motif. It is preserved in Turfan Museum now.

251, Fragment of Woollen Embroidery
10c B. C. Hami

This is a fragment from a woollen robe. On the dark red ground, the bright — colored and beautiful regular design was formed by em-broidering with yellow, blue and green woollen threads, which shows a much developed an-cient woollen embroidery technique in Xinjiang. It is preserved in Xinjiang Museum now.

252, Grass Woven Basket
10c B. C. H. 10cm Ruoqiang

Woven up from the braided grass of splendid achnatherum (Achnatherum Splendens), the basket has a straight neck, swollen belly and round bottom. Fancy weav-ing formed wave design and concentric lines on the neck. Covered on the basketmouth is one piece of brown woollen cloth. It is preserved in Xinjiang Institute of Archaeology now.

253, Wool Knitted Cap and Felt Cap

9c B. C. Qiemo

The left one is the oldest wool knitted cap found in China. Knitted up from black wool thread, the cap has a opoening diameter smaller than the top's, and one hairpin like appentage sticking on the flat top. The cap is very springy and shows a four—petal form fabric structure formed by four different knitted methods. The right one is a white felt cap sewed up from two pieces of felt by white thread. The mouth diameter is bigger than the top's. There is a horn—like decoration on the top and a fasten ribbon on the side of back opening. The two caps are preserved in Bayingolin Museum now.

254, Felt Cap

9c B. C. H. 29cm Qiemo

Sewed up from two pieces of triangular brown felt by white woollen thread, the cap shows an erecting form due to the supporting of the hard material lined inside. It is preserved in Bayingolin Museum now.

255, Woollen Coat

9c B. C. L. 53cm Qiemo

Roughly sewed together from five pieces of twill weave woollen cloth, namely left and right front pieces, left the right sleeve pieces and back piece, the coat has a edge—to—edge center front opening, oval neck line, a fasten ribbon under neck line, short and thin sleeves, no waist dart and no fringe decoration. It is preserved in Bayingolin Museum now.

256, Man's Woollen Trousers

2—3c A. D. L. 115cm Yuli

The plain weave cloth is rather sort and fine, yellowish—colored and vertically wrinkled. Along the trouser leg's bottom are the attached fringes. The waist of the trousers was sewed up with separate pieces. There is a fasten ribbon on the waist opening. It is preserved in Bayingolin Museum now.

257, Woollen Carpet

2—3c A. D. L. 260cm W. 95—100cm Yuli

The rectangular carpet was knitted up with white, red, blue, light green and black threads. On the carpet are the elegant animal patterns in the middle, " 卍 " designs and rhomboid patterns outside, color bands and flower patterns along the border. It is pre-served in Bayingolin Museum now.

258, Brocade Coat

2c A. D. L. 133cm Minfeng

The coat has a edge—to—edge center front opening, long and thin sleeves, clear waist dart and oblique front—back seam. On the coat are the bright—colored and elegant red, dark red, green, blue and white polychromatic deformed cloud pattern and embroidered Chinese characters "万事如意" (means every thing as you wish). At the lower right front part of the coat is an attached brocade piece with auspicious Chinese scripts "延年益寿大宜子孙" (means longevity and having most descendants) on it. The coat is preserved in Xinjiang Museum now.

259, Brocade Belt with Dragon Design

1—2c A. D. Yuli

The belt was damaged into two pieces. On the belt are three rows of bright—colored lively dragon design, woven by green, yellow and red thread and contained in regular checks, and yellow geometric pattern among the dragon motif. With beautiful crown on its raised head, the dragon has a long neck, long jaws, slender body, long tail, and limps in a running posture. It is preserved in Bayingolin Museum now.

260, Cotton Cloth with Buddha and Dragon Designs (Fragmentary)

3c A. D. Minfeng

On the blue ground, wax printing formed white designs with the Buddha's portrait as the motif, which betrays the prevalence of the Buddhist in ancient Yutian Kingdom. At the lower left corner is a decollete Buddha figure in half—length, contained in a band—bordered square, with solemn expression, thin face, a string of beads around his neck, a polygonal container full of grapes in his hands and circular nimbus behind. To its right are the chessboard pattern at upper part, dragon design and bird design below. Further to the upper right is an incomplete pattern with several horizonal rows of color bands and one horizonal row of zigzag design bordered the bottom. It is preserved in Xinjiang Museum now.

261, Part of "Perpetual Prosperity" Brocade

2c A. D. Ruoqiang

On the blue ground are elegant yellow, brown and green polychromatic patterns, namely twisting vine pattern, filled in the blanks with various kinds of auspicious beasts and Chinese characters "永昌" (means perpetual prosperity). From the left to the right, the first vertical row are standing birds. The second row are grotesque beasts with long horns and wings on the back. The third row are docile lambs. The fourth row are ferocious tigers, facing back and in a climbing posture. This is a precious sample for the study of the ancient Chinese silk weaving technique. It is preserved in Xinjiang Institute of Archaeology now.

262, Part of " Longevity and Having Most Descentants" Brocade

2c A. D. Ruoqiang

On the brown ground are yellow and blue polychromatic patterns arranged in vertical rows, i. e. grotesque auspicious beast pattern, deformed cloud design, and Chinese characters "延年益寿大宜子孙" (means longevity and having most descendants) filled in between. The left vertical row beast, lifting their front limbs, are in a climbing posture. The middle row beasts are seemingly in walking posture with their head raising and facing back and their raised tails connecting with the deformed cloud design. The right vertical row beasts have a forward extending head, large and widely opening mouth, raised ears, wings on the back, raised tails, and dot—decorated body. It is preserved in Xinjiang Institute of Archaeology now.

263, Part of " Longevity and Prosperity" Brocade

2c A. D. Ruoqiang

On the blue ground are the yellow, brown and green polychromatic designs, with the twisted branches and vines as the motif and filled in between the branches with lively auspicious beasts and four Chinese characters "长寿明光" (means longevity and prosperity). The left beast has long horns on its head, wings on its back, a large and widely opened mouth, and limps in running posture. The middle beast, raising its head and facing back, is in a climbing posture. The right beast, also raising its head and facing back, is in running posture too. It is preserved in Xinjiang Institute of Archaeology now.

264, Part of the Brocade with Fish and Bird Designs

2c A. D. Ruoqiang

On the brown ground are elegant yellow fish design and blue twin duck design between every two fish. It is preserved in Xinjiang Institute of Archaeology now.

265, Part of Woollen Cloth

1—2c A. D. Ruoqiang

On the purplish red ground are the elegant yellow, green and blue polychromatic patterns. In the center is a complete peach—shaped garland with one three—leaf design inside, dewlike dots above the central leaf and one dewlike dot above each of the left and right side, there is an opened flower design. To the right of the garland is one row of vertical wave patterns. It is preserved in Xinjiang Institute of Archaeology, now.

266, Part of the Woollen Cloth with Wefting Pattern

7—9c A. D. Turfan

On the blue ground are the elegant white, red yellow and green polychromatic patterns, i. e., geometric pattern, filled in blanks with floral design and deformed bird design, bordered by yellow and green triangle design and yellow " 卐 " designs. It is preserved in Stockholm, Sweden now.

267, Part of the Woollen Tapestry with Centaur Design

1—2c A. D. 58×45. 5cm Lop

This precious tapestry was cut into four pieces and then sewed up to form a trouser before unearthed. On its blue ground is the elegant wefting pattern formed by fancy weave with the threads of more than ten kinds of colors, namely a centaur design on the right trouser leg. The centaur motif was often seen in the Hellenic legendary, but never appeared on fabrics before. It is preserved in Xinjiang Museum now.

268, Woollen Saddle Blanket

1—2c A. D. 76×74cm, W. 74cm Lop

Covered on a saddle when unearthed from the ancient tombs, the thick bright—colored blanket was knitted up by " horse—hoof—knot" method. In the middle of the blanket is the red rhomboid pattern on the dark green ground, filled in with yellow or brown fruit and leaf design bordered by black, yellow and red polychromatic band. Outside the band are the green zigzag lines filled in between with yellow leaf design. The blanket is bordered by brown fringe and has one braid at each of the four corners. Being exquisitely knitted and richly ornamented, the blanket shows a strong local craftwork style and is one piece of the precious material for the study of the ancient blanket—making technique in Xinjiang. It is preserved in Xinjiang Museum now.

269, Part of the Woollen Tapestry with Wefting Warrior Design

1—2c A. D. 61×48. 2cm Lop

The tapestry was skillfully made with the threads of more than twenty kinds of colors, thus the pattern has the effect of depth and solidity. It is preserved in Xinjiang Museum now.

270, Restored Tapestry with Centaur and Warrior Designs

1—2c A. D. L. 231cm W. 21—49cm Lop

Showing a strong Hellenic style, the tapestry was ornamented with the designs of a centaur at the upper part and a warrior holding a spear in his right hand below.

271, Blue Cotton Cloth with Printed Patterns

1—2c A. D. L. 11. 5cm, W. 41. 2cm Lop

On the blue ground, wax printing formed elegant, horizonally placed, white patterns, namely floral design, dots, long lines, wave design and circles. It is the oldest wax printing cotton cloth found in Xinjiang, and is preserved in Xinjiang Museum now.

272, Silk with Printed Hunting Pattern (Fragmentary)

8c A. D. W. 30cm Turfan

On the plain weave silk is the printed decorative pattern of a hunting scene, i. e. a hunter on horse back ready to shoot an arrow to a ferocious lion, hounds chasing hares, felcon pursuing birds etc. It is preserved in Xinjiang Museum now.

273, Brocade Decorated with Chinese Character

5c A. D. Turfan

On the red ground are elegant blue and white stripes, checks and thorny bush pattern, filled in between with Chinese character "吉". It is preserved in Xinjiang Institute of Archaeology now.

274, Brocade with Dragon Design

4—5c A. D. Turfan

On the fine and thick blue ground are the Persian style yellow, white, red, green and pink polychromatic twill weave wefting patterns, with the horizonally placed dragon — shaped twisting vine design as the motif. Filled in the blanks are double — horned grotesque beasts and rhomboidal floral and grass designs and serveral attached nipple — shaped copper decorations on it. It is preserved in Xinjiang Museum now.

275, Woven Shoes Decorated with Chinese Scripts

5c A. D. L. 23cm, W. 8. 5cm Turfan

The shoe's sole was woven up with pale yellow flaxen thread, while the shoe's upper was woven up with bright—colored red, white, black, blue, green, apricot yellow, pale yellow and brown silk threads. Displayed in sequence, from front to back, on the instep are elegant yellow honeysuckle design and zigzag lines on red ground; sapphire blue symmetrical honeysuckle design on yellow ground; green dots and symmetrical twin leaf design on red ground; alternating red, yellow and blue mountain pattern on pink gound, filled in beside with red, blue and yellow threads embroidered Chinese characters "富且昌" (means being wealthy and prosperous), "宜候王" (means being prince or duke) and "夫延命长" (means all these being eternal and being longevious). The shoes are preserved in Xinjiang Museum now.

276, Qi (Ancient Chinese silk fabric)

5c A. D. Turfan

On the light red plain weave ground are the elegant dark reddish purple patterns, namely linked garlands, filled in with Chinese character "贵" and twin bird design. The fabric is rather fine and translucent, showing the highly developed Chinese traditional silk weaveing technique of that time. It is preserved in Xinjiang Museum now.

277, Part of the Brocade with Confronting Sheep and Tree Designs

5c A. D. Turfan

On the dark green plain weave ground are the bright — colored and elegant red, yellow, brown and white polychromatic designs. In the middle are one row of tower — shaped tree design, with one pair of the confronting long — horn sheeps under the tree and one standing bird symmetrically on each side of the treetop. Above that are one row of paired confronting birds, each holding one end of the same honey-suckle branch in their mouth. Each pair of con-fronting birds is separated by a small tree standing between. It is preserved in Xinjiang Institute of Archaeology now.

278, **Emboridery with Princess and Child Designs**

9—10c A. D.　17. 5×4cm Turfan

The subject on this very fine, skillfully ex-ecuted embroidery is a Uyghurian princess with her doughter. The artistocratic — featured woman grasps the stem of a flower in both hands. She wears her hair high and bedecked with ornaments. Her robe is fastened down the middle and topped with a collar. It is preserved in Berlin now.

279, **Piece of the Cotton Embroidery from an Armour Suit**

7—9c A. D. L. 17—21. 5cm W. 20cm U-rumqi

Bordered by the attched yellow cotton cloth stripe, the central blue cotton cloth has yellow and green silk threads embroidered flo-ral and grass designs and several attached nip-ple—shaped copper decorations on it. It is pre-served in Urumqi Museum now.

280, **Brocade with Lion and Elephant Designs**

5c A. D. L. 13cm Turfan

On the white ground are the crimson, green, blue and yellow designs. The main de-signs are two rows of coiled circles. Lion and elephant designs are inside the circles. Between the circles are acanthus designs. This brocade, unearthed from the Astana Ancient Tombs, is preserved in Xinjiang Museum now.

281, **The Brocade with the Designs of Double Horses**

7—8c A. D. L. 19. 6cm Turfan

The Fragment of a brocade was unearthed from the Astana Ancient Tombs. Its decorative designs was complicated and elegant. In the center of the circular granulation was weaved the designs of two horses facing each other and the seedpods of the lotus, and leaves, ect.. Now, this brocade is preserved in Xinjiang Mu-seum.

282, **Fragment of A Brocade**

7—8c A. D. W. 70cm Turfan

In this elegant fragment, there are three main kinds of designs, the circular auspicious flowers, the flying phoenixes and butterflies.

It was unearthed from the Sengim Buddhist Temple Site, and now is preserved in Xinjiang Museum.

283, **Part of Brocade**

7—8c A. D. Turfan

On the yellow ground are the horizonally placed red and white patterns, i. e. one pair of confronting chickens, standing on square things, contained in a garland design. Each chicken has a beautiful crown on its head and a ribbon around its neck. The brocade is pre-served in Xinjiang Museum now.

284, **Part of the Brocade Decorated with Myth-ical Bird Design**

7—9c A. D. Turfan

On the yellow twill weave ground is the dark blue, grey and white polychromatic de-signs, namely a standing mythical bird design contained in garland design. With its wings opened and tail droped, the bird holds a string of beads in its mouth and wears a backwards fluttering ribbon on its neck. It is preserved in Xinjiang Museum now.

285, **Part of the Brocade with Garland Circled Deer Design**

7—9c A. D. Turfan

This is a Sasanian style Chinese brocade with black and garland circled male deer pat-tern on yellow ground. The deer has a large multibranched antler, and backwards fluttering ribbon on its neck. Its body was ornamented with zigzag design, friangle design, spirals and mountain design. The brocade is preserved in Xinjiang Institute of Archaeology now.

286, **Brocade**

5c A. D. Turfan

On the pale yellow ground, normal and re-versed jacquard wefting formed, upper and lower symmetrical, crimson and tangerine pat-terns, namely oval garland design, filled in with upright and reyersed symmetrical camels, cameleers and Chinese characters ″胡王″ (means Iranian King). The cameleer holds a long whip and has frontier minority's charac-teristics, i. e. with deep eye sockets and highly bulged nose. There is a four—leaf honeysuckle design filled in the blanks outside the garlands. The brocade is preserved in Xinjiang Museum now.

287, **Part of the Green Gauze with Printed Hunting Patterns**

7—9c A. D. Turfan

On the dark green loose plain weave ground, basic dyeing formed bright — colored and elegant light green patterns of a hunting scene, i. e. hunters on horse back either ready to throw a rope, to shoot an arrow or chasing beasts, startled birds flying above, deers and hares running among trees and flowers below. It is preserved in Xinjiang Museum now.

288, Part of the Brocade with Beast Pattern

5c A. D. Turfan

Showing somewhat Central and Western Asian style, the brocade was ornamented with orderly placed blue, yellow, white, green and brown ox, lion and elephant patterns, which was often seen in Central and Western Asia. The left vertical row are the oxen, facing right, in a walking posture. The middle vertical row are the crouching ferocious lions, with their front legs raised and prepaired to stand up. The right vertical row are walking elephants with people and canopy on their back. The brocade is preserved in Xinjiang Museum now.

289, Brocade with Knight and Twin Beast Patterns (Damaged)

5c A. D. L. 22. 5cm Turfan

On the yellow ground are the dark blue, light blue and pale yellow patterns, namely the garlands connected by lotus flowers, with twin horse pattern, honeysuckle design between the garlands, and with knight shorting deer pattern, twin elephant, twin lion and camel patterns in the garlands. It is preserved in Xinjiang Museum now.

290, Part of the Brocade with Branch Design

5c A. D. Turfan

On the yellow and black bands are the alternately placed red branch design, filled in between with rhomboid form and square checks. This kind of simple decorative pattern is one characteristics of the fabric ornaments of that time. It is preserved in the Xinjang Museum now.

291, Part of the Brocade

10—11c A. D. Yuli

This is the part of an intact brocade robe. On the pale yellow ground are the elegant blue, white and black patterns, with garland circled twin back—to—back divine vutures as the motif. It is preserved in Palace Museum, Beijing

now.

292, Carpet with Wefting Pattern

19c A. D. L. 115cm Hotan

On the brownish red ground are the elegant brown and white polychromatic rhomboid pattern, filled in the rhomboidal blanks with four — petal flower and dots, surrounded by zigzag design, leaf design and floral designs. It is preserved in Xinjiang Museum now.

293, Part of the Silk with Printed Rhomboid Design

18c A. D. L. 310cm Hotan

On the purple plain weave ground were the printed red, dark green, light green, dark blue, light blue and orange yellow polychromatic designs, with the elegant and bright — colored linked lozenge form as the motif, by the Uighur traditional pad dyeing technique. It is preserved in Xinjiang Museum now.

WOODEN ARTICLES

294, Two Painted Wooden Sculptures

3—4c A. D. H. 34. 5cm Minfeng

The two painted wooden sculptures, found at the Niya Site, are legs of the chair which were engraved in the shape of man's figures. The left one is a woman, and the right is a man. Their faces were engraved clearly, and the feet were engraved in the shape of horse's feet. These figures are preserved at London now.

295, Female Half—Figure

9c B. C. H. 57. 5cm Ruoqiang

The wooden figure of a woman, excavated from the Ancient Tombs of Gumugou, near the Peacock River, was engraved with an integrated wood. The woman wears a round hat, and the breasts hang down. The eyes, nose, mouth, ears, hands and legs, etc. , weren't engraved concretely. This wooden figure is preserved in Xinjiang Institute of Archaeology now.

296, The Wooden Bowl with a Bird — Shaped Handle

9—8c B. C. L. 17cm Hejing

It was carved with an integrated wood. The handle was carved in the shape of a bird's head. It was excavated from the Ancient Tombs of Chawuhu Gully, and now is preserved in Bayingolin Museum.

297, **A Man and a Woman**

　　10—9c B. C.　H. 14,12cm Hami

　　All parts of these two wooden sculptures were engraved roughly; but, their genitals were engraved outstandingly and exaggeratively. The left one is a woman and the right is a man. The two sculptures, excavated from the Yanbulake Ancient Tombs, are preserved in Hami Museum now.

298, **Wooden Comb in Sheep Shape**

　　9c B. C.　L. 12. 4cm Hami

　　The comb, carved with wood, was excavated from the Wupu Ancient Tombs. Its handle was engraved in the shape of a sheep with a big horn. Now it is preserved in Xinjiang Institute of Archaeology.

299, **Wooden** *Si*

　　10c B. C.　L. 38. 5cm Hami

　　Si is a kind of farm tool used in ancient China. This one is in the rectangle — shape, and has a handle. There are some repaired and used traces on it. It was excavated from the Wupu Ancient Tombs and now is preserved in Xinjiang Institute of Archaeology.

300, **Wooden Bowl and Ladle**

　　1c A. D.　Bore of bowl 34cm, Length of ladle 28cm Lop

　　The bowl was lothed with wood; the ladle with a long handle was carved. They were excavated from the Shanpula Ancient Tombs, and now are preserved in Xinjiang Museum.

301, **Wooden Bow and Arrows**

　　5c B. C.　L. of bow 121cm Shanshan

　　The ends of the arrows were tied 3 — 4 pieces of feathers. These bow and arrows were excavated from the Subashi Ancient Tombs, Shanshan; and now they are preserved in Xinjiang Institute of Archaeology.

302, **Painted Wooden Comb**

　　1—2c A. D.　H. 9cm Lop

　　The part of the handle was carved in the semicircle shape, and painted in red, yellow, and green colors. The comb has 61 teeth. It was excavated from the Shanpula Ancient Tombs, and now is preserved in Xinjiang Museum.

303, **Sculpture on a Wooden Door—Leaf**

　　2—3c A. D.　L. 30cm Minfeng

　　This is a wooden door—leaf engraved with decorative patterns such as some kinds of the geometric figures, a man, and an elephant car-rying something, a monster with four legs, etc. It was found at the Niya Site. Now, it is preserved in Hotan Museum.

304, **Inscribed Wooden Tablet with Kharosthi Scripts**

　　1—3c A. D.　L. 27. 5cm Minfeng

　　It was cut with wood, and in the shape of rectangle. In the middle of the upper piece, there are three concave lines for tying up the strings and a square concave for sealing the mud. Inside the two pieces and the surface of the upper piece were the Kharosthi scripts in black inks. It was found at the Niya Site, and now is preserved in Hotan Museum.

305, **Wooden Table**

　　1—2c A. D.　L. 36. 5cm Lop

　　It was cut and carved with wood, and excavated from the Shanpula Ancient Tombs. Now it is preserved in Xinjiang Museum .

306, **Bowls and Cups**

　　3c A. D.　H. 6. 4—13cm Yuli

　　These bowls and cups were all lothed with wood, and unearthed from the Yingpan Site. Now, they are preserved in Bayingolin Museum.

307, **Standing Bodhisattva**

　　8c A. D.　H. 24cm Bachu

　　The wooden scupture was unearthed at the Kumuake Buddhist Temple Site, and then preserved at Berlin. The head and hands of Bodhisattva have been destroyed. The parts of chest and buttocks are very full, but the belly is thin. He stands on the lotus throne with bare feet.

308, **Standing Bodhisattva**

　　12c A. D.　H. 9cm Turfan

　　The wooden sculpture of bodhisattva was unearthed from Gaochang Ancient City, and then preserved at Berlin. The bodhisattva standing on the lotus throne wears a crown and dresses a magnificent suit of clothes. His face is full and peaceful.

309, **Seated Buddha**

　　9c A. D.　H. 15cm Turfan

　　The wooden sculpture was unearthed from the Gaochang Ancient City. The Buddha sits on a lotus pedestal. His right shoulder is partly covered by a section of shawl, and his hands rest on his lap. Around the mandorla is a border of addorsed spirals, carved from the full thickness of the wood. Now, it is preserved at

Berlin.

310, A Devata Playing Waist—drum

    6—7c A. D. H. 10. 9cm Baicheng

Found at the kizil caves, Baicheng, this wooden sculpture depicts a devata playing waist —drum. A waist—drum under his left arm, the devata sits with legs crossed. This kind of wooden sculptures are seldom seen among the cultural relics from Qiuci (Kuqa). Now it is preserved at Berlin.

311, Standing Buddha

    7c A. D. H. 18cm Baicheng

The Buddha wearing a long kasaya stands on a square base. His hands hold the kasaya. This wooden sculpture was unearthed at Kizil Cave Temple, and then preserved at Berlin.

312, A Bodhisattva Sitting Cross—Ankled

    7—8c A. D. H. 16cm Baicheng

The wooden sculpture of a bodhisattva sitting cross — ankled was unearthed from the Kizil Cave Temple, and then preserved at Berlin. The bodhisattva's hair is tied together with a ribbon, and the body is bare. The face is full and kindly; there is a nimbus behind the bodhisattva.

313, Head of a Buddha

    5—6c A. D. H. 11cm Bachu

This gilt head of a Buddha is an example of wooden sculptures from Tumshuk. The coiffure of closeclinging spiral looks that continue up into the topknot is one traditionally worn by Buddhist ascetics. This topknot, the distended earlobes, and the round urna in the forehead, which probably once contained a precious gem, are three of the textually prescribed mahapurushalakshanas. In addition to the gold leaf, traces of red and blue paint have survived.

314, Standing Avalokitesvara

    7c A. D. H. 38cm Shanshan

The standing Avalokitesvara, engraved with wood, wears a high crown which was decorated with ten human heads, the necklace and ribbons, and a wide skirt. The face is full and merciful, and the feet are bare. It was unearthed at Tuyugou (Toyok), Shanshan, and now is preserved at Berlin.

315, Standing Vajrapani

    8c A. D. H. 25. 6cm Yanji

This wooden sculpture of a vajrapani, who is the warrior attendant of Buddha, was unearthed at the Buddhist Temple Site, Qigex-ing. The vajrapani wears a small hat, and a long and wide cloak. His eyes glare forward. It is preserved at London, now.

316, Painted Wooden Niche for Buddha's Statues

    7—8c A. D. H. 28. 2cm Yanji

The painted wooden niche, unearthed from the Buddhist Temple Site, Qigexing, is in the shape of a pillar. All of the figures include three parts from the top to the bottom. On the top, there are a standing figure of Buddha and an attendant who holds up a canopy. In the middle, on the left of the standing Buddha are two Bodhisattvas and a man worshipping on bended knees to Buddha. On the bottom, there are two parts: the right is a Buddha, and the left are two donors. The wooden niche is preserved at London, now.

317, The Wooden Sculptures of Desk's Legs

    1—4c A. D. L. 67. 8cm H. 60cm Minfeng

The wooden sculptures, found at Niya Site, include four legs and four flank boards of a desk. They were engraved in the patterns of flowers and plants, such as the four — petals' flower, the eight — petals' lotus, and the pomegranate, etc.. All of these part of the desk were installed by the tenons and mortises. These sculptures are preserved at London, now.

318, Seated Buddha

    3—5c A. D. H. 25cm Bachu

The Buddha sits in the gesture of meditation, with the hands putting the palms together, and the legs coiling. He wears a crown, and there is a back — halo behind his back. This wooden sculpture, found at the Tuokuzisalai Site, is now preserved in the Cultural Center of Bachu County.

319, Reliquary

    8—9c A. D. H. 13. 4cm Shanshan

It was lothed with wood. The lid was made in the shape of the pagoda. On the surface of belly of the reliquary was painted with red, green, yellow, and black colors in the patterns of the lotus flowers. It was found at Tuyugou (Toyok), Shanshan; and now is preserved at Berlin.

320, Buddha's Reliquary

    8c A. D. H. 25cm Baicheng

The reliquary was lothed with wood. On its surface was painted in the geometric patterns. It was unearthed from the Kizil Cave Temple. Now it is preserved at Berlin.

321, Seated Buddha

　5c A. D. H. 16cm Bachu

This valuable wooden sculpture of Buddha was unearthed at Tumshuk Site. The Buddha sits cross — legedly. His head is slightly inclined forward; the hair and the topknot are smooth. The figure is preserved at Berlin, now.

322, Wooden Figure of a Groom

　7—9c A. D. H. 56cm Turfan

This painted wooden sculpture was formed with ten parts of engraved wood. The groom is a man of the non—Han nationalities. He wears a very high hat, a long robe and two boots. His eyes are big and the nose is high, and the hands are in the gesture of leading a horse. This figure, found at Astana, is preserved in Xinjiang Museum .

323, Wooden Ducks

　7c A. D. L. 15, 14cm Turfan

The two wooden sculptures of ducks, painted with red and black colors, were excavated from the Astana Ancient Tombs, and then preserved at London . The left one has a long beak. They were engraved in the gesture of swimming.

324, Wooden Ox and Cart

　6—7c A. D. L. 53cm Turfan

The ox was engraved with an integrated wood, and painted in black color. The cart has two wheels each of which has twelve spokes and a box—like body with two entrances. The wooden figures are preserved in Xinjiang Institute of Archaeology now.

325, Painted Wooden Jar

　7—9c A. D. H. 7cm Turfan

The jar was lothed with wood, and painted in the patterns of flowers, plants, and clouds. It was excavated from the Astana Ancient Tombs, and now is preserved in Xinjiang Museum .

326, A Woman

　7—9c A. D. H. 54cm Turfan

Being excavated from the Astana Ancient Tombs, the painted wooden sculpture of a woman is preserved in Xinjiang Museum , now.

327, A Young Woman

　7—9c A. D. H. 29. 5cm Turfan

The head and body were engraved with wood, and then painted; the arms and the long skirt were made of papers. The young woman wears a very high hair and puts her hands together on the belly. It was excavated from the Astana Ancient Tombs, and now is preserved in Xinjiang Museum .

328, The Wooden Figure of a Lokapala Stepping on a Demon

　7—9c A. D. H. 86cm Turfan

This figure was formed with about 30 parts of engraved wood, and painted with red, yellow green, blue, purple and black colors. The Lokapala wears a suit of armour; his right foot steps on a ugly, small demon. It was excavated from Astana Ancient Tombs, and now is preserved in Xinjiang Museum .

STONE STATUES

329, Stone Statue

　6—8c A. D. H. 160cm Altay

Engraved on a long and slender boulder, the figure has an oval face, prominent cheekbones, highly bulged nose, deep eye sockets, handlebar moustache and shaggy beard. His right hand holds a cup and rests on his chest, while his left hand places on his belly. It is preserved in Altay Museum now.

330, Lushi (Stone pillar engraved with running deer design)

　8c B. C. H. 300cm Qinghe (Qinggil)

The stone pillar has a square section, 23cm in each side. On the two faces of the pillar was engaved with running deer design, five deers on one face, six deers on the other face. Such kind of stone caving are mainly found in the east of the Altay Mountain and the west of the Mongolian Plateau. It is preserved in Altay Museum now.

331, Lushi

　8—3c B. C. H. 290cm Fuyan (Koktokay)

The stone pillar has a rectangular section, with 40cm in length and 20cm in width, and has engraved design on all of its four faces. The uppermost of the stone pillar was engraved with a circle representing the sun, below which are one row of dots and running deer design. Facing the same direction, every deers has a long neck, long jaws, thin waist, large antler and unclearly carved legs. With the first deer turned its head back, every latter deers stretches its head over the back of the former deer. It is preserved in Altay Museum now.

332, Stone Cup with a Beast — head — shaped Handle

6—5c B. C. L. 13—15cm Altay

Made of quartzite stone by chiselling method, it has a flat belly, and a mouth diameter of 13—15cm. The single handle takes the shape of a beast' head, which has long jaws, an opened mouth and erected ears. The decoration on the handle is one of the typical decoration forms used by the ancient nomadic people in northern grasslands. The stone cup is preserved in Xinjiang Institute of Archaeology, now.

333, Stone Female Figurine

18c B. C. H. 27. 5cm Ruoqing

Made of white stone by grinding method, the figurine has a smooth surface and a square head. Her hair, forehead, eyebrows, eyes and mouth are represented by painted black horizonal lines, where as her nose is represented by vertical lines. The three lines around her neck represent the collars of her garments. There are a pair of breasts on her bosom and a girdle around her waist. Her legs were not clearly carved. The stone figurine is preserved in Xinjiang Institute of Archaeology, now.

334, Stone Penis Model

Neolithic Age L. 13cm Mori

With two opposite grooves on the surface, it was roughly engraved out of a cobble. It is a symbol of ancient phallicism (masculine fertility worship) and is preserved in Mori Museum now.

335, Stone Mortar

10c B. C. Girth 12. 7cm Hoxud

Made by grinding after chiseled out a rough shape, it has a contracted mouth (rim turned inward), swollen body, round bottom, and a handle of 5. 5cm long extending from the mortar's body. It is preserved in Xinjiang Institute of Archaeology, now.

336, Macaque—shaped Stone Lamp

1c A. D. H. 30cm Barkol

Engraved out of a greenish stone, the macaque is in kneeling position on a square pedstal. Its hands raise upwards and hold a bowl as the lamp oil container on its head. It is preserved in Hami Museum now.

337, Stone Statue

7—9c A. D. H. 145cm Zhaosu

Carved on a long and thin boulder are only the sketch lines of the figure's head, showing a nearly rectangular form face, acute chin, prominent cheekbones, circular eyes, long nose, slightly opened mouth and handlbar moustache. The engraveing of the face has an solemn and unfeeling looks. It is preserved in Zhaosu Grand Lamasery now.

338, Stone Statue

7—9c A. D. H. 110cm Zhaosu

Engraved on a long and slender boulder the are figure's eyes, eyebrows, nose, mouth and handlebar moustache in proper scale. His hands are shown by incised lines, with the right hand holding a goblet resting on his chest, and the left hand holding a dagger resting on his belly. It is preserved in Zhaosu Grand Lamasery now.

339, Stone Statue

7—9c A. D. H. 108cm Zhaosu

Carved on a long and thin boulder are only the sketch lines of the head, showing an oval face, prominent cheekbones, short beards, big eyes, nose and mouth. It is preserved in Zhaosu Grand Lamasery now.

340, Stone Statue

7—9c A. D. H. 230cm Zhaosu

The statue has a capped head, a nearly rectangular form face, bulged nose, deep eye sockets, handlebar moustache, decorated girdle and long hair in braids extending behindwards to his waist. His right hand holds a cup resting on his chest, while his left hand rests on his belly. His legs have not been clearly carved. Below his body are some Sogdian inscriptions. It is preserved in The Stud Farm of Zhaosu County now.

341, Stone Statue

6—8c A. D. H. 285cm, Wunquan (Arixang)

Engraved on a sandstone boulder, the figure has a rotund face, opened eyes, broad bulged nose, closed mouth, handlebar moustache, a coat with circular turndown collar on his body and a broad girdle around his waist. His right hand holds a goblet, while his left hand holds a tagger. There is also sword worn on his waist. Such kind of stone statues are believed as the remains of ancient Turkic people. It is preserved in Xinjiang Museum , now.

342，**Painted Stone Statue**

　　7—9c A. D. H. 130cm Altay

Engraved in low relief, on a long rectangular shape boulder, the figure has a nearly rectangular form face, long and narrow eyes, handlebar noustache, distinct shoulder and long curved eyebrows extending to the nose. His right hand holds a goblet and rests on his chest, while his left hand places on his belly. It was painted with red pigments on all of raised parts. Unfortunately, this stone statue has been broken into two parts along his neck. It is preserved in Xinjiang Institute of Archaeology, now.

343，**Stone Statue**

　　7—9c A. D. H. 160cm Bole

Engraved in low relief, on a long and thin boulder, the figure has an oval face, bulged eyes, eyebrows, nose, handlebar moustache and a deep groove under his neck. His right hand holds a goblet resting on his chest.

344，**Stone Statue**

　　7—9c A. D. H. 110cm The Stud Farm of Emin (Dorbiljin)

Roughly engraved on a reddish grey sandstone boulder, the figure has a square face, acute chin, prominent cheekbones, highly bulged nose, deep eye sockets, handlebar moustache, and long eyebrows extending to the nose. His torso below the neck has not been clearly engraved. It is preserved in Tacheng Museum now.

345，**Stone Statue**

　　7—9c A. D. H. 90cm Usu

Engraved on a long and thin boulder are only the sketch lines of the statue's head, which has an oval face, slightly opened eyes and mouth, broad bulged nose, thick lips, handlebar moustache, and peach—shaped, carved in low relief, decoration under his neck.

346，**Female Stone Statue**

　　7—9c A. D. H. 60cm Altay

Engraved on a triangular form boulder, the figure has a rotund face, prominent cheekbones, circular eyes, broad nose, slightly closed mouth, and a pair of breasts on her bosom. Her right hand is placed on her chest. Having life—like looks, the rarely—seen stone statue is preserved at Kimqi Township now.

347，**Stone Statue**

　　7—8c A. D. H. 190cm Toli

Engraved on a long and slender boulder are only the sketch lines of the statue's head, showing a reversed triangular form face, highly bulged nose, deep eye sockets and handlebar moustache. The carving of the face has a solemn look. It is preserved at Toli County now.

348，**Stone Statue**

　　7—9c A. D. H. 250cm Jeminay

Engraved on a boulder, the figure has a round head wearing a square cap, bulged nose and eyes, an unclear mouse, and wide and flat shoulders. The body below shoulder takes a rectangular form. This stone statue stands at Shentash, Shawozi Mountain now.

349，**Stone Statue**

　　7—9c A. D. H. 62cm Aheqi

The most magnificent characteristic of this statue is the high — bridged nose. It almost takes half of the length of the face. It was found in Awenku, Aheqi.

350，**Stone Statue**

　　7—9c A. D. H. 110cm Zhaosu

This stone statue is roughly engraved in intaglio out of a rectangular stone. Only its face can be recognized.

351，**Stone Statue**

　　7—9c A. D. H. 90cm Yiwu

This simiply—engraved statue has a round face and apricot—shaped eyes. Now it is preserved at Ketuoguole, Yiwu.

352，**Votive Stone Stupa of Ghaochang**

　　4—5c A. D. H. 66cm Turfan

This stone stupa, made of sandstone, consists of an octagonal base, a cylindrical central portion, and a crown with eight niches surmaounted by lotus. The niches contain eight Buddha figures, one of them is Maitreya. the central portion is engraved all round with thirty — five columns containing the Ekottarikagama in Chinese. Bodhisattva figures are incised into the eight faces of the base. Now, it is preserved in Berlin.

353，**Stone Mask**

　　10—13c A. D. H. 23. 5cm Xinyuan

This sandstone mask was engraved and polished exquisitely. It has deep sockets and protruding pupils with two holes. Now it is preserved in Xinjiang Institute of Archaeology.

354，**Stone Tower**

　　18c A. D. H. 15cm Hejing

This hexahedral tower was carved and polished finely. The total nine storeys descend in diameter from the bottom to the top. There engraved one niche — shaped window in every storeys above the second storey. This tower is preserved in Bayingolin Museum now.

CLAY SCULPTURES

355, Devata

6—7c A. D. H. 31. 5cm Yanji

The devata has a high hair worn in a coil and a full, round face. There are two decorative ribbons intersecting at the chest. This clay sculpture, unearthed at the Buddhist Temple Site, Qigexing, is now preserved at London.

356, Gandharva

6c A. D. H. 14cm Hotan

The gandharva with a head—halo has hair tied together. His body is bare, and the hands are holding a ribbon. The clay sculpture was found at Kadeluku, and now is preserved at London.

357, Pottery Cup

3—4c A. D. L. 19. 5cm Hotan

This yellow, fine pottery water dropper was engraved in the shapes of a man's head and a cow's head. It was found at the Yotkan Site. Both of the ends of it have a hole threading together from the top to bottom. It was called rhyton in Greece. Now, this water dropper is preserved in Xinjiang Museum .

358, Musicians

4—5c A. D. H. 12cm Yanji

Inside the semicircle—shaped niches, sustained with the short pillars of Indro—style, there are two musicians who are playing the different musical instruments (the cymal and the flute). It was unearthed from the Yotkan Site. Now it is preserved at London.

359, Pottery Bird

2—3c A. D. H. 10. 8cm Hotan

The bird has a high crest and a long beak. On its surface was engraved in the patterns of feathers. It was found at Yotkan Site. Now it is preserved at London.

360, Pottery Cup

3—4c A. D. L. 17cm Hotan

This pottery cup is similar to No. 357, but the part bellow the man's head has been destoyed. It was also found at Yotkan, and now is preserved in Xinjiang Museum .

361, Head of a Man

3—4c A. D. H. 13cm Hotan

The yellow pottery sculpture of a man's head was found at the Yotkan Site. The man has the rough features with bushy eyebrows, big eyes, thick moustaches and beards. It is preserved in Hotan Museum now.

362, Pottery Sculpture of a King

2—3c A. D. H. 12cm Hotan

This sculpture of a man was found at Hotan. The man seats on a chair which has a high back, and puts his right hand down the handrail. He was considered as a king. The sculpture is preserved at London, now.

363, The Mould of Buddha's Face

4—9c A. D. H. 25cm W. 23cm Pishan

The plaster mould was found at Duwa, Pishan. The face of Buddha is full, dignified, and kindly. The eyes and eyebrows are long and thin, and the nose is high and long. It is now preserved in Hotan Musem.

364, Seated Buddha

3—4c A. D. H. 26cm Lop

The yellow — brown clay sculpture was found at the Buddhist Temple Site, Rewake. The Buddha sits cross—leggedly and the hands pile up in front of his belly. There is a head—halo behind his bead, and a big, open lotus flower behind the body of Buddha. Now, it is preserved in Hotan Museum.

365, Standing Buddha

5c A. D. H. 20cm Hotan

The Buddha has a head—halo and a nimbus surrounded by the flame. He stands with his right hand holding upwards and the left hand putting down on his left side; under his feet are the wave. This clay sculpture in the Gandhara — style was unearthed at the Karadong Site, and now is preserved at London.

366, Half—figure of a Woman

1—3c A. D. H. 12. 4cm Hotan

The pottery sculpture shows the half—figure of a young woman. Her hairs hangs down her shoulder; the big eyes, high and straight nose were moulded gracefully and vividly. It was found at Yotkan Site. Now it is preserved at London.

367, Pottery Monkey

7—8c A. D. H. 6. 8cm Yotkan, Hotan

The monkey was moulded out of clay first and then burnt. It is in the posture of kneeling with the right hand resting on the breast and the left hand on the sexual organ. It is now preserved in Lushun, Liaoning province.

368, Seated Buddha

7—8c A. D. H. 102cm Yanji

This painted clay sculpture was unearthed from the Buddhist Temple Site, Qigexing, and then preserved at Berlin. The Buddha sits on a high, finely painted pedestal, conceived at the top as a lotus throne with rounded contours. The hair is high and tied together on the top. The left hand puts down on his legs, while the right raises up.

369, Head of a Bodhisattva

4—5c A. D. Bachu

This clay sculpture was found at the Buddhistic Temple in the Tuoguzishalai Ancient Town. Now it is preserved at Paris.

370, Head of a Demon

8—9c A. D. H. 30. 3cm Turfan

This clay sculpture of a demon was unearthed at the Sengim Buddhist Temple, and then preserved at Berlin. A broad cap in the form of a helmet comes down low over the head. The protruding eyeballs, the broad nose, and the large, expressive mouth give the face a humorous air. The mask effect is heightened by the generous application of paint.

371, Head of a Bodhisattva

6c A. D. H. 27cm Baicheng

This painted clay sculpture of a bodhisattva was unearthed at the Kizil Cave Temple, and then preserved at Berlin. With the broad face, the short nose, the leftward glance of the eyes, the individuality of the face heightened still more by the treatment of crown and hair. The crown consists of a red — and — green wreath with two slanting ornamental disks on top.

372, Half—Figure of a Devata

7—8c A. D. H. 52cm Yanji

This is the painted clay sculpture of a devata, unearthed at the Qigexing Buddhist Temple Site, and then preserved at Berlin. The hair is tied together, and there are some ornaments decorated at the neck, shoulders, and chest. etc.

373, Standing Devata

7c A. D. H. 72. 7cm Bachu

This painted clay sculpture was unearthed at Tumshuk Site and then preserved at Berlin. The standing devata has a full and round face with curly hair; he wears a green shawllike garment, which leaves the right shoulder and arm uncovered. The devata stands on her right leg; the left leg raised in a dancer's posture. The right hand raises but the left hand has been destroyed.

374, Standing Clay Monkey

5—6c A. D. H. 23cm Bachu

This personified clay figure has a human's body and a monkey's head. A wooden stick is held by the hands. This strange figure is probably a deity in Buddhist Story.

375, Head of a Bodhisattva

6—7c A. D. Kuqa

The bodhisattva has a long and thin eyes and eyebrows, and curved moustache. This painted clay sculpture was found at Kumtura, and now it is preserved at Tokyo.

376, The Clay Sculpture with Human Head and Elephant's Body

7—8c A. D. H. 63. 5cm Baicheng

This painted clay sculpture was excavated from the Kizil Cave Temple, and now is preserved at Berlin. Under the human head, there is the body in the shape of the elephant, with the head, eyes, ears, foot, and the long nose stretching from the back. There is a rectangle — shaped base behind the statue. Now, this sculpture is preserved at Berlin.

377, Head of a Buddha

3—5c A. D. H. 50cm Ruoqiang

The head of Buddha was unearthed at the Buddhist Temple Site, Milan. The face of Buddha is regular, full and beautiful and the expression is merciful and peaceful. Now, this clay sculpture is preserved in Xinjiang Institute of Archaeology.

378, Head of a Bodhisattva

6—7c A. D. H. 30cm Yanji

This painted clay sculpture of a bodhisattva who wears a golden crown was unearthed from the Buddhist Temple Site, Qigexing; and now it is preserved at London.

379, Head of a Man

6—7c A. D. H. 14cm Yanji

The clay sculpture, unearthed from the Buddhist Temple Site, Qigexing, is a man's head of Brahman. It is preserved at London, now.

380, Head of a Bodhisattva

7—8c A. D. H. 20. 5cm Yanji

This clay sculpture of a bodhisattva was unearthed from the Buddhist Temple Site, Qigexing. Now it is preserved at London.

381, Warrior

6—7c A. D. H. 42cm Yanji

The warrior wears a suit of armour, and holds a sword and a shield in his right hand; but the left hand has been destroyed. His expression is mighty and dignified. This clay sculpture, unearthed from the Qigexing Buddhist Timple Site, is now preserved at London.

382, A Woman

7—9c A. D. H. 56cm Turfan

Being excavated from the Astana Ancient Tombs, the woman's head was sculptured with the clay and then painted; but the body and legs were made of wood, and the arms were made of papers. She wears a suit of brocade clothes. Now, it is preserved in Xinjiang Museum.

383, Head of a Woman

7—9c A. D. H. 16. 5cm Turfan

This painted clay sculpture of the head of a woman wearing a manly hair, was excavated from the Astana Ancient Tombs. It is preserved in Xinjiang Museum.

384, A Woman in Meditation

7—9c A. D. H. 13cm Turfan

The painted clay sculpture, excavated from the Astana Ancient Tombs, is the image of a woman who is in meditation. Her head is propped up by the right hand, and inclined to the right. She dresses a long suit of clothes and sits on the ground. Now this statue is preserved in Xinjiang Museum.

385, Eunuches

7—9c A. D. H. 34. 5cm Turfan

These two sculptures, painted partly, were excavated from the Astana Ancient Tombs. The two eunuches wear the silk robes. The part of heads was moulded with earth, but the chest was engraved of wood; the arms were made of papers and the legs were made of the wooden sticks. The faces were treated by polishing and painting. These figure are preserved in Xinjiang Museum, now.

386, Blue Demon

8—9c A. D. H. 21. 7cm Turfan

The clay sculpture was excavated from the Sengim Ancient Tombs. It gains its fearsome aspect from the protruding eyeballs, peering to the side from under bushy, twirled eyebrows, the large, vertical third eye on the forehead, and the fangs in the open mouth. Now it is preserved in Berlin.

387, Head of a Warrior

8—9c A. D. H. 22cm Turfan

The painted clay sculpture is now preserved at Seoul, South Korea. The warrior wears a helmet, and has a rude face with the protruding eyeballs, big and wide nose, and the stretching mouth, expressing the condition of a warrior who is angry.

388, A Civil Official

7—9c A. D. H. 24. 2cm Turfan

The civil official stands and holds a writing brush in his right hand; a roll of papers is held under his left arm. This painted clay sculpture, excavated from the Astana Ancient Tombs, is preserved in Xinjiang Museum, now.

389, Male Figures

7—9c A. D. H. 24, 29, 28cm (From left to right) Turfan

These painted clay sculptures of three men were all excavated from the Astana Ancient Tombs. The left one is a soldier wearing a suit of armour. A shield is held in the left hand of the middle one. Now, these clay sculptures are preserved in Xinjiang Institute of Archaeology.

390, One—Humped Camel

7—9c A. D. H. 72cm Turfan

This clay sculpture of a standing one—humped camel was excavated form the Astana Ancient Tombs. It is preserved in Xinjiang Museum, now.

391, An Ox

7—9c A. D. L. 31cm Turfan

The painted clay sculpture of an ox was excavated from Astana Ancient Tombs. The ox raises its head and stretches forward, in the gesture of being towed. There is a high protrusion of the bone on its back. Now it is preserved in Xinjiang Institute of Archaeology.

392, A Man

7—9c A. D. H. 110cm Turfan

The painted clay sculpture of a man was excavated from the Astana Ancient Tombs. The man has a high hair tied together on the top, and wears a long gown and boots. He has a high nose and thick beards. All of these express the characteristic of a Hu man, who is the non－Han nationality. The statue is preserved in Xinjiang Museum , now.

393, The Polo Game

　　7－9c A. D. H. 26. 5cm Turfan

The rider raises his right hand and holds a stick, looks attentively at the ground, in the gesture of batting. The polo game, originated from Persia, propagated into China in the Tang Dynasty (619－907A. D.) and became a prevalent fashion in the noble's life at that time. This painted clay sculpture, excavated from Astana, is preserved in Xinjiang Museum , now.

394, Pottery Horse

　　9－13c A. D. H. 13,4cm Turfan

Being found at the Yingshar Ancient Town, the grey－red pottery sculpture is in the shape of a horse that carries a bowl－shaped lamp on the back. The horse raises its head and the tail hangs down the ground. It is a practical handicraft article, and now preserved in Xinjiang Museum .

395, Animal Guarding the Graves

　　6－9c A. D. H. 86cm Turfan

The painted clay sculpture excavated from the Astana Ancient Tombs, is one of the animal guarding the graves. It has a human's head wearing helmet, a leopard－like body, horse－like feet, and a snake－like tail. The statue is preserved in Xinjiang Museum , now.

396, The Animal Guarding the Graves

　　7－9c A. D. H. 75cm Turfan

The painted clay sculpture of the animal, used to guard, suppress, and drive out the demons and ghosts in the underground, was also excavated from Astana. The animal composes with four kinds of animals; the lion's head, the leopard's body, the ox's feet, and the fox's tail. It is preserved in Xinjiang Museum , now.

397, The Warrior Riding a Horse

　　7－9 c A. D. H. 39. 5cm Turfan

This painted clay sculpture was excavated from the Astana Ancient Tombs. The warrior wearing a suit of armour, rides a tall, black horse. It belongs to the kind of the figures of warriors and horses buried with the dead. Now, it is preserved in Xinjiang Institute of Archaeology.

398, Female Half－figure

8－9c A. D. H. 43cm Bachu

The clay sculpture, unearthed from the Tumshuk Site, is the half－figure of a woman. Her hairs are very high and hang down the shoulders. Her face, the eyebrows, eyeballs, nose, and mouth, etc, are very beautiful and full. But under her neck, the body was treated roughly. This statue is preserved at Seoul, South Korea.

399, Acrobatics

　　7－9c A. D. H. 12. 8cm Turfan

The painted clay sculpture, excavated from the Astana Ancient Tombs, show three men who were performing the acrobatics. The man rides on the back of a horse, which is acted by two men. Now, it is preserved in Xinjiang Museum .

400, A Standing Horse

　　7－9c A. D. H. 56cm Turfan

This painted clay sculpture of a standing horse was excavated from the Astana Ancient Tombs, too. The horse holds up its head highly and opens mouth. It is preserved in Xinjiang Museum .

401, A Young Woman Riding a Horse

　　7－9c A. D. H. 39cm Turfan

The young woman wears a high hat with wide border, and rides a tall horse. This painted clay sculpture was excavated from the Astana Ancient Tombs, now is preserved in Xinjiang Museum .

402, A Black Man

　　7－9c A. D. H. 12. 5cm Turfan

The painted clay sculpture, found at Astana, expresses a man who was sporting. He has a short hair and the lip is thicker. He only wears a reddish－orange shorts, and stands on the ground with bare feet. His face and body was painted with black colours. It is considered as the figure of a black, and now is preserved in Xinjiang Museum .

403, Dancers with Lion's Mask

　　7－9c A. D. H. 13cm Turfan

The painted clay sculpture, excavated from the Astana Ancient Tombs, showing the dancing played by the double dancers with a lion's mask, is preserved in Xinjiang Museum , now. The surface of the statue was combed to the crooked, small, and fine lines in the hair－shape.

404, A Dancer

7—9c A. D. H. 10. 2cm Turfan

This painted clay sculpture shows a man who is dancing in the wrestle gesture. It was excavated from the Astana Ancient Tombs, and now it is preserved in Xinjiang Museum .

405, Group of Working Women

7—9c A. D. H. 9. 7—16cm Turfan

These painted clay sculptures were excavated from the Astana Ancient Tombs. All of them are four women who are working at the process of threshing, picking and choosing, milling and rolling (from the left to right). These sculptures are preserved in Xinjiang Museum , now.

406, Clay Sculpture

7—8c A. D. H. 80cm Turfan

This painted clay sculpture was also excavated from Astana. It is the sign of *You*, corresponding to the cock, one of the twelve Earthly Branches. It has a cock's head and man's body, and now it is preserved in Xinjiang Museum .

407, Clay Sculpture

7—9c A. D. H. 75cm Turfan

The painted clay sculpture of a man with the pig's head and human body, was excavated from the Astana Ancient Tombs. It is the sign of Hai, corresponding to the pig, one of the twelve Earthly Branches, used to symbolize the year in which a person is born. Now, the statue is preserved in Xinjiang Museum.

JADES

408, Jade Applique Plate with Twin Dragon in Relief

10—12c A. D. L. 20cm Yining (Gulia)

The white — jade plate has a rectangular form. The twin dragons were engraved in high relief, with their bodies twined around each other, and with many spiral designs on the body surface. It is preserved in Ili Museum now.

409, Jade Inkslab

18c A. D. L. 20. 5cm Turfan

The inkslab was engraved out of a white—jade lump. One side of it is a rectangular pit for grinding the stick of Chinese ink. The other side of it is a lively lying tiger figurine, with the tiger's front limbs extending forwards, hind limbs going down on its knees, head raising and facing forwards, and with prominent

muscle, sharp teeth and claws. It is preserved in Xinjiang Museum , now.

410, Necklaces

1—4c A. D. Ruoqiang

The necklace beads were made of blue, red, green, yellow or black color, cylindrical, spherical or oval shape agate or sheep — fat — like jade lumps by grinding and drilling methods. They are preserved in Xinjiang Institute of Archaeology, now.

411, *Bi* (A round flat piece of jade)

Chalcolithic age, D. 7 cm, Qiemo(Qarqan)

Made by grinding method, this jade article has a yellowish blue color with some brown spots, a round flat shape of 2. 5cm thick, and a hole, 1. 6—1. 9cm in diameter, in its center. It is preserved in Xinjiang Institute of Archaeology, now.

412, Jade Beads

18c B. C. Ruoqiang(Qarkilik)

Either cylindrical — shaped or rhombohedron —shaped, the beads were made of yellowish translucent nephrite lumps. They are preserved in Xinjiang Institute of Archaeology, now.

413, Agate Seal with Human Figure in Relief

4—5c A. D. H2. 2cm Turfan

The half—lentoid seal was made of orange color agate by engraving in low relief. On the seal's surface is a standing human figure, with his head facing leftwards, long hair, highly bulged nose, deep eye sockets, circular earrings, shaggy beards, a short robe on his body, and a girdle around his waist. His left hand raises to the front of his face, while his right hand holds a cup placing on his waist. It is preserved in Turfan Museum now.

414, Agate Seal with Human Figure in Relief

4—5c A. D. H. 2. 2cm Bachu

Showing somewhat Mesopotamia style, on the orange agate seal's oval surface is a human figure, in profile, with a hat on his head, a highly bulged nose, deep eye sockets, an apron —like ornament around his waist, a load on its shoulder, and boots on his feet in a walking posture. It is preserved in Xinjiang Museum , now.

415, Jade Cup with Two Dragon—shaped Handles

18—19c A. D. H. 5. 5cm Urumqi

Engraved out of a sheep — fat — like jade

lump with exquisite craftsmanship, the cup has a slender shape, thin cup wall, open mouth, small circular leg and two dragon—shaped handles. The dragon has its front claws holding the cup rim, head resting on its front limbs, hind limbs placing on the lower part of the cup wall, and its body bent to a bow form. Around the rim surface are one circle of elegant rectangular spirals. It is preserved in Xinjiang Museum, now.

416, Jade *Yu* with Tiger Eating Donkey Statuette

18c A. D. L. 29cm Turfan

It was engraved out of a jade lump. The lively tiger is on bended knees, with its front talons holding a donkey and his teeth biting the donkey's neck, while the donkey wails and struggles. It is preserved in Xinjiang Museum, now.

417, White—jade Armrest

18—19c A. D. H. 34cm Kashi

Engraved out of a white—jade lump in high relief, the frame—fordered armrest has a rhomboid net form structure. The left upper part of it takes a spiral shape, while the lower left part takes the shape of a half—opened flower. It is preserved in Xinjiang Museum, now.

418, White—jade Dish

18c A. D. D. 22cm Hotan

Engraved out of a white—jade lump, the shallow dish has a wide flared mouth (rim turned outwards). Bulged lines on inner surface divids the dish into two sections. There are rows of inscriptions on the inner surface, one in Arabic alphabet, the other in Persian alphabet, meaning "Allah is the only supernatural being. The treasured sword is the only sharp sword for our hero. The omnipotent Allah will bless us and protect us from all disasters and sufferings". It is preserved in Xinjiang Museum, now.

419, Peach—shaped Jade Bowl

18—19c A. D. H. 6cm Kashi

Engraved out of a sheep—fat—like jade lump, the two peach—shaped bowls were connected together by a tiger—shaped connecting handle at the one side, and interlocking branch and flower decoration at the other side. It is preserved in Xinjiang Museum now.

420, White—jade 3—opening Lamp

12—15c A. D. L. 23cm Kashi

Engraved out of white jade lump, the lamp has three protruding opening. The central part of the lamp was carved into a 12—petalled spherical form, with a hole in the middle connecting with the three openings. It is preserved in Xinjiang Museum, now.

ARCHITECTURES

421, Stupa in Loulan Ancient City

3—4c A. D. H. 10. 4m Ruoqiang

The stupa is situated in the Loulan Ancient City. The upper part of it was made of earth—bricks, but the part of the base was hammered with earth. Among each two storeys of the earth—bricks, there is a branch storey, which was used to reinforce the stupa.

422, The Tuguluk—Temur Mazar

1365A. D. Huocheng

Tuguluk—Temur (1329—1362A. D.) is the 7th generation descedant of Genghis Khan. He was the first Mongolian khan who accepted Islam in ancient Xinjiang. The mazar is located at the place 38km northeastern to Houcheng Town. It is also the cuboid structure with a dome on the top, inlaid with blue, white and purple glazed tiles. It is a famous ancient Islamic building in Xinjiang.

423, The Ancient City of Jiaohe

2c B. C.—14c A. D. Turfan

The Ancient City of Jiaohe is located 10km to the west of Turfan City, on an island—like platform which was surrounded by the rivers. It was planned on a cliff without a city wall, but the cliff itself was its best protection. There is a slope path leading out of the southern gate, connecting the only central path from north to south. The eastern and the western parts of the city has a big Buddhist monastery and group of stupas.

424, Niches and the Figures of Buddha

9—10c A. D. Turfan

There is a pillar made by ramming earth in the center of the Buddhist Temple of Jiaohe Ancient City. Niches were made on four sides of the pillar and clay figures of seated Buddha were moulded inside the niches. The figures are all damaged. This kind of pillar, different from that of the Buddhist temples in Inner China, is a transformation of the Buddhist architecture in India.

425, **Group of Stupas**

5—6c A. D. Turfan

The group of stupas, situated in the north-western part of Jiaohe Ancient City, take a big stupa as the dominant factor, distributed with 25 small stupas at four corners.

426, **The Ancient City of Gaochang**

4—14c A. D. Turfan

The ancient city is located 40km to the east of the Turfan City. It is roughly in square—shape with a total circumference of about 5km, built by ramming earth and laying bricks, including three parts: the outer city, the inner city, and the palace city.

427, **City Wall of Gaochang Ancient City**

5—13c A. D. Turfan

This picture shows a section of the city wall in the western part of Gaochang Ancient City. The wall was made by ramming earth. Although being remains, the wall reminds us of the magnificence in the past.

428, **The Stupa of Gaochang**

7—9c A. D. H. 7m Turfan

This stupa, located at the southeastern part of Gaochang Ancient City, is very complicated and advanced in structure. Its base, formed with two storeys square platforms and a round storey, is about 3m high. On the top of it, there is a cylinder—shaped body with three storeys. In the one side of the stupa, there are some rooms, where some wall paintings have been protected. Both of the stupa and rooms are all earth—bricks structures.

429, **The Kizil Caves**

4—8c A. D. Baicheng

The Kizil Cave Temple is located at the northern bank of Muzart River, east of the Baicheng Town. It is the biggest cave temple in the areas of Kuqa, Baicheng, eg. the area of the ancient Qiuci Kingdom. It has 236 caves which have been numbered, including two kinds of caves: the monks' living quarters and those for worshipping and other religious activities. The style of this building is very unique.

430, **The Cave with a Centural Pillar**

4—5c A. D. Kizil, cave 100

This kind of cave with a centural pillar is common in Kizil Cave Temple. This picture shows the front of the centural pillar of cave 100. In the center, there is a big niche with two small niches on its sides; on each side of the centural pillar, there is a path leading to the backroom. The niches were used to lay up the Buddha's statues; wall paintings were usually painted on the surfaces of the pathes, backroom, and the sides of the niches.

431, **Stupa in Milan**

3—4c A. D. H. 3. 5m Ruoqiang

This stupa of earth—bricks structure, situated in the Buddhist Temple Site of Milan, expresses an special style in building. There is a round wall around the cylinder—shaped body of the stupa. On the lower surface of the stupa's body and inside the walls, there are some wall paintings, such as the very famous painting of the Winged Angels, which was found newly in 1989.

432, **Stupa in the Niya Site**

3—4c A. D. H. about 5m Minfeng

The Niya Site is situated in the Taklamalan Desert, 120km north to the Minfeng Town. The earth — bricks structure can be parted three storeys: the two lower storeys are the square base of the stupa, and the 3rd is the stupa's body which is in the cylinder shape.

433, **The Mol Stupas**

5—6c A. D. Kashi

The stupas are located 30km north to the city of Kashgar, including two stupas. One is in the shape of square, which has been destroyed gravely; the other is 12. 8m high, in the shape of cylinder with two square storeys of bases, and a semicircle top. The two stupas retained some clear traces of evolution and was effected by the style of the Indian stupas. They are one of the creams of the Buddhist architectures in Xinjiang.

434, **The Rewak Buddhist Temple**

5—6c A. D. Lop

The ruins of the temple is situated in the desert, 50km north to the Town of Lop. The square temple was built by laying earth — bricks. In the center, there is a stupa which is about 10m high. Around the stupa is a square wall of which each side is 60m long. In the past, many painted clay sculptures have been found in this temple.

435, **Stupa**

6—7c A. D. H. 7. 5m Kuqa

The stupa is situated in the Subashi Site which is 20km northeastern to the Kuqa Town.

The earth—bricks structure has a square base and a cylinder—shaped body which has a semi-circle top on it. This kind of stupas express a style of primitive simplicity on the modelling.

436, Beacon Tower

　　7—9c A. D. H. 13. 6m Shanshan

　　The beacon tower, made of earth—bricks, was located at the northwest 5. 5km to Bagezhuang of Lianmuqin Township. It is in the square shape with a big bottom and a small top. Inside the hollow tower, there is a centural pillar, which has a cave on its southern wall and eastern wall.

437, The Kizil—Kargha Stupa

　　2—3c A. D. H. 15m Kuqa

　　The tall and magnificent Stupa, near the Kizil—Kargha Cave Temple, is located 10km northwest to Kuqa Town. It is a square and rammed structure. In the rammed earth, there are some reed—branch storeys to reinforce the stupa.

438, The Id Kah Mosque

　　1426 A. D. Kashi

　　The Id Kah Mosque, situated in the center of Kashgar City, is the biggest mosque in Xinjiang. Its whole areas is about 16,000sqm, including the worshipping hall, preaching hall, gate, and other subsidiary buildings. The big gate, which has a 18m high minaret on both sides, is 12m high; on the top of the minaret, there is a crescent. The mosque is the typical Islamic structure in Xinjiang.

439, The Worshipping Hall of Id Kah Mosque

　　The layout and structure of this worshipping hall are very complicated. It includes the inner hall, the outer hall, the entrance corridor, the lecture room, and the garden, etc. The entrance corridor is 160m wide, and 16m deep; Its roof is sustained by 140 pillars.

440, The Apakhoja Tomb

　　1640A. D. Kashi

　　The tomb, also called the Tomb of the Fragrant Imperial Concubine, is situated in the northeastern part of Kashgar City. It is the burial ground for Apakhoja, the Islamic ruler of Kashgar, and his family. The cuboid building which was mainly made of bricks, is whole high 26m, 35m long, and 29m wide, and there is a minaret at each of the four corners and the sides of the gate. The top is in the shape of a dome, of which the diameter is 17m,

and there is a minaret and a crescent on it. The surface of the tomb was inlaid with green, blue, yellow, and other color glazed tiles. It is a model of the art of ancient Islamic tomb building in Xinjiang.

441, The Kuqa Mosque

　　Rebuilt in 1935 Kuqa

　　It is said that the Kuqa Mosque has been initially built in the 16th century A. D.. In 1931, it was destroyed by the fire, and in 1931—35, it was rebuilt. The mosque, made of bricks, stone and wood, includes the worshipping hall, minaret, gate, religious court, and hostel, etc. The two minarets are 18m high, and the main hall is propped up by 88 wooden pillars, that were painted and carved in various decorative patterns.

442, The Emin Minaret and Mosque

　　1777 A. D. H. 37m Turfan

　　The Emin Minaret is also called the *Sugong* Minaret. It was built by Emin Holja, the King of Turfan, and his son Suleyman, during the reign of Qian Long Emperor of the Qing Dynasty. The brick—structure includes two parts; the minaret and the mosque. Outside the door of the minaret, there is a stone tablet carved in Chinese and Jagatai (Caqadai) characters on it. It is a famous ancient building in Xinjiang.

443, The Body of the Emin Minaret

　　The body is the main part of the minaret. It is 37m high, and was entirely made of yellow bricks, decorated with fourteen kinds of geometrical patterns such as triangle, rhombus, cross, and ripple, etc. The structure is in the shape of cylinder with regularly contracts from bottom to top. There are 72 steps of spiral stairway inside the minaret to arrive the top.

444, The Tatar Mosque

　　1901 L. 35m W. 10m H. 7m Tacheng

　　The mosque situated in the center of the Tacheng City was formed with two parts. The upper part is the housetop in the yurt shape that was made of the iron sheets and then painted with green paint. The house was made of bricks and in the cuboid shape with 18 windows around its walls.

445, Aimaiertai Tomb

　　About 1934 H. 10cm Berjin

　　The brick—structure tomb is situated near the Dulate Town. Its door faces west; The front part is in the shape of a yurt; but the back is in the shape of a tower with a crescent at the top. Some kinds of patterns of the geomtric figures were used for this building. The modelling of this tomb is very distrinctive.

446, The Tomb of the King of Hami

1840 A.D. Hami

The tomb is 1km western to the Huicheng of Hami City. The whole architectural group includes three parts: the Big Tomb (tomb of the 7th and 8th kings), the Small Tomb (1st—6th, 9th kings), and the Big Worshipping Hall. This tomb in the picture is the Big Tomb, which turns its door to the west. The cuboid structure with a dome which has a column at each of the four corners, was made of bricks and inlaid with the blue glazed tiles on its surface.

447, The Bell and Drum Tower of Huiyuan Town

1882 A.D. Huocheng

The Huiyuan Town is situated in Huiyuan Township, Huocheng, and this famous tower is in the center of the town. The wood—brick structure is three storeys high with three layers of eaves, decorated with carved beams and painted pillars. The bell and drum are hung on the second storey. The Huiyuan Town was the capital of the Ili General Government in the history, and was the political and cultural center in Qing Dynasty's Xinjiang.

448, The Main Temple of the Lamasery

1898 A.D. Zhaosu

The Lamasery is also called the Shengyou Temple, which is located 2km northwest from the town of Zhaosu. It is the biggest lamasery in Xinjiang, including three parts: the fore, main, and rear temples, which were all made of bricks and wood. The Main Temple has a seven—room square layout, and the whole structure has upturned eaves and layered garrets, carved beams and painted pillars that are magnificent and majestic. It is a traditional Chinese building.

449, The Hongshan Pagoda

1788 H. 12m Urumqi

The pagoda, situated in the center of Urumqi City, is also called Zhenyao Pagoda (the pagoda which is used for suppressing the demons and ghosts). It is a octagonal, brick—structured building with 11 storeys. The base is large and the top is small, and the eaves of it is very short. It is in the traditional style of China.

450, The Confucian Temple

1922 Urumqi

The Confucian Temple, situated in the center of Urumqi City, was a God temple at first, where the God was mainly worshipped, and the Confucious was the second. In 1945, the main hall was transformed into the Dacheng Hall of Confucious. The areas of whole temple is 2,800sqm., including the gates, wing—rooms, main hall (the Dacheng Hall), bell—drum tower, and rear halls, etc.

古城遺址文物出土地點示意圖　THE ART IN THE WESTERN REGIONS

撰　　文　穆舜英(前言)　　　張　平(分類文章)
攝　　影　祁小山　王　露　馮　斐
圖版撰文　吳　勇(銅器、木器)　　李文瑛(繪畫)
　　　　　周金玲(岩畫、編織)　　劉學堂(陶器、玉琢)
　　　　　劉文鎖(建築、泥塑)　　于志勇(石雕、金銀器)
　　　　　張强禄(石器)
英文翻譯　肖小勇(前言)　　　　　朱　新(分類文章)
　　　　　張　川(圖版)　　　　　劉文鎖(圖版)
英文校審　胡錦州(前言、分類文章)　朱　新(圖版説明)
漢文校對　劉國防
地圖繪製　楊曉梅
插　　圖　張華君　　王　博　　哈斯也提
總體設計　祁協玉
責任編輯　柳用能
督　　印　程　軍　賈修和
提供部分照片資料者(姓氏筆劃爲序)
王　博　王建林　王林山　呂恩國　劉文鎖
劉玉生　劉國瑞　杜根成　張永兵　李　肖
伊第利斯　陳　戈　陳長庚　宋士敬　何德修
阿合買提　柳洪亮　單衛彤　范明華　武純展
黨　彤　黃時青　黃小江

Contributors: Mu Shunying (Preface), Zhang Ping (Essays)
Photographers: Qi Xiaoshan, Wang Lu, Feng Fei
Entries Writers: Wu Yong (Bronze, Wooden Article), Li Wenying (Painting), Zhou Jinling (Rock Carving, Woven Ware), Liu Xuetang (Pottery, Jade), Liu Wensuo (Architecture, Clay Sculpture), Yu Zhiyong (Stone Statue, Golden and Silver Objects), Zhang Qianglu (Stone Implement)
Translation: Xiao Xiaoyong (Preface), Zhu Xin (Essays), Zhang Chuan (Entries), Liu Wensuo (Entries)
Proof−readers and Revisers (English): Hu Jinzhou (Preface & Essays) Zhu Xin (Entries)
Proof−reader (Chinese): Liu Guofang
Map: Yang Xiaomei
Illustration: Zhang Huajun, Wang Bo, Hasiyet
Disigner: Qi Xie yu
Excutive Editor: Liu Young neng
Other Picture and Material Contributors: Wang Bo, Wang Jianlin, Wang Linshan, Lu Enguo, Liu Wensuo, Liu Yusheng, Liu Guorui, Du Gencheng, Zhang Yongbing, Li Xiao, Idlis, Chen Ge, Chen Changgeng, Song Shijing, He Dexiu, Ahmat, Liu Hongliang, Shan Weitong, Fan Minghua, Wu Chunzhan, Dang Tong, Huang Shixin, Huang Xiaojiang

本書由新疆美術攝影出版社與臺灣淑馨出版社合作出版

中國新疆古代藝術

主　編:穆舜英

副主編:祁小山　　張　平

出　　版:新疆美術攝影出版社

　　　　　(中國新疆烏魯木齊市西紅路 118 號

　　　　　郵政編碼 830000)

制　　版:六景彩印實業有限公司

印　　刷:美達柯式印刷有限公司

發　　行:中國國際圖書貿易總公司

　　　　　(中國北京車公莊西路 35 號)

　　　　　北京郵政信箱第 399 號

　　　　　郵政編碼:100044

版　　次:(漢英文版)1994 年 10 月第一版

　　　　　1994 年 10 月第一次印刷

ISBN7—80547—223—8/J・180

17500

84—CE—731P

版權所有・翻印必究